The LONG JOURNEY

JOURNEY

My Life Story

The *LONG JOURNEY*

My Life Story

Created by
Helena Fąfara Robaszewski

Written by
Lila Ndinsil

Edited by
Danusia Robaszewski,
Sophia Robaszewski,
Michael Robaszewski

THE LONG JOURNEY
My Life Story

Published by Danusia Robaszewski, Edmonton, Canada

ISBN:
     Paperback   978-1-77354-611-7
         ebook   978-1-77354-616-2

Publication assistance by

PAGEMASTER
PUBLISHING
PageMaster.ca

Contents

Part 4
INDIA

Part 5
AFRICA

Part 6
ENGLAND

Part 7
CANADA

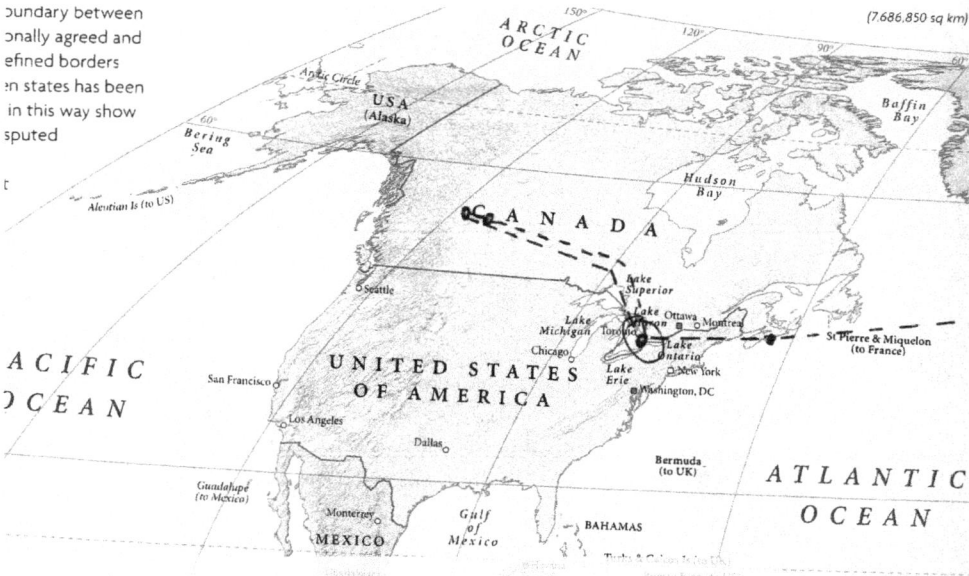

ARCTIC
OCEAN

150°   120°   90°   60°

(7.686.850 sq km)

Arctic Circle

USA
(Alaska)

Baffin
Bay

Bering
Sea

Aleutian Is (to US)

60°

C A N A D A

Hudson
Bay

Lake
Superior

Seattle

Lake
Michigan

Lake
Ottawa Montreal
Huron Toronto

St Pierre & Miquelon
(to France)

P A C I F I C
O C E A N

San Francisco

UNITED STATES
OF AMERICA

Chicago

Lake
Erie

Lake
Ontario

New York

Washington, DC

Los Angeles

Dallas

Bermuda
(to UK)

A T L A N T I C

O C E A N

Guadalupe
(to Mexico)

Monterrey

MEXICO

Gulf
of
Mexico

BAHAMAS

The Journey

» Home - Nowogrodek, Poland
» Cattle Car train, north to Kubalo camp - Kotlas, Arkhangelsk
    Oblast, Siberia, Russia
» Train, south to Kazakhstan
» Boat from north part of Caspian Sea
» To south tip of Caspian Sea
» From sea port by truck to Teheran, Iran (2 years)
» West by truck to Pehlevi, Iran
» South by truck to Ahvaz, Iran
» Train to Karachi, Pakistan (Lived in army tents)
» Mumbai, India
» Boat to east Africa Dar el Salaam – port
» Train north/west to Tengeru, Tanzania
» Tanganyika, Arusha, Moshi, Tanzania
» Until the end of the 2nd world war, 1948
» Trucks back to Der el Salem
» Ship to Arabian Sea - Gulf of Aden - Red Sea -Suez Canal –
    Mediterranean Sea – Strait of Gibraltar   Atlantic Ocean - north
    around Spain - north past France -east through English Channel
    and north to   Port of South Hampton, England
» North to East Moor (Army base)
» Lived in Yorkshire
» Then back to the port of South Hampton
» Ship to Halifax, Nova Scotia
» Train to Toronto, Ontario
» Train to Edmonton, Alberta
» Speden & Vilna, Alberta
» Than back to Edmonton, Alberta and finally Toronto, Ontario

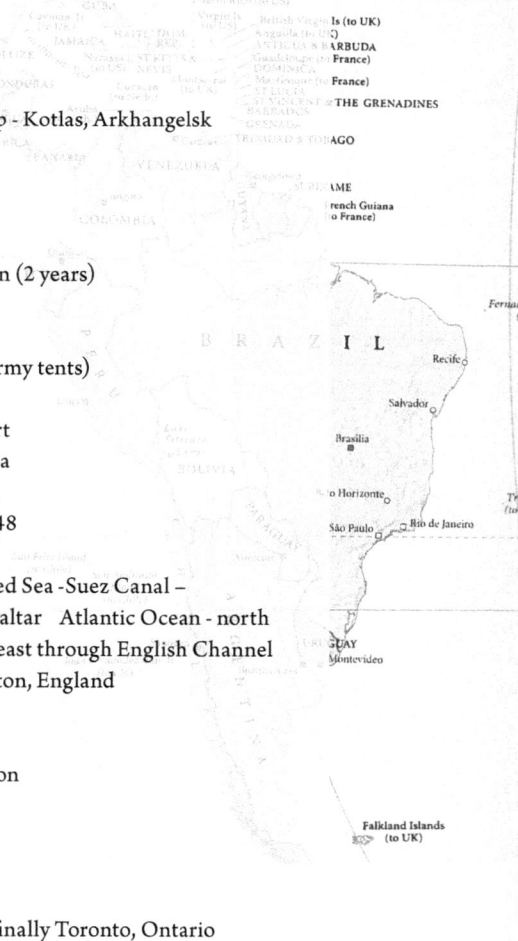

Falkland Islands
(to UK)

About the Author

Helena (Babi) Fąfara Robaszewski

I am thrilled to share the extraordinary tale of my life's journey as a Polish girl navigating the turbulent landscape of World War II. In the pages of my book, I invite you to embark on a heartfelt voyage through the trials and triumphs that shaped my existence and developed me into the person I am today. With each word, I aim to uplift and inspire, shedding light on the indomitable human spirit that can rise above even the darkest of times.

My memoir is not only a testament to my own resilience but also a heartfelt tribute to the unwavering love and support of my family; my parents Ludwik and Anna, and my siblings Janek, Jadzia and Andziej. Throughout the chaos of war, they stood by my side, providing solace, strength, and a reminder of the beauty that can be found amidst the rubble. Their unwavering presence gave me the courage to face each day with hope and to cherish the moments of joy, no matter how fleeting. Within the pages of my book, you will discover the power of family bonds and the extraordinary ways in which love can sustain us through even the most challenging circumstances.

Join me on this remarkable journey as I recount the indelible memories and profound lessons learned during my wartime experiences, before and after. It is my deepest desire that my story will resonate with readers, reminding them of the resilience of the human mind and spirit and the enduring power of love and family.

Danusia Robaszewski

This book is the culmination of listening and learning to my Mother's stories throughout my life. Mama is a woman of deep faith and conviction, a strong devotion to family, with a creative spirit and unwavering determination and strength and resilience. I will forever cherish how resourceful and innovative she is. I believe that this book, will bring you closer to her memory and personality. It will offer insight into the simple and modest but incredibly meaningful life she experienced and enjoyed. Mama inspired me to become the very best version of myself. If I am but one fraction of this incredible Woman and her Mother, I am blessed beyond words.

I love you, Mama, forever and always.

Sophia Robaszewski

My Grandmother is a remarkable storyteller. This is why my family; my Mother Danusia, my brother Michael and I wanted to bring her stories to life. I've learned that all of our experiences such as loss, sorrow, joy, and success will shape us into who we are, who we are meant to be, though it is hope and knowledge that will steer your boat to happiness. This book serves as a tribute to my beloved Babi's courage and determination. She is a true survivour who never gave up in the face of adversity.

Michael Robaszewski

For as long as I can remember, I've been fascinated by my family's history. Growing up, my Babi would tell me stories of this incredible journey. I am fascinated by how someone could survive such unimaginable hardships and still come out the other side with compassion and composure. My Babi taught me to learn as much as I can, because in life, everything can be taken away but your knowledge is always yours to keep. It is an honour and a privilege to put this book together, and I hope you will join me as I celebrate my Babi's incredible life

Lila Ndinsil

Lila Ndinsil has been writing stories since she learned to write and used to sell (yes, sell) books she made to her classmates in elementary school. She later on took part in a few local literary contests and published her first YA novel in French, titled Lorsque Notre Voeu Porte Malheur, in 2018. She is an artist as well as a writer and currently works as a freelance illustrator. Her work can be found on her website: artsyamani.com.

Prologue

The whole house was woken up brutally by pounding on the door. I jolted out of bed, my heart beating in unison with the sturdy gloved hand banging against the wood. My Mother rushed to the front of the house, and we followed her, keeping a safe distance. I checked the clock: a little past midnight. Even though I didn't know what was about to happen yet, I knew nobody would come to give us good news at this hour.

"*Ruki Vierch!*[1]" were the first words addressed to Mama after she opened the door. In the door frame, I saw none other than Russian soldiers, threatening us with their imposing uniforms and heavy guns. They looked at us as though we were criminals. The nasty glare in their eyes sent shivers down my spine, but I managed to stand still, unlike my siblings. My older sister Jadzia and my little brother Andrzej both fainted from fear. I helped Mama lay them down as she whispered comforting words to us, and then she turned her attention to the soldiers.

"You need to evacuate the house. Pack only what's necessary."

The soldier spoke in brutal short sentences.

"Why do we need to leave?" asked Mama.

"This is a big house. We need to search for hidden ammunition or fugitives. You'll come back once we're done."

---

1   "Hands up!"

There was no use trying to argue or retrieve more information. Mother looked at us, and her eyes said what her mouth didn't. Or couldn't. We needed to leave.

"You have thirty minutes. Make it quick!"

Thirty minutes? What could we possibly bring in such a short amount of time? Mama quickly sprang into action and piled things in a bundle. However, the soldiers kept following her around, saying she wasn't allowed to take this or that. I didn't know what to pack, so I just grabbed my school books. Maybe my older brother, Janek, felt the same way because he asked to take his pet rabbits. As if those would be any useful! Nonetheless, the soldiers let him.

"Who is this?" The Russians pointed towards my cousin Lydia, who was trembling. Mother spoke for the young girl who seemed to have lost her voice. "She's my sister's daughter. She came to help me care for my family since my husband's been taken away."

There was a lot of reproach in her tone. Either the soldiers didn't perceive it, or they didn't care. One of them simply declared: "She's not coming with us. She's not on the list."

I couldn't tell if there was relief or despair in Lydia's eyes, but what I know is that she was as frightened as any 18-year-old would have been in front of Russian soldiers.

"Where are you taking us?" asked Mother.

"To the school in the village." The soldier didn't give her an opening to ask more questions, so she didn't.

The clock was ticking, and we had to use the remainder of our thirty minutes wisely. At some point, Lydia came to see Mom and I while we were packing clothes. Her face was grave, and her hands were shaking. She looked paler than ever.

"Ciocia (Aunt) Anna," she whispered, "one of the soldiers... he told me something." Tears welled up in her eyes, and Mama held her close for comfort. "What is it, Lydia?"

She tried to calm herself, but her emotions were taking over. "He said: 'Tell your Ciocia to take as many things as she can because you will never see her again.'"

Thick tears rolled down her cheeks, and it didn't take long for Mother to imitate her. I only tried to understand what was happening. Only twenty minutes ago, I was peacefully dreaming. Now, I had woken up in a nightmare.

"You have to stay quiet, Ciocia," she uttered between sobs. "That soldier could get shot for what he told me. We can't let that happen after what he did."

Mama nodded and packed more things, but soon enough, our time was up. We had to depart. The soldiers put us on sleighs, and we said our goodbyes to Lydia, who now stayed alone in that big house. As the sleighs slid away, everything faded on the horizon. Our big house slowly disappeared in the bitter cold night. I don't think I realized that I would never see it again; our warm and cozy home had been swapped for discomfort and fear.

In half an hour, we lost everything.

Now, all we owned were the meager bundles on our backs.

Part 1

Poland

Osada Miratycze

Wojewodztwo Nowogródek

CHAPTER 1

Capture the Flag

My home in Poland was on a big farm that was owned by my Father. After the First World War, some plots of land were given to polish troops for their service. Tata was one of these troops, and he was given land and even a grant from the Government to buy materials for a big farmhouse, and later, some livestock.

We had three horses on our farm. They helped with every big and heavy lifting job, plowing fields, and pulling the carriage or sled in the winter. One year in late winter, a foal was born. I remembered that night. Tata brought the whole family to the stable to welcome the new baby and announced, "He shall be named Tytus."

Over the months that came, I watched Tytus grow up. One day I heard my little brother Andrew calling to Tytus, "Tesz! Tesz! Tesz! (Tesh)..."

"What are you doing?" I asked. His name is Tytus.

"Well, I thought it would be a cute nickname to call him. Since his name starts with a T." Andrzej said.

"Oh, that's creative, I like it!" "Tesz! Tesz! Tesz!" we both tried to lure Tytus over to us for a treat and a scratch behind his ear.

Baby Tytus was already on his feet, prancing around the field. His coat was beige with dark brown fur.

"Tata says that Tytus will soon have a dark chestnut coat just like his mother. It will take about a year," said Andrew.

June came along, and it was time for me and my siblings to change rooms. Tata and Mama had decided a couple of years ago to rent our rooms for vacationers and travelers. I didn't really mind having people over; they were usually nice and always had good stories. Our family hosted this one man named Aleksander Boruki. He came every summer to get a break from the city life in Warszawa.

"Mr. Ludwik, you have a real foal here? This is incredible; you must show me at once!" Mr. Boruki exclaimed to Tata.

Yes, of course, Alek! Tytus will love the attention.

Let me get some sugar cubes for him and his mama." Mr. Boruki replied.

The men went off to the paddock and greeted the horses.

"Oh, he is magnificent! And so large!" Aleksander exclaimed.

"Yes, he is a late winter baby. It's not very normal for a foal to be born so early, but Tytus looks happy and healthy."

Tytus did indeed love Aleksander's attention, especially his sugar cubes. This is where their relationship bloomed. Mr. Aleksander would often make a seat for himself with a book near Tytus's paddock. I don't think there was ever much excitement like this in Warszawa. Maybe Mr. Aleksander was a farm boy at heart. I later realized that watching a young foal grow up was a very rare and special opportunity.

My house was built so that some rooms opened directly outside and were connected by a long porch/veranda; Almost like a motel. This made it convenient for the renters to have their private rooms. Coincidentally, Mr. Aleksander's room looked right out over Tytus's paddock. Sometimes it would seem as though Tytus missed Mr. Aleksander when he wasn't seated near the paddock. However, Tytus was a smart horse. He watched where his friend went after spending the afternoon with him.

Mr. Aleksander heard a noise by his bedroom window. *scratch scratch*

It must be some leaves or the wind, he thought. But it happened again. *scratch scratch*

Mr. Aleksander went to the window to inspect. "Tytus? What are you doing here?"

The young horse had studied his friend's movements and figured out where his room was.

"Ah, I know what you want. You came for some sugar cubes. Hahahaha!"

In previous years, while peace still remained in the country, our farm was home to many others. We lived in Osada (County) Miratycze, Wojewodztwo (Community) Nowogródek. The Scouting Association has always been a big part of Polish culture. We hosted about sixty girl scouts who regularly camp in our region. This visit, in particular, consisted of girls aged 18 or 19 years old who had just graduated from high school.

We helped Mama push the dining room table and chairs to one wall to make room for them, where they slept on the floor in their sleeping bags. They were very independent and went out to explore the region during the whole day, or sometimes even camped out. They went into the forest on hiking expeditions, identifying and admiring the different types of trees, flowers, and other plants nearby. Where I grew up, nature still reigned, with its tall cedar trees and branches intertwined together to filter in the sun. Various mushrooms populated the ground, creating white, brown, and cream-colored spots contrasting with the rich emerald-green grass.

"You really live in a beautiful area," one of them said as we ate dinner.

"Oh yes!" her friend added. "I especially love the lake!"

My eyes lit up, and I turned around at the mention of my happy place, my straight blond hair whipping the air. "Me too! We go there to play all the time!"

My family and I lived near Lake Świtez[2]. Every year, it attracts many tourists. I often went there with my siblings, and since my brother, Janek, was old enough to watch us, we didn't need adults to chaperone.

"But you need to be careful," my brother said. "The lake can be dangerous. I heard many stories of people who drowned there." He squinted and smirked, clearly trying to spook us.

I noticed some of the girls widened their eyes, but his tactics didn't work on me.

"Rumour says the lake is... cursed!" One girl let out a small cry, to Janek's satisfaction.

"Don't tease them!" Mama scolded him, but he probably didn't hear her because he was laughing too loud. We quickly moved on from the subject since the girls really liked the lake and didn't want Janek to ruin the beautiful image they had of it.

"So Helena? What grade are you in?"

"I'm going to be in fourth grade!" I said proudly. Happy to receive some attention, I rambled on and on about how I was always one of the smartest students in class and that my teacher often congratulated me for my accomplishments. The girl scouts were impressed, which made me want to show off even more. However, Jadzia didn't let me enjoy the spotlight much longer.

"Do you know how much she begged Tata[3] to let her go to school? You should have seen her. She was always crying whenever Janek and I left her behind for school. She couldn't understand because she was still too young."

"Jadzia!" A rosy tone crept up my cheeks as I remembered the embarrassing memory. Indeed, when I was five years old, I begged and cried because I wanted to go to school so badly. Thankfully, Father was good friends with the principal - they went hunting together - so he was able to talk with him, and the principal let me enroll.

---

2   Probably current-day Belarusian lake Verovskoye, located in the Grodno region of Belarus

3   Tata means "Dad" in Polish

"Don't worry, Hela, I was the same!" said one of the girls with a smile. I turned to look at her. "Hela?"

"Yeah, it's your new nickname. Do you like it?"

I completely forgot about Jadzia and her effort to embarrass me, simply happy with my new nickname. "Yes! I love it!"

I was happy every time people called me Hela. I thought it was cute.

The girl scouts were lovely; we had a wonderful time with them. I remember one special time when we went to the lake. Even though I didn't know how to swim, I wasn't going to let that stop me from having fun, but I also had to be mindful of playing safely in the water. After all, I would come there all the time with my siblings.

"Hey, Hela! Hop on!"

One of the girl scouts turned her back to me in the water, and I understood by her gesture that she wanted me to climb on. Overjoyed, I hopped on her back, and we swam around; I'll never forget that moment. We laughed with the other girls and played around in the water and summer sun, splashing each other or having contests to see who could hold their breath underwater the longest. The more experienced swimmers raced, and I cheered them on.

I didn't know then that a secret plan had already been set for us. The clock was ticking, and unbeknownst to us, we were enjoying our last smiles for a while.

We sat joyfully in front of the dinner my Mother had just prepared, and we hastily took our first bites. Most of us sat on the floor, and a few were on chairs since the dining table had been pushed to the wall to create space for the scouts,

"You know you don't have to do this," said one of the girls. "We can make our own food."

Mama nicely hushed her as she tucked away a blond strand of hair behind her ear. "Don't say that. I feed everyone who comes under my roof."

She always had a big heart, so to her, giving was as natural as breathing. I believe her inner beauty was reflected on the outside, for she was a lovely young lady with fair skin and nice blue eyes. She was the kind of woman I was proud to call Mama.

The atmosphere was festive, and many conversations animated the group.

"You know, I heard there are boy scouts in the region."

"Boy scouts?" said two girls in unison.

"Yes! And they aren't too far from here."

The girls smirked and exchanged glances as if the mere mention of boy scouts in the region was a secret code they all knew. Confused, I asked what was going on.

"Don't you know? Each scout group has a special flag they need to guard against other groups, or else it'll get stolen. Since the boys are around, that means we should try to steal their flag. It's like a game."

I was excited about the idea of this secret game, and my Mother was too; because she quickly joined the conversation. A few seconds later, they were already brainstorming ideas to capture the flag.

"I know!" someone finally said after a long deliberation. "Janek and I can go explore the area to locate the camp. After that, we'll need someone to figure out when they'll be gone. It might be too risky for Janek and I to ask them ourselves."

"I can go," said Mama, "and I can bring Rzenia, our housemaid. We'll pretend we're selling something and casually get information about their activities and outings."

"Yes! That's a great idea!"

Things got more exciting as the plan took shape. Eventually, all the preparations were ready, and the girls took action. Two of the scouts; Janek and Amelia, managed to locate the camp. From there, Mother and Rzenia took the lead. They dressed up as innocent villagers and went to the camp, pretending to sell eggs and bread.

In the evening, we waited for their return and report. When I heard the front door open and close, I rushed to the front of the house, followed by about twenty other girls, to welcome Mother and Rzenia.

"So?!" I asked impatiently. "How did it go?"

They kept quiet for a bit, which worried us. However, after a few seconds, we could see a smirk creeping up their lips. "They'll be gone the whole day after tomorrow… Hiking."

The girls giggled and grinned, already imagining how easy it would be to carry out their mission with the boys out of the picture.

Mother sat down, began telling her story, and shared more details with the girls. "They were very nice; didn't even suspect a thing. They looked pretty hungry too. I'm guessing that since they live outside, they need to make everything themselves. It's no surprise they jumped on the occasion to get produce. We pretended to be interested in their activities, and they naively told us everything they were planning to do for the rest of the week."

By then, we were all laughing at those poor boys who didn't know what was coming for them. Capturing their flag would be a piece of cake if no one was guarding it. Soon enough, the day after tomorrow arrived, and the girls quickly went to the boys' camp. As expected, no one was around, and no one was watching over the flag they came for. That night, they returned home giggly and proud of what they had accomplished.

A few days later, a knock at the door interrupted our evening. My Mother went to open, and there stood none other than the boy scouts.

Mama invited them inside, and right away, they noticed the girls - who were pretty hard to miss since there were so many.

"We came to retrieve our flag."

"Who said we have it?" asked one of the girl scouts.

"When we came back from our hike the other day, our flag was gone. We asked around and discovered there were girl scouts here, so we figured you must have it."

I looked back and forth at the two speakers, not knowing what would happen next.

"Ok, fine. We'll give you back your flag."

The boys were already rejoicing, but Mama quickly rained on their parade. "Under a few conditions, boys."

Their movements froze, and they stared at her in anticipation.

"Number one: you need to pick a lot of mushrooms for a social night we're going to have. Number two: you need to gather enough wood to make a bonfire. Number three: you'll need to provide entertainment for the social night by singing and reciting poems."

There was a bit of clamor, but the boys' leader calmed them down. He then turned toward us.

"Alright then, Pani (Ma'am). You have a deal!"

The social night was also to celebrate the last night the girls were staying with us. I was sad because they had to leave, but they kept reassuring me they'd come back by next year. It was near dusk and we waited for the boys to arrive with the wood and mushrooms. After some time, they finally showed up.

"Took you long enough!" Jadzia whined, brushing away the curly hair strands from her forehead.

"Sorry. Mushroom picking took longer than we thought."

Immediately I heard them speaking of mushrooms, I started getting hungry. I excitedly opened the bags they brought and backed away in fear. "Eww! They smell so bad!"

Some other girls came to take a look and, just like I did, quickly backed away due to the stench.

"These mushrooms are all bad!"

"What? No way!"

The girls took a closer look and realized the boys had mixed together good *and* bad mushrooms, so the whole lot was no longer edible.

"Don't you know how to differentiate them?"

The boys scratched their heads and avoided our gaze, which gave us the answer we needed. Unfortunately, we couldn't eat any of the mushrooms anymore and thus had to throw them all away.

"Can't we keep some? We worked quite hard to gather them."

"Unless you want to have some serious indigestion, I suggest you don't."

The boys and I were disappointed, but we quickly moved on. Thankfully, it didn't take an expert to pick wood, so we were able to light the bonfire. We gathered around, and the boys entertained us with songs and poems. Some of the songs were very good, and we encouraged them to continue, but others were so bad that we mocked them. Everyone had a great time, and it truly was a wonderful night. In the end, the boys got their flag back and exchanged contact information with the girls, which made quite a few of them happy.

Despite the joyful night, there was a melancholic undertone; The girls were leaving.

"And you promise to come back next year, right? You said you'd promise!"

"Yes, Hela, we'll come back for sure!"

"Come on, let them go now." Mama pulled me back as I sent my last goodbyes to the scouts.

I could tell they were just as sad as I was with this separation. However, they loved the region so much that they said they'd come back. I finally let them go, clinging to their promise.

But we never heard from them again.

Barely a week later, the first invaders arrived.

CHAPTER 2

In the dark

Dates can mean nothing and everything. For us, September 1st, 1939, would forever hold a totally different meaning.

"The Germans invaded us!"

Right away, I didn't understand the panic in Mother's eyes. She cranked up the volume of the radio to learn more. I felt I should listen too, so I came closer to the small machine.

"Germany has just declared war against Poland. Chancellor Adolph Hitler is moving in from the west, north, and south."

Mother's face grew paler by the second, and I heard the word "war" escape the low mumbling of my Father.

"What's going on?" Andrzej came next to the fireplace, and Mama held him close, stroking his short blond hair.

Father rubbed his blue eyes and sighed heavily. "Not again. Not this again!"

It was the beginning of a very long nightmare.

"What about Janek?" Andrzej asked.

My parents suddenly realized my older brother was in danger. He had recently started high school and chose to attend a military one located near the German border. It only took me a second to recognize the risk he faced.

"They'll kill him! They're going to kill my son!"

"Calm down, Anna."

"How could I calm down? My son… they'll…"

"Anna."

"My son… no…" Tears ran down her face, and soon enough, Andrzej and I were also crying. How was all this happening? Why was it happening? The situation seemed too surreal for me to acknowledge it.

"I just heard France and England declared war against Germany."

That was probably the first good news we'd heard in the last two days. Everyone was still in shock about Hitler waging war against Poland. Especially since we had just gotten our freedom and independence not too long ago after having Russia, Germany, and Austria take turns ruling over us. However, we now had allies: France and England.

My parents knew more about war time than we children, since they were born before the First World War. During this time of panic, we turned to them, not knowing what to expect. The problem was that no one really knew what to expect during such a massive conflict. Anything and everything could happen during a war.

"They're going after the Jews!" I heard someone say in the village.

"Yes. They were already treating them badly in Germany."

As expected, the recent events were the talk of everyone in Miratycze[4]. Many would speculate about Hitler's intentions, and some decided not to stay to find out, fleeing to Lithuania, among other countries. The atmosphere was very troubling, and I was getting more worried by the day. What was going to happen to our country? To us? Would France and England interfere soon enough? The same questions I pondered were the ones weighing on everyone's mind.

A week passed, and our anxiety grew. Germany was ravaging our country, and even though they hadn't come to our side in the east of

---

4   Now, the Miratycze village is probably a Belarusian village near lake Verovskoye

Poland, we feared it was only a matter of time before they did. The radio constantly remained on, with our ears trying to pick even the smallest details that could offer some sort of relief. On September 10th, we learned that Canada also joined the war; Another ally.

Just like everyone else, I hoped things would settle quickly and the good guys would win. After all, we hadn't done anything wrong, so why was this happening to us?

Time went by, and we still had no news of Janek. Our anxiety grew every day, and Mama started losing it. I, too, was getting scared, but I wanted to believe everything was somehow going to work out. My parents tried to comfort us, yet the grave look in their eyes told us otherwise. Father had fought in WWI, and inevitably flashbacks started haunting him again. All I knew about the war was what he had told me, and all I had seen were the sword and boots he kept from his fighting days. The accessories Janek used to parade in, which I always admire, now made me fearful. I didn't want Father to have to put those boots on and wield that sword once again. However, it seemed like fighting was the only option left.

Two days before my tenth birthday, it was Russia's turn to invade us from the east. They infiltrated Poland on September 17th, 1939.

"As if things weren't bad enough with the Nazis, now we have the Red Army here too!" Mother couldn't stop shaking her head. Everything was going so fast - too fast. "What are we going to do now? We have invaders everywhere!"

Tension kept rising in the village and everyone was scared. People spoke in hushed voices, carefully selecting their words. No one stayed out too long, and everyone avoided the soldiers' gaze. The Russian soldiers were terrifying in their imposing uniforms, and their stone-faced expression sent chills down my spine. They walked around with huge guns that I always feared they'd shoot someone.

When the Russians came, everything changed. In schools, they converted Polish classes to Russian, so now we had to learn their language. They also closed banks, and we couldn't get money anymore. Since they didn't believe in God, they didn't allow us to go to church either. What a punishment for a mostly Catholic country! My village was a small community with very few shops, but even those few ones had been completely taken over. The corner store where we used to buy candy wasn't as jovial anymore. Intimidating Soviet Union flags dissuaded us from eating at local restaurants. The big Catholic church in the middle of the village was now quiet, its bells were forbidden to chime.

Steadily, our country was being taken over, and our culture was washed out. Everything converted to Russian, to the point where I barely recognized my birthplace anymore. All I could see were soldiers that weren't from here, and all I could hear was a language that wasn't mine. The Polish government had already fled, leaving its people to fend for themselves. They were safe and sound in England, whereas our lives were constantly threatened. Many Poles tried to fight off the Russians; but all to no avail. On September 29th, Germany and Russia had a meeting and declared that Poland ceased to exist as a state. All hope of survival and Polish independence vanished.

Just when things couldn't get worse, my Father disappeared.

"It's already so late. Why isn't he home?" Mama was getting worried, and her worry was contagious.

Where *was* Tata? None of us had seen him nor heard a word about him. Just like that, he simply didn't come back home one night.

"Something must have happened to him. I'm sure of it!" Mama paced around in the living room, and all we could do was watch torment eat her away. It was then we heard a knock on the door. We hoped to see Father appear and ran to open it. Unfortunately, we were utterly disappointed when we saw one of our neighbours.

"Good evening, Anna. Sorry to come by so late."

"It's OK," said Mama, trying to hide her disappointment.

She invited the man in, but he politely refused. "I only came to tell you one thing. It's about Ludwig."

Her eyes lit up and ours too. However, something was off. The neighbour certainly didn't seem excited at all. He was troubled and worried. He fidgeted a lot, and his eyes kept checking his surroundings.

Finally, he uttered the dreaded words in an ushered and raspy voice: "The Russians arrested him. I saw them take him from the street."

Everyone paused; No one talked, and no one breathed. Father was...

"Arrested?! For what?"

Our neighbour didn't have any more information to give us and wouldn't dare say anything else. He simply told us what he saw and knew nothing else about the matter. With that, he quickly left. The house felt emptier the minute Tata wasn't present, and we stayed alone. At least he was still alive. But arrested?

"How dare they!" burst out Mama. "How dare they take my husband from the street like some worthless criminal?" Tears flooded her cheeks, and Jadzia tried to comfort her. Andrzej stayed close to me, also about to start crying. Mother's sobbing pierced my heart, and it didn't take me long to imitate her. Everything was going horribly wrong. The Germans came, and now the Russians. We had no news of Janek, and now Tata got arrested. I simply couldn't believe this horrible chain of events.

After a while, Mother suddenly stopped crying, and her red eyes looked more determined than ever. "I'm going to the police office."

We didn't say anything, and she repeated herself. "I'm going to the police office. I'm going to ask about Ludwig." She was definitely not asking for our approval. She got ready quickly and stormed out of the house. I followed her.

At the police station, she had trouble controlling herself. "I am looking for my husband, Ludwig Fąfara. He hasn't come back home, and I want to know where he is."

The soldier before her looked completely uninterested in her troubles, but still pretended to try to help her. He looked through some files, his movements unbearably slow, then finally came back to us. "Ah yes, Ludwig Fąfara," he mumbled as if he hadn't heard Mother say his name. "We just need to ask him a few questions. After that, we'll release him, don't worry."

The glare in his eyes and his crooked smile punctuated by yellowed teeth didn't feel reassuring, but what could Mama do? She was now a helpless woman without her husband and oldest son. Together, we reluctantly left the office.

It is really true that we only realize the value of what we have once we've lost it. Now that Tata was gone - or should I say *away*, since it's less macabre - everything was different. The house was emptier, and quieter. Obviously, we also missed Janek, but Tata was the pillar. He was the one who knew the war, fought the war, and could help us get through this one. We were very scared now that he was gone- *away*. It was especially hard for Mama to take care of her children alone. Thankfully, we were helped by some villagers who came at night to bring us a bit of food. They did everything in secret, fearing they might become the Russian soldiers' next target. We were thankful for their generosity and kindness. It was also around that time that Janek came back.

Sitting by a tree, in one of our many orchards, I saw a figure on the horizon. Instinctively, I thought of running back home but I felt like I knew the person. I waited until he came closer and closer, and then...

"Janek!"

When he heard my voice, he ran up to me and pulled me in a warm embrace. Tears streaked our cheeks, and we laughed uncontrollably.

"Helena! Oh Helena!" was all he could say.

We stood there, laughing and sobbing in the middle of our orchard-filled field. After that, we went inside to share the good news with the others. As soon as she saw her son, Mama burst into tears.

"Janek! It's really you!" She held him tight, to the point of almost choking him, so he begged her to loosen her grip. Mama checked him all over, noticing how dirty and beaten up he was. His black hair was as messy as ever, and his clothes were tattered.

"What happened to you?"

"Long story. But first, I need some food!"

Mama took another look at him and shook her head. "You need a bath. *Then* some food."

As Janek cleaned up, Jadzia and I helped Mama set the table. At least now, all the children were reunited. Maybe soon enough, we would be setting the table to dine with Tata too.

We sat at the dining table to enjoy the meal, but with a bittersweet feeling.

"Where's Tata?"

We lowered our heads, and Janek probably feared the worst, so Mama quickly reassured him. "He's alive. Just... The soldiers arrested him."

"Arrested him? Why?"

"We don't know... we really don't know..." Mama's voice trailed off, and my brother didn't inquire further.

There was a short moment of silence, and then Andrzej asked what we were all wondering.

"So what happened to you, Janek?"

The spoonful of soup making its way to my older brother's lips stopped right in front of his open mouth. He put down his spoon and began his tale.

"You probably know that my school is close to the German border. The Nazis found out we were a military school and started bombing us."

At the sound of the word "bombing," Mama's face went pale.

Janek quickly reassured her. "But I was able to escape, as you can see! I don't know if everyone made it out alive or uninjured. The Germans chased us and often shot at us, so we had to be hiding constantly. Thankfully, some people helped us along the way, and that's how I was able to come back home. Even so, it's a miracle I made it back safe."

I could hardly imagine having soldiers chasing and shooting me. Janek talked a bit more about his perilous adventure, which only increased my fright. What if the Germans came here and started shooting us? Unless the Russians did it first? I tried to drive those thoughts from my mind, but they haunted me in my dreams, which quickly became nightmares. Nightmares of matching uniforms and big guns, loud voices, and scared people. Some of them disappeared without a trace, others died on the spot. Because of this, I really feared the night.

Mama went back to the police office to receive news about her husband. It had already been over a week since they took him, and he still wasn't back. Once again, a Russian soldier - the same as last time - told her they were questioning him and he would return home soon. Little did we know, he was never going to come home again.

There is no peace or joy during a war. Only anguish and terror. There was a perpetual fear lodging down our stomach which shocked us if we ever wanted to start getting accustomed to our situation. Nights were rough and short; sleep was desired but suppressed. Food was tasteless, and tears constantly threatened our eyes. Uncertainty troubled us day and night, and we started wondering if there was much left to hope for.

One day, we heard loud noises coming from outside. Soon enough, we realized those were gunshots. Immediately, I remembered Janek's story, and panic seized me.

"Everyone, stay down! And stay close!"

We followed Mama's orders, not knowing what else to do. I could see the shots being fired from the window. Heavy metal planes circled above, and tiny dots rushed out of some sort of mechanism. Frozen in fear, I couldn't look away. I saw how they were shooting persistently and aggressively. Our property was big, and on some parts, we had bundles of buckwheat that were tied up. They probably looked like people from afar, so the planes wouldn't stop attacking them. I kept watching, horrified. All they were shooting at were bundles of wheat, but that also meant they could - and would - do the same to a real person. That person could be me. Us. Anyone.

I sobbed uncontrollably as I realized the horrors of my new situation; During war period, soldiers shoot people as if they were mere bundles of buckwheat.

Mama decided to call her niece over to help her around the house now that her husband wasn't there - and might not be back anytime soon. Lydia was a lovely cousin of mine, around 18 or 19 years old. She brought a bit of warmth to our household, but her stay with us was brief. We didn't know that since December 1939, our time in Poland was counted, and now time was up.

The night of February 10th, 1940, was the night of goodbyes. A little past midnight, we were brutally forced out of our sleep by the alarming sound of a pounding fist on our door. Russian soldiers barged in without an ounce of concern for the time and the rest they woke us from. The worry and uncertainty on our faces meant nothing to them as they coldly spat orders. "Pack your things! You have thirty minutes! Make it quick!"

Even as we fussed around trying to obey their instructions, there was always something we weren't doing right.

"No, don't bring that! Leave that here, you can't take it with you!"

No papers, no food. Barely any clothes. It was the most stressful half hour of our lives.

"Where are you taking us?" Mother dared to ask what we all wondered.

"To the school in the village. We need to search your house."

It's not like we were hiding anything. Or anyone. Thankfully, there was one good soul among the brutes. He pulled aside my cousin, Lydia, to whisper what we didn't want to hear but needed to know.

"Tell your Ciocia to take as many things as she can because you will never see her again."

She sadly repeated the words to Mama, who tried to control her tears. Time ran out, and we had to leave. We said goodbye to Lydia because her name wasn't on the list, so the soldiers weren't going to take her away. Honestly, I can't really say if she was the lucky one or if we were. Gloomily, we trudged to the sleighs waiting for us, the sorry-looking bundles on our backs being our only luggage. The sleighs started moving at the same speed our home disappeared on the horizon. Goodbye Lydia. Goodbye house. And soon enough, goodbye Poland.

We arrived at my school, but it seemed alien to me. All the desks, chairs, and other furniture that used to be there were gone. The only thing left inside were desperate people with sorry-looking bundles on their backs, just like us. Panic was palpable. Everyone here was confused and anxious. The Russian soldiers knew how to torture us psychologically, keeping us in the dark for as long as possible. Some were crying, while some were whispering. Words were too scary to hear and too dangerous to utter. Many speculations circulated about what was to become of us. The older ones, who had the war experience, were the most pessimistic and fully aware of our fate.

I clung to Mama as the only source of comfort and hope I had left; my siblings did the same. Mama started praying vehemently, fiddling with her Rosary. I decided she knew best and didn't take long to join her in prayers.

There were many, many Poles in my school that dismal night. It seemed like all the families in the village had been woken up to be brought here. Sure enough, I recognized some of them - we lived in a small community after all. I hadn't realized it at the time, but it wasn't just anyone that had been brought here at such an unusual hour. Those gathered were all educated and established people. They were those with means and knowledge - later on, I learned we also referred to them as "intelligentsia." We had all been targeted by the Soviet Union as potential threats. By getting rid of the smart and rich, the USSR would have less reason to fear opposition from their captives.

I don't remember how long we stayed in the school, but it wasn't a pleasant time. I didn't know what was going to happen to us, and Mama could hardly hide her own uncertainty. Everyone was distressed and fatigued. The night had always been long, and we barely got any sleep. It was hard to find a place to rest in the crowded building, and even if we did, apprehension kept us awake. Then finally, it happened.

"Everyone listen up! You all need to evacuate the building and make your way to the train waiting for you!" The soldier spoke so loud that his voice rang in my ears. He gave instructions, and as soon as he finished, everyone started moving, hustling and complaining. The Russians had no regard for us, so they simply executed their evacuation plan with barking orders. My family and I moved as one unit, making sure we stuck close together. After much elbowing, we made it to the train.

"These are cattle wagons." My brother Janek made the remark, and I realized he was right. However, we didn't have time to pause because the soldiers were pressing us on.

"Come on! Move it!"

Reluctantly, we boarded. The inside was horrible. Big shelves hung wearily on the sides, coated with the thinnest layer of hay. There was also a small hole in the middle. I didn't know why that was there yet, but I'd discover it soon enough. A few translucent windows hung at the top of the dirt-covered walls.

"They're treating us like cattle," Janek said.

The expression on his face was that of a revolted, upset teenager. Being a rebel at fifteen was a typical phase, but he had to wait since submission was the only option left at the moment. Everyone was pressed inside, and in minutes, we were densely packed, squished like sardines into those shelves, bodies to bodies. The wagons started moving, and we left; For good.

I am not sure how long the trip was, but I remember it wasn't pleasant. I found out that the hole in the middle of the car was supposed to be our bathroom. That meant we had to do our business in front of everyone; That was the beginning of the dehumanizing process. We had to put our pride aside and lower our trousers with witnesses all around unless someone was there to cover us with a blanket. Others didn't have that courage and urinated right on their shelf, but the problem was that the liquid would drip down if that person were on top of the shelf. Needless to say, it was troublesome for the individual on the bottom bunk.

There was a small window that allowed us to speak with those in the next wagon, but there wasn't much to say. Some gave us encouraging words, but most were conquered by discouragement, and their pessimism quickly gained more and more captives. Our light started fading away; our world turning grey.

We were locked up the whole time. Only once a day, the soldiers opened the doors, and at that moment, some ran outside to relieve themselves. However, they couldn't go far because the soldiers watched them, so it was all the same whether they did their business in front of us, in front of the soldiers or in the wagon in front of the other Poles. We had no privacy or dignity, but by that point, it didn't matter anymore; we were simply trying to survive.

It was also when the soldiers unlocked the door that they fed us. Well, "feed" is probably too strong a word. We were only given a watery "cabbage soup." Quickly, the first changes started to occur. Thinner bodies and hollow cheeks. Grief clung to everyone's face like a new layer of skin. Also, the temperature getting colder wasn't helping at all. The train was even heading north, and we didn't have the proper clothing to endure the extreme weather. The pile of our excrement would freeze, and we'd use a small stove to melt it and clean up a little. Despite the horrible hygiene conditions, I didn't witness anyone get sick in our wagon.

One day, something caught my eye. I was looking at one of the ladies in our wagon, and her dress seemed curious to me. I stared at her for a few seconds before my suspicions were confirmed. Right away, I elbowed Mama, waking her from her precious sleep.

"Mama, Mama! Look! It's your dress!" I whisper-shouted.

She rubbed her eyes and tried to look in the direction I pointed at. She kept quiet for a while, and I knew she recognized the garment from her gaze. That lady stole it. At the time, clothes weren't massively produced like they are today, so it was easy to know to whom a piece of clothing belonged and that dress was my Mother's.

I waited for her to say something, to get mad and go yank her dress off that lady, but she didn't. She simply laid back down on her hay.

I was confused. "Why aren't you going to see her? She stole your clothes!"

Mother opened her eyes and looked tenderly at me. "You see how worn-down everyone looks. Now's not the time to start problems. And besides, she probably needs it more than I do, so I'll gladly let her have it."

She smiled at me, but I had trouble understanding. Didn't *we* need clothes too? This was war, and we had to think about ourselves! But that wasn't Mama. She was the kind of person who would gladly let a stranger steal her dress. A real angel.

Eventually, there were no more train tracks, so we continued the journey on sleighs. About 200km separated us from our destination. The winter was harsh, at its epitome in February. We moved like prisoners on their way to die. The analogy wasn't too far from our reality. Mother had a boil on her big toe, so walking was hard for her. Honestly, I don't know how we survived that trip. Four young children and a thirty-six-year-old woman. We had such little food, and I know it's a miracle we made it since many others perished on the way, their bodies tossed on the sides and stripped of their clothes to offer a bit more warmth to the living.

Then finally, after the most exhausting trip of our lives, we made it to Siberia.

Part 2

Russia

Kubalo Camp

CHAPTER 3

Survival of the fittest

In Siberia, there was nothing. Grey engulfed us, and the sky and snow mixed together creating one huge void. It was a frozen desert. As we were trying to take in our new environment, a soldier stepped forward, calling our attention.

"Everyone listen up! You are now in the Kubalo camp, in the Oblast Arkhangelsk.[5] You will stay in those barracks. You get showers once a week in the steam bath over there. Make sure you're in your barrack every night because we will count you. You will get 600 grams of bread a day, but only if you can afford it. Those above 16 will go to work."

After that, we were organized into our barracks. They were old, rusty and looked just like cattle wagons. Our beds were two levels of shelves hung on the wall, covered with some hay. We were all put in one big room, once again packed like sardines; there were more people than the space available. The place looked like it had formerly housed prisoners and refugees, and we were the next wave. Families stuck together with whichever member they still had. We were mostly women and children since the men had been taken away early in the war. Everyone was worried about what would happen to us, and I, too, was perturbed by our uncertain future.

Mother saw how scared we all were and took us aside.

---

5   Arkhangelsk is a province in northern Russia, next to the White Sea

"Listen to me," she said. "Listen carefully. Right now, we are in a bit of a bind. I know our situation seems desperate, but we will make it out of here."

"What do you mean?" Jadzia asked angrily, tears already welling up in her blue eyes. "Look around us! There's snow everywhere, it's freezing, we'll barely get any food, and we have the worst possible lodging! Our situation is hopeless!"

Mother looked at her sternly. "Jadzia, I said we'll make it out of here, but to do that, you have to trust me and do as I say. Understood?"

My sister was still crying but slowly nodded. Mother took a deep breath and then turned towards Janek. "You'll have to go to work, my son."

"How come? You heard the soldier. Only those above 16 can work, and I'm still 15."

"But they don't know that."

Janek soon understood what she was getting at.

"The soldiers back home didn't allow me to take any papers," she continued, "so we have no proof that you're 15."

"Yes, I guess you're right."

"We'll need whatever income we can get. The only way to get food is to pay for it, so every single ruble[6] counts."

With this understanding, Mama continued to instruct her children on what to do. After that, we went and "settled in" our new home. Heads hung low, and many were crying. A lot of refugees were already in a severe state, with washed-out skin and tattered clothes due to the harsh trip. Looking around, I couldn't see the hope Mother was trying to light in us. Could we really make it out of here alive? There were already so many who perished on the way. However, I wanted to trust her. She was my Mother after all, and she had to be right.

The showers were horrible. It was a community mixed bath, so men and women, old and young, bathed together. Once again, our dignity was

---

6   Russian currency

stripped from us, but what could we do in this case? We had to keep clean somehow, especially to avoid diseases such as typhoid and dysentery.

Soldiers yelled orders, and we followed. Like animals obeying their masters, we had no say whatsoever. It's crazy how quickly the refugees stopped caring about each other's nakedness. They dragged their bodies around like carcasses and lazily took their showers, enjoying the hot water as much as they could; At least there was that. We froze seven days a week simply to enjoy an hour of warmth. At this point, it was a pretty good bargain.

Janek started working as a woodcutter, so we rarely saw him. The soldiers didn't question him when he affirmed he was sixteen and immediately gave him the job. Actually, my brother wasn't the only one lying about his age. Some boys as young as twelve also worked because they had to support their families. Their weak arms were forced to handle dangerous axes, swinging them against the sturdy bark. With Janek's wages, we were able to have a bit of money to buy food. The 600 grams of dry bread were barely enough to keep us alive, but it was still better than nothing. Unfortunately, Mother couldn't work because her foot still hurt, so she stayed with us in the barracks.

There was nothing to do. We lived in one of the "free settlements" in Siberia. They were called that because, unlike other Siberian camps, there wasn't any forced labour. However, we quickly understood we'd have to work if we wanted to survive; no work meant no money, and no money meant no food. Our living conditions were atrocious enough, so we definitely didn't need to add starvation to our long list of problems. We also received some parcels from Poland; Mama's sister sent us food - dry bread, bacon, grain - that helped us survive in such a rough and harsh place. Mama stocked the provisions and fed them to us bit by bit in order to make them last. We were never fully fed, but we didn't starve either.

Oftentimes, we don't fully recognize the gravity of a catastrophe before it gets out of hand. I probably thought that soon enough, we'd be delivered by either the French, or English, or Canadians, or anyone fighting for our cause, and we'd safely go back to Poland and live as we used to. My Mother also knew how to reassure me, and I trusted she could and would get us out of this situation. I also prayed with the other refugees, begging God to deliver us and trusting that soon enough, He would.

However, not everyone was as optimistic. Some refugees had already lost hope. The look in their eyes was always dull, their skin grey from the cold. Life and vigour slowly abandoned their bodies with hunger eating them away.

"We're doomed, you know?" one lady told me. The look in her eyes scared me, but I wanted to give myself a certain countenance.

"No, we aren't. We'll make it out of here."

She turned to face me as if I had just said the strangest thing. Then she chuckled, a wicked smile twisting her lips. "Out of here? We aren't leaving. We'll either freeze to death or starve to death. Once we're sent to Siberia, there's no going back. We're sent here to die."

Shivers crawled up my spine, and I quickly left.

Winter was still at its most brutal stage, and we started losing refugees. When someone died, their family members took care of the burial. Discouragement quickly lowered the morale, and the fear of death soon became just as unbearable as death itself. Knowing we couldn't continue this way any longer, some of the older people came up with a plan for their survival.

"Steal grain?"

We looked at Edward, one of the few men in our camp, puzzled. He and two other men came up with a plan to help us survive the winter.

"There are farms not too far from here," he said. "We can sneak out at night and go steal some of their grain."

"But how are we going to do that without getting caught?"

"We'll head out after the soldiers count us at night. Someone will keep watch while the others are in the field. As long as we're careful, everything should be fine."

Edward explained his plan further, and more and more people were willing to join him, including Mama. She turned towards Jadzia, who was also there. "Do you want to come with us? We'll need some help."

My sister barely let her finish her sentence when she vehemently shook her head. "No way! It's too dangerous. And it's still really cold outside."

Mother was disappointed but didn't say it. That's why I decided to offer the help needed. "I'll go."

They both looked at me with surprise in their eyes.

"You're barely ten, Hela. Maybe it's a bit too much for you," Mama said.

This time, I was the one shaking my head. "I'll be fine, don't worry."

Looking back, I was very brave for my age. Even though I was just as worried as the others, I didn't want to rot away in this hole. I was aware that many had already died of disease, starvation, and even grief. Mama said we were going to make it out of here alive, so if I wanted that to happen, I had to do my part also.

Seeing the determination in my eyes, Mother didn't argue any longer. It was set, and I was going with them.

Two days later, we set our plan in motion. The soldiers came to count us as usual, and then abandoned us in our dark room. We waited a little before we began to move. Mama made bundles of clothes and put them on our shelf under our bed sheets to make it seem as if we were sleeping there. Jadzia was going to stay with Andrzej since she was afraid and he was only nine.

In single file, we left our barracks and quietly hiked to the fields, our watchmen were behind us to keep an eye out for soldiers. We had a few leaders who knew where the fields were, so the rest of us simply followed. Our group was composed mainly of men, but there were also a few women - and a child - among us.

The snow was up to our waist, and the night was brutally cold, but we had to advance. At this point, we were choosing between warmth and food. I bit down my lip in an attempt to tame the pain spreading through my body and pressed forward. I tightened the curtain that Mama wrapped around my body and torso, and the other fabric overtop to keep me warm; thankful Mother brought it with us when we evacuated our house. She had taken beautiful white curtains, which helped me feel somewhat at home in this foreign land. Eventually, we made it to our destination.

"Alright everyone, you know what to do," Edward whispered loudly, the moonlight reflecting in his dark gaze.

Swiftly, we bent down and dug through the snow until we discovered bags containing barley grain. We hit them with sticks, and since it was frozen, the grain poured quickly into our bundles. We didn't take everything, just enough to keep us alive another week or two. When Edward signaled us to start moving again, we quickly left.

The way back didn't seem as long and arduous. We marched once again in a single file to get back to our barracks as soon as possible. No one talked, and the night was quiet, our footsteps were the only sound. We were more than happy when our barrack was in sight and even happier when we laid down on our haystacks. Smiles crept up our lips, and I'm sure many regretted not being able to express their glee outwardly. For the first time since we got here, joy filled the room.

"We did it!" Edward whispered, and his joy contaminated all who were still awake.

That night was a small victory, and the first one that really mattered to us.

The next day, Mama cleaned the barley grain and crushed it with stones. She then cooked it, and it was a nice change from the dry bread we usually ate. She didn't use all of it and stored some. I learned in Siberia the importance of keeping food for tomorrow.

"Mama, how is it that you know so well how to survive?"

She looked at me tenderly as I tried to understand where all her wisdom came from. We were losing our bulk and flesh by the day, but somehow Mama knew how to keep us alive.

"This isn't my first time going through a war." Mama squinted, as if she remembered a time that was far back in her memory, opening a box she wished she could have kept sealed forever.

"During the war of 1914, my family was taken to be sent to Siberia."

"Really? So you already came here before?"

Mama slowly shook her head, a faint smile stretching her lips.

"Thank God, no. The Russians were intercepted before they carried out their plan, but it was still a tough time."

Her eyes were sad, and I wanted to comfort her but didn't know how. Mama turned once again to look at me.

"War can really change people; for better or for worse. I want you to come out of here stronger and better. Wars already kill so many soldiers, and we don't need to let it destroy civilians too."

I didn't fully grasp what Mama meant but figured it out soon enough. Many were scarred by those troubling times, traumatized and transformed forever. Even if we weren't fighting on battlefields, we had to fight on the inside. Fight to stay alive, to stay strong, to stay sane. It was a long battle, and if it hadn't been for God and my Mother, I would've died, one way or another, in that abhorrent Siberian camp.

Janek finally got a day off - they had about two each month, and he came to spend time with us. He seemed different every time I saw him, growing and maturing at a frightening speed.

"You'll never guess what happened to me."

We all sat together in our barrack, enjoying one of the rare, fleeting moments of peace we could hope to get in such a place.

"This one time, I was bored and decided to carve a gun out of wood. I would work on it when I had free time during my shift. It was a small project to pass the time. I kept working and working until I finally finished it, and the final product was pretty good!"

"I don't believe that," Jadzia said, with a tone full of skepticism and sass.

Janek turned towards her and continued his story. "Oh, but it's true! And I got in trouble because of that gun. One of the other employees thought it was real and reported me. Then one morning, it's still quite early and I'm in bed when I hear violent banging on my door, and the next thing I know, two Russian soldiers stare at me with a menacing look."

He imitated the look they made, which did seem pretty menacing.

"One of them tells me to show him where my gun is, and I'm confused. Remember that I just woke up! I don't answer quickly enough, so he repeats his question in a meaner tone. Then I tell him I don't have a gun. He says someone reported that I had, and finally, I connect the dots and show him the replica I made. They were so amazed and could hardly believe it was a fake!"

Jadzia still looked a bit skeptical. Andrzej was simply full of admiration for his big brother being able to carve realistic guns. I wondered why he chose to carve a weapon out of all the things he could have made. I then remembered how he used to parade in Father's military boots and wield his sword. He would admire himself in the big mirror we had near the entrance, feeling proud like a peacock; I guess he always had that military itch.

"Where's the gun now?" Andrzej asked.

Janek shrugged. "The soldiers confiscated it and told me not to make any more."

Andrzej was disappointed; he really wanted to see the work of art.

"You better be careful," Mama said. "They went easy on you this time, but if they sense any form of rebellion or disobedience on your part, they could punish you much more severely. Look out for snitches too!"

Janek nodded. We were always watched, so one wrong move could mean the end for our family.

We were interrupted by a loud noise coming from outside. Alarmed, we rushed out of the barracks where others had already gathered, heads turned to the sky. They were focused on a plane passing by.

"We're saved!" said one lady, and her excitement quickly contaminated the others.

Everyone waved and yelled, trying to get the attention of the pilot.

"They came to free us! We're getting out of here!"

I started believing in the hope of leaving Siberia and frantically waved my arms over my head. We screamed as if our very survival depended on that plane landing; but it didn't land. The metal bird continued in a straight lane, not even noticing us at all.

"Mama! The plane didn't come," Andrzej said.

I also turned to Mama, searching for a faint hope to cling to.

"Maybe it'll come back or send people on foot to rescue us. I doubt it could land in this forested area."

We went back inside, convinced. We clung to her words like a revelation from God Himself with lowered heads, followed by many others. The plane didn't come back, nor was anyone ever sent on foot to rescue us.

A few more times, we snuck out at night to steal grain. Spring was afoot, so we went on our last nocturnal excursion. I had become accustomed to the thrill of our nightly escapades and thought I would miss them. The coming of spring didn't only mean the end of our venture. It also meant we had been here for about three months. We've spent three months living in cold and shame. Three months of scarce meals and sleepless nights. Our constantly frozen bodies were becoming more ragged each week, removing fat layers until all that was left was skin and bones. It was a horrifying spectacle to witness.

Our group continued our midnight excursions as we needed to; for food. We also learned we had an opportunity to find frozen potatoes left over in the fields from harvest time. The villagers did not like us trespassing on their land and set out every night to patrol their land and protect it from poachers. Mama and I would hide under the evergreen trees, where the very large lower branches spread out on the ground, and the space becomes an opening near the trunk. This is where we hid when the villagers on horses came by, because if anyone got caught, they would be fiercely beaten by the villagers with their horse whips. As soon as they passed, we sneaked on the same path they took but in the opposite direction, returning to our barracks.

During our last outing, we got caught. A woman from the nearby village spotted us. She was probably as frightened as we were, and no one moved for a few seconds.

Eventually, she spoke. "So you are the ones stealing our grain and potatoes."

She knew we were from the camp, which meant she could report us.

Edward cautiously stepped forward. "We only take what we need. This is our last outing."

My heart was pounding in my chest as I watched the events unfold. The woman shot us a glare, and her eyes landed on Mama. My chest felt tight, and I forgot to breathe. She marched forward, and everyone's senses were on high alert, ready to pounce if necessary. The woman came so close to Mama that only a few inches separated them. She raised her hand, followed by about ten pairs of eyes.

"These are nice."

The woman touched the buttons on Mother's coat and gazed at them with admiration. None of us moved, confused by what was happening. There was a short silence before she spoke again.

"We don't have this in the village. Many would like them."

She looked at Mother straight in the eyes, and they stared at each other for what seemed like forever, as if they were communicating in a language that didn't require words. I was totally confused, trying to figure out what I was witnessing. Mama slowly nodded, and satisfied, the woman left without adding another word, abandoning us with our perplexity.

When she was out of sight, Edward spoke first.

"What was that?"

Mama slowly turned to face her, a sweet smile stretched across her lips. "She's a very nice lady," she said, as if they had gotten to know each other after talking for hours.

I was able to pick up that she wouldn't report us to the soldiers, but I still didn't understand what had happened. Aware of the questions bubbling in our minds, Mama answered them without any of us pursuing the interrogation.

"She was hinting at the fact that I can sell these buttons in the village. She knows we need money to get by."

"So not only did she decide not to rat us out, but she even helped us? Wow. I didn't think I'd find such a nice Russian," Edward said.

Mother shot him a glare. "Not all Russians are bad. It's the government that is corrupt. Even with the soldiers, some of them can be kind."

I know she was thinking of the soldier who told Lydia about her never being able to see us again. I knew Mama was right, and we couldn't assume a whole nation was bad, but when our only encounter with Russians had been through soldiers and their orders, it was hard to think they could have a heart. We didn't stay there much longer and returned to our barracks. Jadzia seemed relieved when she saw us arrive.

"You took so long; I was scared something happened!"

"Something did happen. Something good." Mama didn't add anything and went to sleep.

Contrary to what I expected, we didn't stop sneaking out at night. This time, however, we were a much smaller group, and the weather was warmer. Prisoners were forbidden to go to the village, or else they would be shot on sight. So, the villagers and prisoners would meet in the forest at dark in secret. Mama cut out the buttons from our shirts and brought them to the meeting spot nearby to sell them. Just like the lady said, the villagers were amazed by the buttons. Their clothes were dull, so they were excited to see something so colourful. Mama decided to sell the beautiful white curtains too. I didn't know if I felt sorry for them being excited over such a trifle or if I felt bad for us having to cut out parts of our clothes just to get by. We made a bit of money that way, which helped us buy food from the camp. Eventually, there were no more buttons to cut out, so we stopped going to the village forest.

CHAPTER 4

Summer interlude

If winter was scarcity, summer was abundance. Food wasn't a problem during the hot season, as berries and mushrooms grew like weeds. It was hard to believe that only a month ago, snow was the only thing we could see all around. Now, healthy plants emerged from the unfrozen ground, and the grey sky finally adopted shades of blue.

As usual, Mama was a genius. She knew which mushrooms were edible and could discern between the weeds. It really was thanks to her that we were able to survive that frozen hell. The soldiers allowed us to go to the forest nearby since it was very dense and never-ending. They probably thought we could only get lost in there and die, so they didn't care if we went; It would just be one less problem on their hands.

I remember how eagerly we filled our bundles with the many berries we found in the woods. Fruit was the sweetest food we could get our hands on, so we valued it like gold. Summer brought hope, and hope brought ease to our constantly tired state. People smiled a bit more often, and even laughed at times. Our weariness seemed to fade just a little, and we could believe once again in a better tomorrow.

"We need to believe." Amelia, one of the refugees, looked at us with a glint in her eyes. Some women had gathered in a barrack to pray, since there wasn't much else to do.

"We need to believe God will save us. He will get us out of here and back to our homes!"

A few ladies acquiesced, and others barely moved. Amelia was as frazzled and shabby as the rest of us, but was distinguished by an aura surrounding her. She had charisma, and her words were convincing, so I was quick to imitate her in clasping my hands together and shutting my eyes tight.

"Pray ladies! Pray that God may help us!"

Right away, voices rose in frantic prayer. We clutched our rosaries in our trembling hands, and our lips rambled on and on, mumbling desperate pleas. Some held their tattered Bibles or holy pictures firmly; anything that could provide hope. During our moment of devotion, we were brutally interrupted by soldiers.

"What is this? What are you doing?"

The prayers stopped suddenly, and the ladies who were just a moment ago so bountiful in words now couldn't say any. The soldiers looked around at us in the only way they could: menacingly. Thankfully, Amelia had enough composure to answer them.

"We are praying to go back to our home country."

The soldiers immediately turned to look at her, still glaring. However, this time there was a hint of mockery in their eyes. Without them telling us, I knew they didn't believe we could one day go back to Poland.

"And praying to who, the devil? Don't you know there is no God?"

"It's OK," Amelia continued calmly. "We brought our own."

This time, the men were furious. In the span of an instant, they ruthlessly took away our rosaries and Bibles and broke them, with the beautiful beads spilling on the ground; they took away our hope.

"If we ever find you praying again, you will be harshly punished, and it will be your last prayer!"

With that, they abandoned us, trembling in our decrepit barrack.

The next day, one of the soldiers returned to see us in secret. He was alone and seemed vigilant. However, yesterday's events left us fearful and angering, so some ladies were ready to scream. Noting their intentions, the man quickly tried to calm them down.

"Ladies, please stay quiet. Please."

The desperation in his eyes immediately suppressed our agitation. He checked behind him, as if fearing a great danger and breathed a sigh of relief when he realized there was no one. He turned his attention to us, showing a serious yet concerned expression.

"I heard about what happened yesterday. And I know that your faith means a lot to you."

He spoke so softly that we almost had to hold our breaths to hear him properly. Again, his eyes nervously glanced at his surroundings before returning to us.

"My parents believe in God, and I do too."

Those were probably some of the most reassuring words I had heard in a long time. I felt less alone, as if we finally had an ally among the enemy.

"At home, we have an *ikona*[7], but it is hidden, so no one knows it. No one knows our faith."

There was empathy and gentleness in his tone, and for the first time ever, I felt I could trust a Russian.

"You can pray if you want, but it has to be in secret. I beg you to do as I say," he said, glancing behind him for the umpteenth time. "If you don't, I could also get in trouble, and the others will shoot me. So please, if you want to pray, do it in secret; pray in your mind and heart."

We simply nodded in unison at every one of his words. His uneasiness was palpable, and we fully understood the gravity of the situation. Seeing we were all willing to cooperate, a smile finally broke through his lips.

"You don't need to gather to pray. It can be alone, or with one or two people. God is everywhere, so He will hear you."

From that moment on, we only prayed in silence.

***

7   Holy picture

"I want to go! I want to go!" Andrzej wouldn't stop pestering me, so I finally gave in and let him join me on my mushroom-picking excursion.

"Fine! But if you get tired, I won't carry you!"

"Oh, come on! I'm almost ten years old. I can take care of myself."

I rolled my eyes; He thought he was so tough, yet he hadn't even lived a decade. But then again, our harsh conditions had strengthened all of us, so maybe I should have given him more credit.

We set out to the forest in search of all the edible mushrooms. I tried my best to remember the ones Mama showed me. We didn't need to add food poisoning to our list of problems. Our bundle was filling up nicely, and I wanted us to pick a few more before we headed back.

"Helena."

"What is it?"

"Helena, look!" My brother was tugging my sleeve, and I looked at him with annoyance.

"What?" I followed the direction his left hand pointed at and spotted a pheasant learning how to fly, its feathers flapping in hesitant and irregular motions. The scene was beautiful, but we didn't care about that. Only one thought popped into our heads: meat! I glanced at my brother, and simultaneously we nodded before carefully approaching the bird. Unfortunately, it sensed danger and started flying away.

My brother and I didn't need to say anything and immediately sprang into action. We ran towards the winged animal, eyes locked on our prey. It kept flying away but wasn't old enough to fly into the sky, so it stayed close to the ground. We ran after it as fast as we could. It had been so long since we last had meat, so we definitely weren't going to pass up such a delicacy!

We had reached the state of hunters, where our only desire was to seize our prey and enjoy every last bit of it. Our washed-out clothes floated over our rugged bodies. Youth and determination were the only explanation for this much energy; this much ferocity. Both the hunters and the hunted were desperate, so this was a battle of grit.

Andrzej and I chased that pheasant so long that it eventually grew tired, started slowing down and was finally captured by our triumphant,

grubby hands. Tears of joy welled up in my eyes as if this animal repre-
sented a seven-course meal. I wrapped it in some cloth so it wouldn't run
away, though I couldn't kill it.

"Quick! Let's go show it to Mama!" Andrzej said with excitement.

Somehow, we also had the energy to run back to the barrack.

"Mama! Mama! Look!"

Mother turned around, and her face lit up as she contemplated our
prize.

"Oh my! Did you two catch it?"

"Yes!" Andrzej said proudly. "We chased it in the woods!"

Mama was overjoyed at the fact that we would finally have some meat.
She took care of finishing off the bird and joyfully plucked it.

"I'll be able to use this for about a week or two!"

I was so pleased to have been able to contribute to our survival. Even
though Andrzej was the one who spotted the bird, I caught it! I had done
my part to allow us to live a little longer. Luckily, Janek had gotten a day
off a few days later and was just as delighted to eat some of the pheasant.
Mama would use its meat bit by bit and every part of its body; bones for
soup broth and meat for other meals, making our hunt last longer.

"I'm finally going to start working," Mama said with mixed feelings.

Her toe didn't hurt as much anymore, so she would help harvest hay.
Jadzia would help out too, reassured that Mama would be there. She was
fourteen now, and girls her age - or even younger - were already on the field
trying to get by, sending her away to work like Janek. I was sad Mother
wouldn't be able to spend as much time with us as before. She probably
sensed it; because she smiled at me.

"Don't worry, Hela. This is a good thing. We need to make as much
money as we can if we want to survive."

Everything was about survival here. Work was to survive. Money was to survive. Food wasn't supposed to be enjoyed anymore, but its sole purpose was to keep us alive. I learned early on that all my childish desires would be tossed aside to make way for real priorities. I learned to swallow the tears and bite down the pain. To keep quiet for all the words of frustration, sadness, and hurt. Bottled-up emotions were so dark that they could drive me crazy. But in this frozen hell, I still had my angel sent from God; My Mama.

"OK."

Mama nodded and went on to work, Jadzia following closely behind.

The next day I decided to do one of the only things I could do during summer: mushroom picking. I made a few friends in camp, but we couldn't do much since the soldiers constantly watched us. Even when we were outside, we couldn't gather because the Russians might suspect us of plotting something. That's why the only semblance of freedom we could get was in the forest.

"Hey, Adam! (Adam Miak, our actual neighbour from home!) You want to come mushroom picking with me?"

The young boy looked up, and his blue eyes pointed straight at me. He was two or three years older, but we got along well.

"Sure."

He wasn't going to pass up the opportunity of doing something productive with his day, so he went to grab a bundle and followed me outside. Before we left, I instructed Andrzej to wait for us in the barrack, as we planned to be back soon, and he simply nodded in response.

Adam and I chatted a bit on the way. It was always as if there was too much and not enough to say. We wanted to talk about our situation, but at the same time, we wanted to forget it at all costs. I was glad I didn't have to constantly blow on my frozen fingers to warm them nor feel goosebumps all over my skin anymore, but I was still thousands of miles away from the comfortable room I used to share with Jadzia, and we didn't have any news of Father either. Nonetheless, I tried to focus on the positive; at least one of our basic needs was met since we weren't starving anymore. Adam and

I picked a few mushrooms and were going to continue until something stopped us.

"That's…" I didn't finish my sentence, too horrified by the scene. A pony lay dead in front of us, its carcass fresh and blood still hot, dyeing the surrounding flora in red. Flies were circling it, eager to decompose this heap of meat. It was probably one of the most horrendous scenes I'd ever witnessed.

"I think a bear killed it."

Only then did I remember Adam was next to me, and immediately, my emotions rushed in.

"A bear?! I can't believe it! We have to get out of here!"

"Shhh! Be quiet. It could still be around!"

Painfully, I tried to hold back my scream, but I wasn't strong enough to keep the tears from streaming down my cheeks. Uncontrollable sobs escaped my lips, shaking my whole body. Adam came closer, trying to comfort me as best he could.

"Don't cry. It's OK. All we have to do is leave quietly, and we'll be fine, alright?"

I nodded, and he grabbed my hand. We quietly left the scene, but I was still very frightened. It took me a little while to calm down properly. Adam's warm hand and composure helped a lot. Neither of us had said a word since we left the carcass, so I decided to tell him a story to break the silence.

"Back in Poland, when I was around seven or eight, I always played with our closest neighbours. They lived in a big house, and I snuck out to play with their children. I always had a lot of fun there, especially because they had a hammock. One day, Mama found out and said she didn't mind me going there, but I had to tell her first. I continued until I played too long one day, and it was getting dark. I was scared she'd get mad at me, so I had to go through a forest to get back home, and I remembered how someone told me that we could see wolves at night because their eyes were shiny."

Adam paid attention to every syllable of my words, not interrupting me once. A shiver ran down my spine as I recalled the incident that followed.

"We had a lot of wolves in the area, so I kept checking my surroundings in case one came out of the forest. I ran quickly to get home as soon as possible, but then something happened. I fell into a ditch, and something was coming out of it. I was so scared that I nearly fainted. Later on, I realized I had fallen into a rabbit hole, and it was the rabbits who came out, but that night I thought a wolf or a dog had jumped on me, so I went home shaking. Mama got mad, and I was crying, trying to justify myself. She still punished me, and since that day, I never went to my neighbours' house in the evening ever again."

"Wow! That is a pretty scary experience."

Hopefully, Adam was able to better understand my fear of the forest and all the scary creatures it held. He then went on to tell me the story of when he got lost in the woods as a child, and his older brother had to come to find him. Speaking of being lost, we soon realized we didn't really know where we were going.

"We should have been back at the camp by now!" I said with a trembling voice.

Adam pondered quietly, which confirmed that he also didn't know where we were. Since he was the older one, I relied on him, but now we were both clueless. The thought of getting lost in the forest brought back the fear I had just tranquilized. Another flow of tears rushed down my cheeks, following the streaks their predecessors left.

"This is exactly what those stupid soldiers want, for us to get lost in the forest and die. No wonder they allow us to come here!"

Adam hugged me tight and caressed my back to calm me down. "Don't worry, Helena, we'll get out of here. I promise."

His soothing voice brought a stop to my sobs. His rugged hand brushed my rosy cheeks, wiping away the fat tears which had left my face damp and crestfallen. At that moment, I looked up and noticed his calm smile.

"We'll get out of here," he repeated with more assurance this time.

I nodded and followed him. He held my hand a bit tighter, and I could sense his determination to return to the barracks. Then suddenly, he stopped walking.

"What's wrong?"

Adam signaled me to be quiet, and I obeyed. All my senses were alert, and I feared he heard a wild animal. As my body already started shaking, a smile crept up his face.

"Water!" he declared, all proud.

I didn't understand, and he didn't give me time to. He guided me through the forest, until we reached a small stream of water. I still didn't understand why he was so excited.

"Don't you get it? Water always goes down the hill, so if we follow this stream, maybe it will guide us back to the camp."

I smiled, happy to know we finally had some way of knowing where to go. We walked for a while, following that stream of water like the road to heaven itself. I was getting tired, but I tried to ignore my fatigue because I had to focus my energy to get back. To pass the time, I decided to continue talking about my life in Poland.

"You know, back home, we had a lot of orchards. Maybe 120, no, 150, and they were huge! There were fields of wheat, barley, and oats. We had horses with stables, and barns with chickens, turkeys, and pigs. We had a lot of lands and a nice big white house!"

Adam listened quietly, also pleased to be distracted in some way.

"We had cows and chickens like most people, and we also had a nice house by Lake Świtez. In the summer, we would rent it out to tourists. Some of them were really nice. I remember a couple from Warszawa who rented two rooms then, and every morning whenever Mama opened the barn, a rooster would run out and sing right next to their window. I thought it was funny, but the man didn't like it and complained, so Mama stopped opening the barn."

By the time I reached the end of my story, we had arrived at a road! We looked both ways, hoping to find some clue to guide us, but there was nothing.

"Now what?"

"Hmmm…" Adam pondered again, scratched his head, and looked from side to side. There was absolutely no indication whatsoever of where we were nor where we had to go. He decided to take a wild guess.

"I say we go left."

I knew he wasn't sure, but I didn't have a better idea, so once again, I followed him. We had been walking for a long time, and I became very tired. Also, the weight of the mushrooms slowed me down.

"I think I'll need to leave some behind."

Adam looked at me with hesitation. He didn't want to leave food behind, and I felt the same way, but all these mushrooms were too heavy for me, and his bundle was already more than full.

"Alright then," he simply said.

Reluctantly, I took out a couple of mushrooms from my bundle and threw them on the ground. I knew how precious food was during these harsh times, so it really pained me to throw some away. I tried getting rid of as few as possible, convincing myself I could carry the rest. This was also an opportunity for us to take a short break since we hadn't stopped moving since we realized we were lost.

"Ok, let's continue," Adam said once I finished.

We had never been so eager to return to our barrack. At some point, we came across a woman picking wild strawberries with her children. Perplexed, she stared at us, obviously surprised to see two kids wandering around in the forest.

"Children, where are you going? Where are you from?" she spoke in Russian.

"We are from Kubalo," Adam replied. "We got lost in the forest and can't find our way back."

"Kubalo?" The woman shook her head and pointed in the direction we had just come from. "You are going the wrong way. Kubalo is over there."

We were annoyed that we have to retrace our steps but also happy to finally receive real directions.

"Thank you," Adam replied before we set off.

Then he turned towards me, smiling once again. I didn't know how he could keep smiling when I felt like my legs were about to fall off.

"Just a bit longer, Hela. We're almost there." His optimism was contagious and gave me the motivation I needed to finish this long journey. We walked and walked, until the decrepit barracks came in sight. We were as happy as we were exhausted when we finally made it to our lodgings. However, when I arrived I found Andrzej sitting on the floor, crying.

"Andrzej, what's wrong?"

As soon as he saw us, a huge smile spread across his lips. "Hela! You're back!"

I had never seen him so overjoyed to see me again. He hugged me tight, and in one breath told me all that had happened while I was gone.

"We received a parcel from Poland, but I couldn't tell anyone because they were all gone and I was waiting for you to come back, but you were taking so long, and I got worried!"

I ruffled his short blond hair, and he didn't stop me, simply laughing like any nine-year-old should.

"Well, what are we waiting for? Let's open this parcel!"

CHAPTER 5

Liberating news

Winter returned too quickly, and our moods dropped in sync with the temperature, foreboding about the upcoming cold season. Before we knew it, the sky readopted its grey tones; the setting we found when we first came to Siberia rapidly settled back in. My mind was troubled at the thought of scarce meals and icy nights. It then started to snow, and snow and snow. The healthy green grass was completely covered by a heavy white blanket; Winter was here.

We relied heavily on the parcels my Aunts sent us; that little bit of food, combined with Mama's survival skills allowed us to see tomorrow. Their letters also helped keep our hope alive. Unfortunately, they never talked about the political issues in Poland, most likely out of fear of punishment. Because of that, we were completely cut off from our homeland. We had no idea how the war was progressing or if Poland could regain its freedom and independence. We blindly prayed, ignorant of the situation outside our, once again, frozen prison.

Matters got worse when the parcels grew scarce. We hadn't received anything for about a month now, and our food stock was running low. We also hadn't received any money from Janek, and Mama didn't work in the winter. All in all, things looked pretty dire. We had no idea that the Russians closed the borders because of this and all related information was kept secret from the prisoners.

One day I found Mother crying in our barrack, sitting on one of the shelves.

"Mama, what's wrong?"

She looked at me with eyes full of sorrow. 'Oh Hela! What am I going to do? We have no food and no money to buy bread!"

Despair was evident in her tone, so I could sense the gravity of the situation. My Mama had always been a strong, dedicated, and hard-working woman. She was my hero, and I felt like having her by my side meant I could overcome anything. However, she seemed so broken and devastated; it made me panic.

"It's OK, Mama. We'll figure something out."

It was at that moment I noticed a patch of white hair growing on the side of her head. Had it always been there? I couldn't remember. Now that I looked at her well, she seemed much older. Mama was only 36 when we were brought here, but now seemed to be in her late forties. I realized then how much stress must have been put on her since the beginning of the war. She had to take care of her four children alone, somehow finding food and clothes when there were barely any available.

I hugged her tight, trying my best to comfort her. Mama always lent us her shoulder to cry on, her ear to listen, but who was there for her? At eleven, I realized parents give everything to their children, but children don't give much in return. We stayed for a long time in that position, and my Mama was crying like a baby as I cradled her head in my arms and held her hands in comfort. Mama needed to be vulnerable, to let out the feelings she bottled up in order to tend to our needs. Nothing existed outside of this moment, where all I wanted to do was console her.

That night, it took me a long time to fall asleep. My mind was troubled by a thousand thoughts, and I really wondered if we would still be able to make it out alive. *Please God! Please help us!* It was the last thing I thought of before dozing off.

My prayers were quickly answered, as we received an unusual request from the soldiers a few days later.

"Mrs. Fąfara, we need you to deliver this document to the nearby village. We'll pay you for this errand, of course"

My Mother blinked in surprise, clearly not expecting such a request. The soldier speaking to her was the one who had told us to pray quietly. There was no malice in his voice, and I believe he truly wanted to help us. Since Mama hadn't gone to buy bread for a few days, he probably figured out it was because she didn't have the means to.

"Well, I wouldn't mind going but…" Mama regretfully looked down at her leg. "I have a problem with my toe, so it's hard for me to walk. Oh! But maybe Jadwiga can go?"

My sister immediately shook her head left and right.

"No way! It's too scary to walk through the forest alone."

Mother was visibly disappointed, but Jadzia didn't care. I then remembered how we seldom did anything for our Mother, so I stepped forward. "I'll go."

Everyone looked at me in surprise.

"No, you can't. You'll get lost in the forest. And besides, you're only eleven." Mama completely disapproved of my going, but the soldier interfered.

"Don't worry, I'll show her the way. It's really not that complicated."

"But…Hela is so young!"

"Mama, I'll be fine. I can do it!"

I smiled at her, hoping to offer some relief. She still didn't want to let me go, but we also needed the money, so her hands were tied. After a short pause, she sighed heavily.

"Fine. But you really have to be careful, Helena. You have a good head on your shoulders; use it. Don't fool around and follow the soldier's directions precisely!"

I nodded and prepared to depart.

"All you have to do is stay on the path, and you'll eventually see the village lights."

I nodded once again and left. It was pretty chilly, so I found some extra layers. Now that I was alone in the forest, my bravery was slowly fading away, and I started regretting volunteering for this errand. Why couldn't Jadzia have a bit more courage and go herself? At this point, all I had to do was to get over this.

I stayed on the path like the soldier told me, but I had walked for a while already. I then remembered my outing with Adam back in summer, when we got lost in the forest, and that fear came back to haunt me. The village was farther than the man made it seem, and I became tired. The cold wind nipped at my ears, and the wind was strong, but I was wearing a big scarf over my head, and at least walking kept me warm.

Eventually, I made it. I saw lights from afar, which gave me a renewal of strength. Houses began to appear, and I rejoiced all the more. Once I arrived in the village, I asked around to know where to bring these documents, and was redirected to the police office.

"Ah yes," said one of the police officers. "Dimitri told me someone would bring these. Wait just a minute."

The man left, and I stood still among all these Russians in uniforms. They didn't seem to notice me though, because they were too busy with their own tasks. After a short while, the officer came back with a letter and a bundle.

"Here. You'll deliver this letter back to your camp. And this is for you."

I opened the bundle and was pleased to discover bread, dried meat, and barley grain. The officer winked before letting me go. Surprised and relieved by his kindness, I left with a skip in my step. Well... I was skipping until I made it back to the forest. It was dark now, and the dense woods seemed even more daunting.

I walked quickly and carefully, following the path as if my life depended on it. I feared for bears, and the traumatizing image of the massacred pony flashed in my mind. At that moment, I didn't know if my brain played tricks on me or if I really heard strange sounds. It sounded like a squeaking noise, and I was too scared to imagine what could have made it. I kept my mouth shut and tried to walk quietly, but then I heard something crack behind me.

"Who's there?!"

I turned around furtively, seeing only creeping shadows in the night. All of this was too much for my eleven-year-old heart, so without a second thought, I booked it! My legs sprinted as fast as they could, and in my race, I lost my hood but didn't care. The only thought that occupied my mind was to get back to camp.

Out of breath, I walked the remaining way back to the barracks. Thankfully, I wasn't too far and was thus able to return quickly, only to find Mother in tears.

"Mama, what's wrong?"

She promptly turned around, her eyes open wide at my sight. "Hela! You're back!" She rushed towards me and hugged me tight, still sobbing. "I was so scared! You were gone so long I feared you got lost."

"Don't worry, Mama. I told you I'd be fine!"

I smiled at her, and she smiled back. I then showed her the bundle I brought back, and her smile grew even larger. We then brought the letter to the office, and as promised, the soldier paid us for our errand. Mother was so happy she kissed me, kissed the money, and danced around. I had never seen her so… expressive! She almost seemed crazy!

"We can buy bread now, Hela! We can survive a bit longer!"

"Yes Mama!"

Survival, that's all that mattered. Surviving one more week, one more day. That money certainly came in when we needed it most.

***

"School?"

"Yes. The soldiers just announced that they had finished building another barrack to be designated as a school. All children under sixteen need to attend."

Mother didn't seem pleased to give us the news, and we weren't happy to receive it either. I was indeed displeased that my studies had been interrupted, but I certainly didn't want to continue them under Russian influence. I still remember how everything had been converted to Russian after they invaded us.

"But the village is far, and we don't have the proper shoes for that."

"Jadzia is right. It's very cold now, and we won't be able to walk those long distances without proper shoes."

Actually, my sister and I had boots we brought from Poland, but we outgrew them over time. Even if we were undernourished, somehow our bodies kept growing, so now those boots were too small.

"Then that means only Andrzej can go. He can wear your boots."

"What? But I don't want to go to school!"

"You have to! It's the soldiers' order."

My brother pouted in discontent, but Mother's decision was final. With that, Andrzej began going to school. He walked to and from the school barrack daily, so we only saw him in the morning and evening. He seemed so grown up, being barely ten and going off alone like that. I guess these harsh times didn't give him much of choice.

Just as I feared, everything was in Russian at school. I was glad I didn't go. Andrzej had to learn the language, the culture, and the history; All of it. It was almost as if they wanted to brainwash him in order to change his nationality to Russian. Thankfully though, he never forgot his Polish heritage.

Winter was not only harsh because of the frigid weather and scarce resources, it was also the season of diseases, and my siblings and I got sick with typhoid. It wasn't anything uncommon, considering the poor hygiene and horrible health conditions we lived in. Soon enough, Jadzia, Andrzej, and I had high fevers with bad rashes eating up our skin.

Thankfully for us, our Mama was still healthy and able to take care of us. I feared she might contract the disease, but she seemed immune to it.

"Back when my family was taken to be sent to Siberia, I got sick with typhoid, and I think it's something you can only catch once."

Her explanation satisfied us, especially since we desperately needed urgent care. Our bodies had been weakened by the bacteria, making it difficult to even walk. Therefore, we always needed to support ourselves when going from one place to another. I don't remember how long we were sick, but I remember it being painful. Also, there was a particular incident that scarred me.

I was laying on my bed, having nothing better to do, and noticed something strange on the shelf in front of mine. A lady sat there with her baby, and neither of them moved. In fact, they had been quite still for a while now. I then heard a weird squeaking noise. To my horror, two rats appeared and… were eating the baby's fingers! Shock paralyzed me, and it took a few seconds for the urgency of the situation to hit me in the face, so I started to scream!

"Mama! Mama!"

"What is it, Hela?"

"The baby! The rats!" I didn't know how to articulate my distress and simply pointed toward the infant. Mama looked over, and immediately, her eyes opened wide.

"Dear Lord…" Quickly, she shooed the rats away, but it was too late. The damage had been done, and the baby was now mutilated. However, that wasn't the worst of it.

"He's dead."

I didn't want to believe her words, but I knew she wouldn't joke about this. Nobody joked about death here.

"Actually, they're both dead."

"What? The mother too? But I thought she was sleeping. I thought they were both sleeping!"

Mama covered her mouth in order to hold back a sob. Her shoulders were shaking and so were mine. We had lost a lot of refugees so far, but witnessing this was simply too much. Uncontrollable tears rolled down my cheeks, and I just wanted to scream. To yell my frustration, my pain, my sorrow! So much had happened. Too much had happened! And I didn't know if I could handle it any longer.

It was also at that moment a thought popped into my head.

"Wait a second. Didn't this lady have typhoid?"

Mother simply looked at me, which confirmed my suspicion.

"Then if she died, does that mean I'll die too? Because I also have typhoid?" More tears welled up in my eyes, and Mama quickly hugged me.

"No, Helena! No way! You won't die here. I said we'd make it out alive, didn't I?"

This time, I wasn't so sure of her words. This lady died in front of us, and no one noticed. She suffered in silence and left this world unannounced, her baby following suit. What if I died the same way? Forgotten and abandoned? I would simply be added to this Siberian camp's long list of deaths.

"You won't die. You won't die Helena!"

The sound of her voice was like a lullaby rocking me to sleep. I started feeling groggy, and then everything went black.

Mother was right; I didn't die; We didn't die. Somehow, she managed to nurse us back to health, and we were as healthy as any undernourished children could be. I started taking part in our nightly escapades to steal grain again. The Russians had built more barracks elsewhere in Siberia, so some refugees were sent there. It was sad to part from those we got to know, but it also gave us more space in our own barracks, and we weren't packed like sardines anymore. Sometimes, we would spot airplanes and wave frantically at them, hoping they'd come to deliver us but all to no avail. Eventually, the cold-harsh winter turned into spring, and the faint glimmer of anything positive was in view.

Then one day, we received shocking news.

"From now on, there will be no more letters and parcels coming from Poland!"

"What?"

"How come?"

"No more letters?"

Confusion arose among the refugees, and the soldiers quickly silenced us. They didn't provide explanations as to why this sudden change occurred. As a result of this, many speculations emerged in the barracks.

"Maybe there was some sort of revolt in Poland, so this is a way to punish them?"

"Or maybe the post office was attacked?"

"Whatever the reason, something big must have happened."

I didn't know who to listen to, so I turned to the one person I had trusted since the beginning of this nightmare.

"Mama, why do you think we can't receive letters and parcels anymore?"

She pondered my question for a while before answering. "I think the Soviet Union is afraid, and that's why they are tightening their regulations. I'm just not sure what - or who - they are afraid of."

We had been kept in the dark since we were brought here, and now more than ever, we were desperate to know what was going on in the outside world. Was Russia losing the war? Was Poland getting back on its feet? Were we going to be liberated soon?

Though we wanted to stay positive about this turn of events, we couldn't hide our sadness. From now on, we had no way of communicating with our families back home. Not only that, we had lost a precious means of survival.

"I won't lie to you, children. It will be tough now that your Aunts can't send us food anymore," Mama said, looking dismal, and her stress was palpable.

The patch of white hair on her head seemed to grow more and more. At least now, it was summertime, so we could still eat berries and mushrooms, but we didn't know how much longer we'd be here. Once winter came again, our resources would be scant. Little did we know, however, we wouldn't spend another winter in the Kubalo camp.

Weeks went by without us receiving anything from Poland. We kept ourselves busy with our usual activities, unaware of the developments of the war. Things were getting worse for the Russians, though we had no way of knowing. A major turning point was about to happen. Then one day, the soldiers gathered us outside to make an announcement.

Everyone was jittery, expecting more bad news. Agitation was apparent, and we were all anxious to find out why we had been summoned. Finally, one soldier stepped forward to give us the explanations we had impatiently waited for.

"Certain events happened lately, and now the USSR needs more fighters. We have signed a pact with the Polish Government-in-exile, which agreed to give us soldiers if we free their families. That being said, whoever is able to fight will be enrolled in the army, and their family will be able to leave the camp[8]."

There was a short pause, quickly followed by a commotion. Mixed emotions filled the people. Some rejoiced while others were angry. After many attempts, the soldiers calmed them down and explained that there

---

8   On June 22 1941, Germany launched Operation Barbarossa, the code name for their invasion of the Soviet Union. The U.S.S.R. was not prepared for the attack and suffered great losses. They seeked the help of the Polish Government-in-exile, promising to release their men if they joined the Red Army. Many negotiations took place, and on July 30, 1941 the Sikorsky-Mayski agreement was signed, which also stipulated that the families of military members be released from Siberian camps.

were two reasons for them to stay in the camp: either they weren't in the army or didn't have a family member in the army.

After that, we all returned to our barracks, holding heated discussions all the way back.

"I will never fight for these Russians! Why should I help the enemy?"

"You're right! I won't go risk my life for those who ruined it!"

"But don't you see? This is our only opportunity to make it out of here!"

Opinions diverged, and there was a lot of back and forth. I stayed close to Mama, asking her what we should do.

"We're going to leave, obviously."

"But we don't have a family member in the army. We don't know where Tata is, and Janek and Andrzej are too young."

"You're right about Andrzej, but not Janek."

She looked at her eldest son, who had also come for the announcement, and smiled.

"You're 19 now."

He was confused at first, but then simply nodded. Janek accepted this call as he stepped up to the plate and responsibility of the Eldest Boy. It was his duty to fill in when Tata was gone. I then remembered that we didn't have any papers, so it was easy for my brother to lie about his age. With that, Janek enrolled in the army, and soon enough, we were packing our bags to leave, imitating many others who would finally escape from this camp. That year, fall didn't bring dread of the cold, but rather hope for the future. It was as if spring came for a second time. With God's Grace, our family's survival trajectory came to be.

Part 3

Iran

Uzbekistan & the Caspian Sea
to Pehlevi-Persia-India

CHAPTER 6

Road to nowhere

Though the Soviets had now set us free, they gave us no means to travel. Since we had been brought to Kubalo, the closest train tracks were about 200 kms away. Over time, more tracks had been built, but there was still a considerable distance to travel on foot before we could hitchhike a train and hopefully sneak a ride for lack of any money for tickets. Another problem was deciding whether or not we wanted to leave. Mama had made it clear that this was our chance to escape this frozen hell, but not everyone felt the same. We either left for uncertainty or stayed put and continued to live through our inhumane conditions.

Not everyone was fit to travel either. The past year and a half had weakened many of us, to the point where some families were torn apart, having to leave a few members behind. There was a certain family, composed of a mother, a son, and a nephew, that would have suffered the same fate if Mother hadn't intervened. Mama was like that, she always thought of everyone and cared for all.

Soon before our departure, I found Mama and Nella, our neighbour and friend, talking.

"What am I going to do? My son can't walk, but I don't want us to stay here!"

Mom rubbed Nella's back the same way she did when comforting her children. "Don't worry. I'll find a solution."

"What solution! It's about 200 km to travel on foot. Dominik will never make it."

More tears flooded Nella's cheeks, and her nephew sat next to her in the barrack to console her; the scene was heartbreaking. Nella's son had a severe handicap preventing him from walking, so now she was torn about what to do. I doubt she would have the courage to leave her son behind, but then again, did she have enough strength to carry on in this place? Mom kept trying to reassure her, saying she'd help her and that everything would be alright. Either Nella truly believed her or simply ran out of tears because she stopped crying.

"Mama, I overheard your conversation with Nella earlier, and I was wondering..." I stopped packing the grain we had and looked at her. "How are you going to help her? You can't carry her son all the way to the train tracks."

"You're right. I've become too weak for that."

"Then how?"

I still couldn't understand Mama's behaviour. This was a crisis and everyone had to care for themselves. However, I knew Mama's mind was not changing whenever she decided to help someone. She was working on making shoes for Jadzia and me, out of the bark of a birch tree, and suddenly, she stopped in her movement.

"This has to stay between us, alright?"

Andrzej and Jadzia were also with us, and suddenly became very interested in Mama's words.

"Right before the war, my brother came to visit us from New York in America. Do you remember?"

We all nodded in unison.

"Well, he gave me something before he left." She pulled three gold coins out of God-knows-where.

"What the..? Since when did you have…?"

Mama didn't let Janek finish his sentence.

"Shhh! Keep quiet. Everyone is on edge right now because of the news we received, and I don't know what some are ready to do to get their hands on this."

Indeed, I had grown weary of some refugees. In a crisis, people could become unpredictable, so we always had to be on our guard, not only of the soldiers but also of our own people.

"I'll use one of the coins to rent a sleigh and horse. Nella's son will be able to rest on it while the horse pulls him to the train station."

"Why didn't you tell us you had this?" Jadzia asked, feeling betrayed.

"It wasn't the right time." was all Mama said.

"Don't think wartime is when you only think of yourself. Instead, it's when you have to think of others more than ever. It's by helping each other that we'll make it out of here, not by being selfish."

With that, my sister didn't add another word, and we continued to pack silently.

Departure day arrived, and we finally left the camp; For good! I couldn't describe the joy I felt when I walked away from that prison, knowing I wouldn't ever have to go back. Siberia really changed me; Changed us. Some for the better, and some, unfortunately, for the worse. Nonetheless, we were out. Mama had fulfilled her promise. We all made it out!

Behind me, I left frigid nights and frozen tears. Waist-high snow and grey skies. No more fingers turning blue, heavy coughs brutally waking us from our precious sleep, 600g of dry bread carefully broken into four pieces so as to not waste a single crumb. No more rats running around the barracks or soldiers' mocking tone and ruthless orders. No more solitary and silent prayers to avoid reprimand. No more frozen hell. All of it was to be buried in the most profound corners of our memory.

We were like the people of Israel leaving the oppressing Egypt for an unknown land. Many families had been broken over there. Groups of five had become groups of two, or maybe only one survivor remained. We marched on with mixed feelings. Happy to leave, but sad about what we left with or without. Nella hadn't stopped thanking Mama for her kindness. Her son Dominik, who was heavily handicapped, was able to journey with her, sitting comfortably on the sleigh she rented. Surely, Mama was an angel sent by God.

"Mama?"

She lowered her gaze to look at me.

"I understand why you wanted to help Nella, but I don't understand why you chose to help just her. Is it because she shared our barracks?"

"Not necessarily."

"Then why? I know we should help each other, but there are too many people to help."

"That's true, and I know I can't help everyone. But it doesn't mean I shouldn't help anyone."

I paused for a second, pondering her words. Mama always had a big heart, ready to give and sacrifice herself for others. She had also gone through WWI, so maybe that's what made her the woman she became; Strong and supportive of others. She was more aware than I of how powerless she was to help every suffering person. However, that didn't stop her from lending a hand; I really admired that.

As a child, I didn't know who led our group nor how they knew where to go. I simply followed the multitude. Mother had made dresses out of potato sacks for my sister and I since our old clothes no longer fit us. There were thousands of refugees who left Siberia. Some decided to go their own way, but there weren't many different routes, so a vast majority of us ended up journeying in the same direction. We also had to walk in birch tree shoes, which weren't comfortable at all. We spent the whole day on the road, thousands of us trekking to better lands. It was very tiring, so Andrzej and I took turns resting on the sleigh next to Dominik.

The trip was extremely arduous, and because of our withered state, many didn't make it to our destination. It was the same as when we were on our way to Siberia; bodies were tossed on the side of the road because they had succumbed to the harsh weather and starvation. A lot of us were sick or getting there. Coughs were our chants, sneezes our hymns, tears our lullabies and shivers our dances. It was a horror show to watch children clutching bundles thicker than themselves, women constantly foraging to the point where they had bags under their eyes, and men collapsing as soon as we stopped to rest for the night.

For weeks, we followed the same cycle. We walked all day, stopped by a village at night, begged for food and shelter, and then headed out again the next morning. The whole thing was exhausting, especially for us children. The road and the snow were all we knew, along with bits of food and diseases ready to pounce and kill; Dysentery, typhoid, and swelling were the common killers. Now that the soldiers weren't there anymore to threaten our lives, a load of other issues arose to complicate our situation. Each day was a battle to be won in this never-ending war. We woke up in the morning to make it to the evening, and at dusk, we fought traumatizing nightmares, eagerly awaiting the dawn. We left villages with a slice of bread or two potatoes. Just enough to sustain us until our next stop.

Anxiety arose, and many of us wondered if leaving Siberia was the right choice. All the soldiers had told us back in Kubalo was that the trains would bring us to the south of Russia. We didn't know what would await us there, and if it was worth all the casualties. Being such a huge group, food was scant, so we stopped in villages in order to replenish our resources. The villages weren't far from each other, but the heavy snow slowed our pace, which prolonged the journey. Finally, we saw lights and smoke, and we all breathed a long sigh of relief.

"Come children. Let's hope God favours us and incites the villagers to be generous."

Andrzej, Jadzia, and I followed Mama, as we hadn't stopped doing since we left Poland. Her Russian was perfect, so she was our spokesperson.

"Please help us! We've been walking all day, and my children are hungry and tired!"

Mama would plead and beg until someone let us in their house. One lady was particularly nice and let us stay with her for a little while. She lived alone with her daughter, since her husband had passed away. I was surprised by how nice and welcoming Russians could be. Since the only ones I had encountered were soldiers, it was hard to have a good representation of them. But as we stopped in this woman's house and others later on, I realized the people weren't the problem; The government was.

"It is a tragic thing you went through, being brought to Siberia and locked in that camp. But then again, being here isn't much better."

"What do you mean?" Mother asked.

The woman sighed and took a sip of tea before continuing.

"No one owns anything here in this village (all of Russia because of communism), and everything belongs to the government. They have total control, even over the amount of food we eat. We can only receive a certain amount that is proportionate to the number of people in the house; everything is calculated."

I couldn't believe a government could be so controlling. However, it didn't surprise me much after spending nearly two years in Siberia. Even we were only allowed 600g of bread per day for the 4 of us.

"There aren't many crops either, so everyone's always hungry. It's hard to be happy and enjoy life when everything is so constrained. Yet somehow, we're managing. Maybe one day things will get better."

Mama came close and put her hand on the lady's lap. "They will."

She spoke with assurance, and we couldn't do much except believe her.

One day we all went into the village. We had decided to split up in order to find food more efficiently, so Mama and Jadzia went one way, and Andrzej and I went the other. As we walked, a young man I didn't know came to me. I have to admit he was quite good-looking too, so I wasn't very weary of him.

"Excuse me, but... do you have a brother?"

I understood Russian enough to answer him. "Yes."

"And is his name Ivan?[9]"

"Yes."

His traits loosened, and a smile crept up his lips.

"Ah, I knew it! You look so much like him!"

"How do you know my brother?"

"I was his supervisor at work when he was cutting wood at the barracks."

"Oh, OK. And where is he now?"

The smile on his face slowly disappeared, and I became weary. "Actually... there has been an incident."

"What do you mean? What happened to my brother?"

I was already prepared for the worse. The man scratched his head before he answered.

"Well... it's a bit of a long story, but he's in prison right now."

It took a little while for Mama to calm down after she heard the full tale. In addition, all of us were just beside ourselves in amazement, since we happened to meet that nice lady who took us in, and that she actually

---

9   Ivan is the Russian translation of the Polish name Janek

lived in the exact same spot where Janek was. This certainly was created by the hand of God. How on earth could this coincidence be??

"So let me get this straight. Janek was accused of cheating on the amount of wood he cut by saying he cut more than the actual amount he did, and because of that, they put him in jail?"

"The man said it's a *temporary* jail. Just until his superiors figure out what happened."

Mama let out a long sigh. We hadn't seen Janek for many weeks. It had been a very long time since they reunited, and the fact that the family happened to walk to the same area as Janek was a miraculous Heaven-sent co-incidence. Now that we finally received news of him and knew that he was imprisoned, I showed Mama where he was detained; It was in an isolated building without too many guards.

"Did you see the huge opening under the door? It's letting all the cold air in. My son must be freezing!"

"The man I spoke with told me he didn't believe Janek cheated the amount of wood. It was probably some other worker, but they blamed him because he's the youngest."

"In that case, he should be released soon enough."

Mama decided to do whatever she could to help her son, and the first thought that came to mind was to feed him. The guards most likely didn't give him much attention, so he must have been quite hungry. Mama made him some slim pancakes using only water and flour.

"Do you think you could sneak them to him, Hela?"

She knew I was the brave one, and I accepted the mission right away. I crept to where he was detained. Sure enough, there were no guards.

"Psst! Janek! It's me, Helena." I quietly knocked on the wooden door with my frail knuckles.

"Helena?"

It was the first time in a while I heard my brother's voice.

"Yes. We heard about what happened to you."

"I didn't cheat the amount, Helena! You know I wouldn't do that!"

"Don't worry. Your supervisor said he also doesn't believe you're the culprit. The guy who did it probably just blamed you since you're the youngest."

I heard him sigh of relief, and then I remembered why I came. "Here. Mama made you these." I slipped the pancakes under the door, and he took them.

"Thank you so much! I was wondering if the supervisors were really trying to sort my case out or just wanted me to freeze or starve to death."

"We'll stick around for a little while to see how things go. I'll try to come back."

"Thank you, Helena."

Though I couldn't see him, I knew he was smiling. I stared at the door for a bit, as if hoping to see my brother's face through it, but then remembered I had to leave before a guard spotted me. With that, I went back to join the others.

As we hoped, Janek's supervisor testified for him, and soon enough, he was released. The real culprit was also found and arrested. From there, Janek journeyed with us. We continued to travel from village to village until we finally arrived at the train station. Janek asked around about Tata, hoping he was also part of the thousands of refugees heading south; but to no avail. We decided not to waste more time and boarded the train. Mama had already used her second gold coin by then, though I can't remember what for. That meant she only had one left, and she used it to buy train tickets.

"It seems we have a problem," she told us as she returned from the ticket booth.

"We sure do," Janek said. "We can't find Andrzej."

"What?"

We looked around and realized our youngest sibling wasn't with us, nowhere to be found.

"My boy! Where's my boy? Andrzej! Andrzej!"

We all walked around the train station, yelling and searching. The train was about to leave, which only made our worries grow.

"Please! Could you wait just an extra five minutes? I can't find my son."

The conductor looked down upon Mama and let out a grunt. "We leave at 2:30 sharp."

"But my son..."

"2:30!"

It was hopeless; no one was going to wait for him. Jadzia's anxiety quickly turned into frantic irritation. "Wasn't he with you? Why didn't you watch over him properly? Now look at the mess we're in. The train is about to leave, and we'll have to stay back for Andrzej."

Janek was clearly offended by her remarks.

"So you're saying this is my fault?"

"Yes! Why weren't you watching him?"

"Because I was asking about Tata!"

They kept arguing, which irritated Mama, but she didn't have time to scold them.

"Mama!"

She turned around swiftly, her eyes wide open. "Andrzej!"

He ran to us, his face beaming, a large bag flung upon his shoulder. Mama's mind debated between anger and relief. "Where were you?" she asked in a semi-reproachful tone.

"I was nearby and heard you all calling, but I couldn't come right away... Because of this!" He opened the bag just enough for us to see all the bread inside. We were as happy as we were astonished.

"Where did you get that? God Bless you, child!"

He raised a grubby index finger to his sealed lips. Mama was about to inquire further, but Jadzia reminded her the train was about to leave, so we quickly boarded. I was disappointed to see that there were bunk beds inside, since it reminded me of Kubalo and the cattle wagon in which we were brought to in Siberia. However, I was ready to endure almost anything to escape this Russia.

"I'm so glad we all made it safe and sound!" I said with a smile. "So, where are our tickets?"

"Yes, about that…" Mom looked down, and we became worried once again. "I only had enough money for three tickets."

"Three? But… we're five." Mama, Janek, Jadzia, me, and Andrzej (It turned out Mama used two gold coins for the horse and sleigh, and one was left; her generosity was that great.)

My heart started beating faster as I tried to understand what Mother intended to do. She came to Andrzej and me, looking us dead in the eye.

"You'll have to hide in the compartment on top. It's the only solution."

My brother and I didn't say anything and simply nodded. We were the thinnest of the group, so it'd be easier to stay hidden there. Nonetheless, I did not want to spend a whole train ride in a compartment. But what choice did we have?

Andrzej and I squeezed together in the tight space, and Mama was about to cover us with rugs.

"You absolutely cannot make noise, alright? And don't move either."

Once again, we nodded, then everything went black as she put the rug on us and closed the compartment. The train began to move, and we stayed as statues in our cramped position. We were both afraid to make any movement or sound whatsoever. Then at some point, we heard voices right outside the compartment. I could hear Mama's voice but couldn't make out what she was saying. Then the darkness was filled with light. The compartment opened.

We stayed still. However, when the rug was removed from us, we had to move. I was scared we had been found out, but instead of a conductor's angry face, I saw Mama smiling, tears in her eyes.

"Come down, my children. You don't need to stay there anymore."

"Did we already arrive?"

"No, not yet."

Andrzej and I were confused, so Mama explained to us what had happened.

"When the conductor came, he asked if we were *bezhentsy,* which means refugees, and I said yes. Then he told us we didn't need tickets because we could board for free."

I was glad to know I didn't have to spend the whole ride confined in the dark with my brother, but Mama didn't seem to share my joy.

"What's wrong?"

"Ah, well…" Silent tears rolled down her eyes, and I became concerned. "I just wish I knew that before I spent our last gold coin. It was kind of our last hope, you know? Now, we really will only have God to rely on."

Anything that could contribute to survival was precious, so I understood Mother's distress. I wrapped my arms around her in an effort to comfort her. "Don't worry. We'll all make it out alive."

She smiled at the familiar words.

The trains weren't much faster than we would've been on foot. It wasn't that the vehicle was slow, rather, we almost never got to ride it since the tracks were used for the military, leaving us on standby; Sometimes even for weeks! It was now February, so there were snow banks on both sides of the track and a constant shivery breeze. Thankfully, we were allowed to stay inside the train instead of freezing outside. Families were squeezed together on the bunks they claimed, trying to keep warm and make it through the journey.

We could see smoke from afar, meaning there were villages nearby. Mama and Janek went to beg for food, returning with meagre results. Once again, we were lucky to receive bread or potatoes. Just enough to make it through a day or two.

After a week of standby, the train was finally about to depart again. It was at that time some Jews tried to board.

"Could you please let us on? We've been walking for weeks and are trying to head south."

"No way! Can't you see the wagon's already packed?!"

"It's your fault we're in this mess!"

"Get lost!"

The moody passengers showed no compassion for the Jews seeking refuge. They only focused on their own problems, unable to see beyond their situation.

"Please! We just need a bit of food and a place to stay."

"Stay away, you filthy Jews!"

"We don't need vermin like you!"

"Please! We are human just like you! What does it matter that we're Jews?"

Anger had hardened their hearts and deafened their ears, so they were numb to these pleading strangers even though they were in the same situation as us. Those refugees were just like us, fleeing and scared. Yet the Poles in the train acted as if they were much better. At that moment, Mama and Janek returned from the nearby village.

"What's going on?"

I filled her in on the recent event, and she was indignant. Mama turned to face those in the train, her expression full of reproach.

"What is wrong with all of you?! For heaven's sake! Can't you see they are people just like us? You had the chance to come on this train, so give them that chance too."

No one dared defy her, and Mama didn't give them the opportunity to anyway. She turned towards the Jews, extending a welcoming hand.

"Come."

A smile crept on their lips, and they eagerly accepted the invitation. They were maybe five or six and squeezed into the already overly packed wagon.

"You must be hungry."

They nodded, and Mama unpacked a small loaf of bread from a bundle. It was the food she had just gotten from the village, and she gave it to them.

They seized it with their frail hands and ate it as though it was the world's last delicacy. No one said anything in the train. The other Poles watched the visitors with distance and scorn, clearly bothered by their presence. As for my siblings and I, we simply stayed on our bunk, waiting for the train to move. From my position, I noticed little black things crawling up the sides of the wagon.

"Mama, what's that?"

She looked closely, and her eyes widened. Mama then spoke with the Jews. "Do you have lice?"

They seemed alarmed, then ashamed, and then slowly nodded. They were probably afraid Mother would throw them away for that, but she didn't. Instead, she went to notify the other passengers so that they could watch out.

"What? You're telling me you brought in Jews full of lice?"

"Look at what you've done, Anna!"

In an instant, clamour rose again. The people were agitated and irritated after hearing the news, but the trip's fatigue added to their frustration.

"Throw them out! Throw them out!" they started chanting.

I was at a loss and looked at Mama to know what we should do. She stayed calm and didn't give in to the peer pressure.

"I will not throw them out. They need help!"

"Throw them out!" the people continued.

Mama ignored them and ignited the small stove in the middle of the wagon. (Each passenger cabin had its own coal stove to make central heating in the cold February weather) She then turned to look at the victims of this riot.

"I'll need you to remove all your clothes."

"What?" The Jews blushed, but saw that Mother was serious. "But… then we'll be naked."

She cracked a smile in order to reassure them.

"Don't worry. We all have the same bodies. I have a plan. Just trust me."

They still seemed a bit reluctant, but since she was the only person who had shown them any kindness, they decided to trust her. Slowly, they removed their clothes, revealing ragged and worn-out skins sticking close to exposed thin bones. They then went to take refuge in a corner of the wagon, trying to avoid curious and angry gazes. Mama put their clothes on sticks which she held above the stove. At that moment, lice started falling down one by one.

"Mama, the lice! Are they dying?"

"Yes, Andrzej. This is a trick I learned during the last war."

The heat killed the lice, and they all fell out until the clothes were completely cleaned. After that, Mama gave back the clothes to the Jews, who were more than grateful for what she had done.

"Thank you so much! Those lice were eating us alive!"

"Well, we've all been there. That's why we need to stick together during these tough times."

She gave a side glance at the people around her. The passengers had kept quiet since the lice died and now pretended they weren't furious just moments ago. The trip continued without too many incidents, and then finally, we made it to our destination: Uzbekistan.

CHAPTER 7

Across the sea

Pitchforks welcomed us to the Uzbek village. Angry faces stared at us menacingly, with furrowed brows and glaring eyes. The people yelled words we couldn't comprehend, accentuating our fear. Thrilled to have arrived from our hellish journey; had I known this sort of treatment awaited us, I might have preferred to endure our hellish trip a bit longer.

"We are just looking for a place to stay! A place to stay!"

Edward desperately tried to explain our situation, but it was no use. Every time he spoke, the villagers replied with shouts and pointed their weapons towards us to keep us at a distance.

"I can't understand what they're saying. I thought they spoke Russian, but clearly, this is another language!" Edward let out a long sigh, discouraged.

Due to fatigue, dark circles surrounded his eyes, and our current predicament exhausted him even more. We had come all this way seeking refuge, and now had to deal with this hostile group.

"What are we going to do now? We have nowhere else to go!"

"Maybe we should have stayed in Siberia after all. These people obviously want to kill us!"

"I told you all that we should have taken a different route!"

Clamour arose from both sides now, and the dispute quickly escalated.

"Everyone, calm down. Please!"

A few men tried to bring back peace, but people were too tired and irritated. Rough situations can really bring out the worst in people, so not many of us had patience left. Upon seeing that we argued among ourselves, the villagers were confused. I clung to Mama, because now I feared both the Poles and the strangers. It was in the middle of this chaos that a voice emerged from the opposing group.

"What is going on here?"

Some of us turned around, happy to hear the familiar sound of Russian. One of the villagers discussed a bit with his people before turning his attention to us.

"I'm so sorry this is the welcome party you received. There seems to have been a misunderstanding."

Edward stepped forward, quickly remembering the lines he'd been repeating since we got here.

"We are refugees and are looking for a place to stay. It'll just be temporary."

"Yes, I understand. For some reason, the villagers thought you were evil. Actually, they thought you were the devil's people! I have to admit they aren't used to strangers around here."

The devil's people? How could we, catholic Poles, ever associate with the enemy? The man turned around to speak to his group. I noticed them lowering their weapons and their shoulders easing up. After a few exchanges, he turned back to us with a smile.

"I explained to them you're just regular people, and that the only difference is language. Now, follow me. We'll see what we can do to help."

A few of us trudged cautiously, and the rest followed suit. The villagers didn't stop staring at us, as if we were aliens invading their territory. I know we didn't look that presentable, with our raggedy clothes and dirt-covered skin, but we were still human. Right?

As we walked through the village, I gazed around, discovering the new environment. Their houses were huts made of clay, and there weren't a lot of trees.

"Look, Mama! Look at their big cows!" I tugged at Mother's sleeve and gestured in the direction of a cow with big horns, which I thought fascinating.

"They are quite different from the ones back home," was all she answered.

The man brought us to a big church and told us to wait there. I felt more at ease being in the house of God. The building had no windows, and there were no chairs inside, so we were just standing around. Those who got tired simply sat on the floor.

"What's going to happen now?" asked Mama.

"I think the villagers are trying to figure out where to put us. After all, we are quite a big group of people."

I looked around and saw hundreds of Poles, clothes falling apart and skin hardened by the harsh weather and living conditions. Some still had enough strength in them to smile, but most just shivered in a corner, somber expressions stretching their faces where tears had long frozen and dried, leaving pale streaks on their grey tones.

Everyone was tired; exhausted actually. The constant uncertainty of our fate had consumed all our energy. We weren't living, just surviving, so we were desperate for any shelter, comfort, or reassurance we could get.

A few hours passed, and we stayed in that church until evening, trying to rest from our long journey. We were disturbed by a brutal knocking at the door at that moment. Everyone turned towards the entrance, alarmed and alert. I suddenly remembered the knocking that interrupted the last night I spent in my home in Poland. Did the Russian soldiers find us? Were they taking us back to Siberia?

The banging was followed by shouting, and our unease intensified. We couldn't understand what was being said, and were too scared to find out.

"I think we should block the door," Edward suggested. "The villagers already tried to kill us earlier, so maybe they still haven't eased up."

The others agreed and blocked the door and all the other exits using the pulpit and whatever other heavy accessory was in the cathedral. They also found axes - which were both relieving and alarming - and armed themselves in case they'd have to fight. Outside, the shouting continued.

"*Chlebo (hlebo) nada! Chlebo nada!*"

We had no idea what they were saying and imagined the worst. Many women were already on their knees, praying and crying. Children clung to them, fat tears rolling down their decolored cheeks.

"*Shhh!* Stay quiet!" some of the men whisper-shouted, silencing the others.

My heart was pounding heavily, its beat reverberating throughout my whole body, and sweat drops gathered on my forehead. I was scared to die. After all we'd been through, from the strenuous trip to Siberia to the horrible living conditions in the camp, finishing with the terrible journey we endured coming here, starved and frozen. Had we gone through all of that only to die here, slaughtered by aggressive villagers and their pitchforks? I clasped my hands firmly together, reciting every prayer I knew. "I will not die at twelve years old." "My life is far from over."

About an hour had passed, and we were more than fatigued by the pounding and shouting.

"I can't take this anymore! Let's just open the door and fight them like men!" someone said.

"Are you crazy? Our lives are at risk!"

"You're right, but I also think this has been going on for too long."

The discussion continued until the men agreed to open the door. Women and children stayed back, trembling. The huge doors opened, and we saw the villagers armed with...

"Bags? Wait. Is that bread?"

The villagers were happy we finally let them in, and they showed us the big bags of bread they had brought for us.

"So all this time, they were trying to bring us food?" Their words meant, "Do you want bread?"

A huge weight fell off our shoulders, and we all breathed a long sigh of relief. I couldn't believe we spent nearly an hour cowering in fear of... bread! It suddenly seemed so ridiculous! Later on, the man who spoke

Russian explained to us they weren't expecting so many refugees, so they put us in the church while they figure out how to provide shelter for us. Eventually, we all had a place to stay in the villagers' huts.

"Well, this is goodbye for now. Take care of yourself, OK?"

"Yes, Mama."

Mama's eyes filled with tears as she held him tightly. Janek left to join the Polish army in Italy under the English and American supervision. He was about to be sent to Italy, which meant we would now continue without him for a little while. Janek walked away in his uniform, looking more mature than ever.

"Next is your turn." Mama turned towards Andrzej, who was now around eleven years old.

The Polish government encouraged refugees to enroll their children in the army - or in the cadets if they were too young - as soon as they arrived in Uzbekistan. They feared Stalin wouldn't keep his word of letting civilians go. Mother, like thousands of others, enrolled her son in the cadets. Right away, he was sent to Egypt to be trained. The women were also told to enroll, but unfortunately there had been an outbreak of typhus among the female cadets, so the recruiting center was temporarily shut down, and only the women of the family remained. We had already left before they reopened.

We stayed in Uzbekistan for a few more weeks, and I got used to a certain routine. We were always hungry because we still didn't have much food. That's why nearly every day, I would pester the women in the village for something to eat. They used to make flatbread using special stoves. The bread clung to the top and fell down whenever it was ready.

I sat there in silence, with my eyes pleading. The women understood what I wanted without me having to say a word, which irritated them. They tried to chase me away, shouting what I guessed were insults in their language. I left, weary of their cooking utensils converted into weapons, and then came back a few moments later when they calmed down. Like a bird preying on someone's food, I kept coming back with my pleading eyes. Eventually, they would give me something just so I'd leave them alone. My mission was a success, and I went back to Mama and Jadzia with some flatbread. Whenever the women weren't so aggressive and had some compassion bestowed upon them, they'd send me back with a boiled egg. My little maneuver is what kept us alive for a few weeks.

I didn't only depend on those villagers, though. Near where we stayed was a military camp composed of Polish, English and American soldiers; It was just a few kilometers away. I had found an aluminum tea kettle to boil water somewhere, and every morning I went to the soldiers' camp with it, pleading for food. They weren't too stingy and usually gave me some bread and soup.

"I don't know how you can do that every morning, Helena. I'd never want to walk up to soldiers like that."

"Well, we can't both be cowards. At least I'm brave to help us get out of here, right?"

Jadzia shot me an evil glare, but I didn't care and went out as I usually did. Even if I talked big, I was pretty terrified of my daily trips. Since the war began, I grew to dislike men in army uniforms because I was never sure of their intent, even if they were supposed to be our allies. However, my hunger conquered my fear, giving me the courage to carry out my task each morning. On the way, I constantly prayed to God to protect me, and He definitely didn't let me down! Despite the fact that I was a young girl walking a long distance alone, and right into a camp full of grown and strong men, nothing bad happened to me.

That day, just like many others, I decided to walk close to some of the passersby. The Uzbek men usually walked around with donkeys, so I would walk not too close for them to be suspicious of me, yet not too far so people would think we were together and wouldn't attack me. I was both brave and careful.

"There she is! Our little kettle girl!"

I didn't understand English, and only half smiled in response when the English or American soldiers said something to me. Thankfully, there were also Polish soldiers, and it was easier to communicate with them.

"Always trying to get some of our food, aren't you?"

A shiver ran up my spine, and I was scared they might harm me for always soliciting them. However, my shoulders loosened when I saw one of the soldiers bring me a piece of bread. I was surprised, though, when I noticed it was much bigger than the usual amount. I stared at him, perplexed, and he winked before saying: "You might get hungry on the trip back."

As I returned to the village, I found Mother in panic. "Helena? Oh Helena, I'm so glad it's you!"

"What's wrong, Mama?"

"We have to go now!"

"Go?"

"Yes, the army trucks are here to take us! Come, we must go now!"

Confused, I let her drag me along a mad race to the trucks. Immediately we arrived, I noticed all the other refugees were already on board. We quickly found Jadzia, who was relieved to see us. We sat down, and soon enough, the trucks started moving. After Mama caught her breath, she explained what happened.

"This morning, not long after you left, Polish and English soldiers came to take us away. It seems as though the Polish government wants us to leave Russia as soon as possible because they fear Stalin might change his mind and keep us all captive. We had to leave right away, and I was so scared you wouldn't make it back on time, but thank God you're here!"

I still couldn't believe we were actually leaving Russia! That jail of a country would finally be behind us, so with each kilometer we travelled, we only made it closer to freedom, to a life that wasn't tainted by fear and anxiety. When we crossed the border, all the refugees cried joyfully. We were out, really out! I simply couldn't believe it.

"Oh, I almost forgot!"

Mama and Jadzia looked at me, puzzled. I pulled out the big piece of bread from my kettle and smiled.

"Are you hungry?"

We were brought to a military base as a pit stop before we continued our journey. Over there, we received real showers for the first time since forever! On the downside, however, our hair was cut in a close-cropped style to ensure we didn't have any lice. At this point, our vitality mattered more than our vanity, so we didn't care as much. Lastly, the soldiers threw out all our clothes, since they could be infected with diseases, and gave us new ones. Well, "new" is probably not the right term. They were all second-hand; donations, actually. They didn't always fit, but at least they covered our bodies.

As we were changing, something caught my eye.

"Look, Mama. Why does that lady have an apron?"

Mother glanced in the direction I was pointing, her eyes grew wide, and she scowled at me.

"That's not an apron, Hela!"

"It's not?"

I looked closely and realized Mama was right. What I thought was an apron was actually the dangling remnants of a previously fat belly. Once I realized I was staring at skin and not cloth, my cheeks grew red, so I quickly looked away. For some reason, that was an incident I still remember till date.

After we had gone through the disinfection process, it was time for us to leave. The soldiers put us on a huge ship that would sail through the Caspian Sea. We were thousands of refugees on that boat, and of course, very cramped. It wasn't sanitary, either. Rust ate up the walls, and a foul odour permeated the air. I wondered why they bothered cleaning us if we'd only end up in a place full of bacteria.

"Are you ok, Dziecko (child)?" Mama caressed my short hair, inquiring with a worried look on her face.

"Not really; I feel sick."

"Maybe you're seasick? Do you feel nauseous?"

"Yes, Mama."

I looked around at the boat, which didn't help because the sight of growing mold conquering dark corners and dilapidated walls covered in cracks with layers of dust only worsened my condition.

"This place is disgusting. Maybe that's what's making me sick."

At that moment, I spotted two rats crawling out of a hole and running into another one; This sent shivers up my spine.

"I know these aren't ideal conditions, but the soldiers are simply trying to get us to safety as soon as possible. Do you think you can bear it just a little longer?"

I looked at my Mama and noticed the dark circles around her eyes, and the patch of white hair on the side of her head. We were all in the same boat. Literally, what was hard for me was just as hard for her; Probably even worse.

"Yeah, I think I can."

She smiled faintly, then left to go find Jadzia. I stayed alone for a bit, or at least, I didn't talk to anyone. There were people all over, screaming, laughing, sleeping, and crying. Resting was hard for me, and my nausea only worsened. Sure enough, I felt the urge to throw up rise from my stomach and force its way through my throat. I looked around for something to contain my vomit, and that's when I found a... a bra?

I walked closer and realized that indeed, there was a woman's bra laying on the floor, no one seeming to notice it or care about it. I didn't have much time to inquire further about the reason it was there. I simply grabbed it and puked into one of the cups. I immediately felt much better, now emptied of whatever was upsetting my stomach. A few seconds later, a voice startled me.

"Did someone see my bra? I think it fell from my bag."

A woman I recognized was walking and looking around on deck. I lowered my head to see the vomit-filled bra in my hand which I knew was hers. She was quite an unpleasant lady, and most refugees didn't like her or her husband because they wouldn't stop complaining about everything; that's why I didn't feel bad about what I did. Since she was getting closer and closer, I quickly got rid of the evidence and threw it into the sea.

"Hey, you!"

She came towards me, and I was scared she saw what I had done. I was standing still, my skin tone getting paler and paler.

"Did you see my bra? I think I dropped it around here... unless someone stole it." Her voice had a lot of reproach, and I feared she was accusing me. I tried my best to remain calm and muster an answer.

"I didn't see it, Ma'am."

She looked at me dubiously before letting out an "Oh, OK" and moving on. I never told anyone about that incident, especially not Mama, because I knew she would scold me. It became a secret I kept to myself for quite a few years.

After a few days, our horrible cruise finally ended, and I was more than pleased to set foot on land again. We were dumped on the sandy shore with the night sky being the only roof above our heads.

"Where are we now, Mama?"

"I believe this is the seaport of Pahlavi,[10] (beach/sea port, once known as Persia in 1942- Iran."

"Persia?"

The name itself sounded too exotic and foreign for me to imagine setting foot in such a place. The sandy beach was filled with thousands of refugees. We exchanged the Siberian snow banks for the Persian sand banks. I didn't complain. As a matter of fact, I wasn't the only one rejoicing about this change in environment; many refugees kissed the ground as they landed, enjoying their first taste of freedom. We were set free from the clutches and chains of the Russian. A new world lay before us. A new life was possible.

We were marveled by the food stands and warm welcomes of the locals. It felt like we wouldn't just survive here, but actually live! However, I noticed the glare in some of the refugees' eyes, speculating everyone as a potential enemy. There were those who still - somehow - possessed something, so they guarded it with their lives. Most of us didn't care though; too drunk by so much fresh air and opportunities.

As we arrived at the seaport of Pehlevi, I noticed Mother wasn't doing too well.

"Mama, what's wrong?"

"Nothing. I just have a bit of a fever, but it should be gone soon enough."

As I tried reflecting, I realized Mama didn't look so well since we were on the boat. Maybe she had also been seasick. How could I not notice? In all cases, Jadzia and I decided to believe her and trusted she would get better.

Unfortunately, a lot of refugees died soon after their arrival. Their bodies succumbed to their decrepit state worsened by disease. It was sad to see when they just made it out of Russia. Burials were speedy and numerous. The corpses were wrapped in white blankets and buried with whatever few possessions they owned, unless one of the living claimed it

---

10   Now known as Bandar-i Anzali

for themselves. The authorities clearly weren't prepared to receive so many of us - alive and dead - so there wasn't much accommodation. White tents were provided for us as a semblance of shelter, while others had the starry sky as their blanket.

Mother still wasn't doing so well; Her fever was rising, and she spent a lot of time laying down.

"I need some rest, so leave me alone for a little bit, OK?"

We nodded as she disappeared under a thin blanket. Jadzia and I stepped away to give her some space.

"I hope Mama gets better soon," my big sister said." Seeing her like this is just so sad."

"I know I shouldn't be thinking this way, but I can't help but fear she might be the next to pass away. There are already so many sick people here and barely any treatment. Plus, Mama has been through so much already."

I glared at Jadzia.

"There's no way she's going to die! Mama is tough! This is the second time she has gone through a war. How dare you speak or even think like that!!"

"That's exactly my point. After two wars, her body is sick of it. She's been doing everything she could to take care of us, but now she's at her limit."

"She's not at her limit! She just has malaria, which is curable, so she'll be fine."

Our argument went on for a little while until Jadzia heard Mama talking.

"Did you hear that?"

"Hear what?" I asked.

We listened and realized it was our Mama's voice.

"Is she talking to someone?"

My sister went to go find out, and we followed suit. Once we reached her, we noticed someone pulling at her boots.

"Who is that guy?"

There were some teenage boys roaming and scanning the beach, calling out, "Kishmish, Hoorma, Varone Jajka, (Dates, Raisins, and Boiled Eggs)." This was their hook, their trick, but certainly not their main goal. They were really scouting out for things they could steal from the poor, defenseless, and exhausted refugees or corpses.

"What guy?" I asked.

I turned in the direction my sister pointed at and noticed a boy pulling Mother's boots.

"Children, stop. I really like this pair, and I told you to let me rest."

Mother, who was still laying under her blanket, didn't realize we weren't the ones pulling her. It was...

"Who are you?" Jadzia asked.

The teenage thief immediately let go of the boots and raised his hands innocently. "I'm just someone who sells boiled eggs."

"Boiled eggs? So what were you trying to do with our Mama?" Jadzia inquired.

"I was just pulling her away, since she's dead."

"Dead?"

Mom sat up, despite her fever. The boy jumped in response, as if she indeed rose from the dead.

"You're not... But I thought... because of the blanket..."

"Didn't you hear me speaking?"

"I heard a voice but didn't pay much attention since there are a lot of people here."

"So you just go around grabbing people's feet?"

Jadzia was boiling mad, and the boy became scared.

"Only if they're dead! Part of my job is also to clear away corpses to make room for other refugees."

"And you don't bother checking if they're still alive?"

"Well... most of the people here are already dying anyway."

That was the last straw for my sister as she tried to hit the boy, who swiftly dodged her fist before making a run for it. Jadzia didn't bother chasing him, deeming it wouldn't be worth her time, and instead turned back to Mama.

"I can't believe that guy. You may not be very healthy, but you certainly are alive."

She said that mostly to herself than to us. I clung to her words as if they were straight out of the Bible. Mother was alive. We were alive, and that's what mattered.

We didn't stay long in Pehlevi, maybe two or three days. We received medical examinations, proper documentation - our first papers since we left Poland - and provisions. Once again, we endured another round of showers from the whole disinfecting process and "new" clothing. They burned our old clothes, including the potato sack dresses Mama made for myself and my sister. Then we boarded Persian army trucks where we were to be shipped to Tehran, the capital of Iran. We drove through the Elburz Mountains, and I remember the ride being horrible. The drivers didn't seem to care much about our well-being, or the roads were in too bad a shape to be properly driven on. Whatever the reason, the ride was pretty reckless and definitely unpleasant. On the plus side, however, the scenery was very nice. I enjoyed gazing at the big mountains on the side of the road whenever my head didn't hurt too much.

Mama also didn't appreciate the ride. As a matter of fact, she seemed to be doing worse and worse. Her fever was rising, and she felt very weak. One of the ladies among us checked her over and asked her a few questions before coming to a conclusion.

"She has malaria."

"Malaria?"

"Yes. Some Middle-Eastern countries – like this one – have it. I can't do much now, but hopefully, she'll receive proper treatment once we arrive."

I was even more worried after I heard the name of the common disease, but Mama tried to reassure me.

"I'll be fine, Helena. After everything we went through, a small fever isn't what's going to stop me."

I tried to believe her.

CHAPTER 8

Taste of freedom

A welcome party awaited us as we entered the capital. The locals greeted us by throwing fruits in the trucks, waving frantically, and smiling all the while. We were astonished by such hospitality. They seemed genuinely happy to have us here. We couldn't understand what they said, but it didn't matter because their hearts spoke better than words. Many of us cried - tears of joy this time. For two years, we had forgotten what kindness and generosity were. For two years, we had been moved around like dead weight. And now, for the first time in two years, we were treated like humans again.

"Alright, everyone, we're here!"

"Finally!" I hurriedly jumped out of the vehicle, excited to have my feet rest on unmoving ground. We stretched and wiggled around, trying to bring life back to our numbed limbs. We showed the same amazement as when we arrived in Pahlavi. Tall buildings stretched towards the cleared sky, sandy ground produced a crispy sound under our feet, and hot air warmed our hearts and rejuvenated our souls. Thousands of us arrived in this foreign land having nothing more than a few rags for clothes. Many of us perished along the trip, so I counted myself blessed to still be alive.

Everyone disembarked, and we followed the soldiers' orders. An ex-American air-force base in Tehran became our refugee camp. There were large buildings surrounded by fences and stones. The buildings were all empty because the American army had been relocated to Europe, allowing us to use the space as shelter. My sister, Mother, and I walked with the large group through the gate and were brought to a halt by a child's cry.

"Mama! Mama!"

We immediately turned around to find Andrzej, waving and smiling at us.

"My son!"

Mama elbowed her way through the human sea to embrace her boy. Tears streamed down both their cheeks, and I was also moved by the scene. After the initial euphoria faded, Mother inquired my brother about his presence here.

"The cadets weren't sent to Egypt right away because it's far, so they brought us to Tehran first. I heard some Polish people were coming, so I came to see if you'd be here."

I could sense the relief in his voice to see us all alive and somewhat well.

"This was God's will for us to be reunited, my son, a true miracle and blessing. A lot of people didn't make it, and we weren't better than them to deserve to live."

Indeed, I realized any one of us could have perished on the Siberian snow banks, or in the Russian villages, or right as we docked at the Pehlevi seaport. I was more than happy to see that we survived this long.

We followed the protocol to settle in the camp. Once again, we were disinfected and given new clothes. Thousands of us had emerged from Russia in desperate need of food and medication. The place was full, and we were densely packed, but at least we were clothed and washed.

Many carried diseases, especially the children. For those who survived the trip, they were battling against typhoid, cholera, smallpox, and typhus. Resources were scarce, therefore not everyone was able to receive proper treatment. There was also a shortage of qualified nurses, so cemeteries filled up quickly. Every day, death plagued us, so it was hard to stay positive when we could be the next corpse wrapped in a white blanket. I was glad hunger was my only problem, but it wasn't the same for

Mama. She was still suffering from the symptoms of malaria and couldn't do much.

We arrived right before Easter in 1942, so some of us tried to forget our hardships to invest ourselves in the festivities momentarily. We were mostly catholic, though there were also a couple of Jews with us. Together, we remembered Christ's death and resurrection; his victory over Satan. In a sense, we were also being resurrected that Easter. We had escaped our inhuman conditions, overcame diseases and hunger, and now arrived in our "land of the free." A land that allowed us to live. Life didn't look so grim, dull, or cold, but had colour and beauty. On Good Friday, since we are not supposed to eat meat with respect to Jesus' death, all kinds of cakes and hard-boiled eggs were brought to us in the camp by the members of the Red Cross. We rejoiced at this feast, crying at the sight of so much generosity.

I couldn't help but remember how we used to celebrate Easter in Poland. We had to fast prior to the holiday, and we also had coloured eggs. We decorated baskets before bringing them to church, where the priest blessed them. I remembered some ladies being quite competitive and wanting their baskets to look the best. The meals we ate and the laughs we shared during that special occasion seemed to belong to another era.

Despite the number of refugees at camp, the Red Cross provided food for all of us. Many drooled at the sight of so much provision, barely re-membering a time when they only had to wonder *what* to eat and not *if* they'd eat. Lamb and rice were the common meal, which was a luxury for us.

"Do NOT eat it."

Jadzia, Andrzej, and I froze, not sure if we heard properly.

"What?"

"I said don't eat it." Mother was serious, which only made us more confused.

"Why not? We've been starving for months! Years even!" Jadzia replied.

"I know the food seems great, but you really shouldn't eat it."

We couldn't understand her reasoning. Here we were, survivors of a brutal Siberian camp and horrible frozen country, starved and tired and presented with proper food, only to be told we couldn't eat it. This was definitely a new form of torture.

We reluctantly watched the other refugees feasting upon savory meals while we only ate the bare minimum.

"Please, Mama! Can't we just have a bit of lamb? Or a bit of rice?" Andrzej pleaded.

"No, it can be dangerous to eat such rich foods after you've been undernourished for so long. Look at how skinny you all are! You might get sick if you eat too much."

Indeed, we were only skin on bones - like everyone else in the camp. Nonetheless, we didn't want to admit defeat. Our childish desires overcame any rational thinking, and all we could preoccupy ourselves with were those lavish meals.

"But it smells so nice! Please, Mama!"

She sighed heavily and rolled her eyes but wasn't about to give in. Instead, she went to see the soldiers and asked for crackers, which they gave her.

"Here. You can have these."

The disappointment was clear on our faces as our shoulders slumped and our lips curved downward.

"It's for your own good,"

She insisted, but we didn't really believe her and grudgingly nibbled away at our crackers.

However, as the saying goes, Mother knows best. While Mama slowly fed us more and more food, many refugees got sick because they ate too much - some even perished! We, on the other hand, maintained a semblance of health. I say a semblance because diseases were everywhere in the camp. People were constantly hospitalized, and medicine was quickly running out. Also, we kept getting more and more shipments of refugees nearly every week. More than what the authorities were expecting. The camp was packed with thousands of Poles, half alive and flirting with death.

Actually, death was constantly roaming around, seeking its next prey. People were so accustomed to losing loved ones that they cried dry tears.

"Here. I want you to have these."

Nadia, a good friend of Mother's, handed her long black leather boots.

"Have them? But I thought you were keeping them for..."

"My husband or son, yes. It was in case they ever came back, but I learned the other day that they both passed away, so there's no point in holding on to them anymore."

There were records of all the refugees, and many men were coming back from work camps in Siberia. Unfortunately, we couldn't find out anything about Tata, but some had been reunited with family members. Others, including Nadia, however, received the sad news of their loved ones passing away under the brutal conditions of their camps.

"I... I don't know if I can accept these. They're for your family."

The lady shook her head, wiggling her blond hair around with each movement. Her eyes were wet, but no tears slid down.

"Don't you get it? I have no family anymore!"

She was shaking, and the pent up emotion was getting to her. Nadia pushed the boots towards Mother.

"Please. Just take them. I can't... I don't think I can keep these anymore."

The pair now held painful memories, so I understood why Nadia couldn't - or wouldn't - keep them anymore. Mother also understood because she accepted the gift.

"Thank you. I'll make sure to take good care of them."

Nadia simply nodded before turning away.

"Oh Lord... You're leaving?!"

Andrzej slowly nodded, but we couldn't believe it. He had only been with us for two weeks and already had to go. The cadets were finally being sent to Egypt.

"But... don't you think you should stay with us now?" Mama inquired hesitantly. "I think it would be best if we all stuck together."

"I would like to stay with you, but..."

"But?"

"Well... I made a lot of friends in the cadets, so I think I'll stay with them."

I was disappointed he chose friends over family, and Mama probably felt the same way, yet she didn't show it.

"And you're absolutely sure about that? Won't you get lonely?"

"I'm not five anymore, Mama."

Indeed, he was now twelve. Though to today's standards, he'd still be considered a child; he had matured quite a lot at that time. Mama knew he had thought this through, so she let him go.

"Alright then, but be careful out there!"

He nodded and joined his group.

"It's back to just us, girls."

"Why didn't you make him stay?" Jadzia seemed more mad than confused. Mama stroked her hair tenderly and answered:

"We can't make people do what we want. We can only encourage them to do what they should."

With that, she laid down to have a rest.

Eventually, Mama slowly recovered until she felt no more symptoms of malaria. We were more than happy about her well-being, and our situation was also improving. Despite the fact that the refugee camp was still overpopulated, we had enough to survive. Also, when we looked back on Siberia, we realized that anywhere was better than there, so we didn't complain much. Mama, my sister, and I were among the first wave of people to arrive. They were transporting people very quickly, and the organizers were trying to figure out where to place all the refugees. We mostly stayed in the refugee camp and didn't interact much with locals, especially since we were located on the outskirts of Tehran, but others often went to the city and enjoyed it quite a lot.

More and more people arrived, and it seemed like we'd be here for a while; It was at this time that school started. Since our studies had been interrupted due to the war, the Red Cross organized a temporary schooling system. Hearing such news made me remember the school books I took with me when we were evacuated from our house, which I ended up abandoning along the way because they were dead weight and our priorities had quickly changed.

A lot of educated people had been deported to Siberia, so it wasn't hard to find teachers - or maybe should I say ex-teachers - among the refugees. We followed the Polish curriculum, and since I had finished fourth grade before the war, I was now entering the fifth. Unfortunately, we had no actual building for the school, and simply sat on bricks alongside the wall of the building.

"Well, Mama, we're heading out."

"Where are you going?"

"To buy notebooks, remember?"

Mother let out a faint "Ah, right" but didn't seem too keen on letting us leave. "You girls better be careful out there. I'm sure you've heard recent stories of…"

"Yes, of locals kidnapping girls in the big city."

Jadzia rolled her eyes as if such incidents only bothered her.

"And do you have a pass? You know you need one to leave the camp."

As a response, my sister waved the pieces of paper in front of Mama. She was sixteen and always thought she knew what she was doing. Now that she had regained her figure and became a well-built young lady, I envied her curly blond hair - contrasting with my straight hair - which quickly grew back after having been close-cropped. Before we left the camp, we went to pick up Jadzia's friend, who also happened to be called Helena. We walked out into Tehran together, seeking a store to purchase notebooks for school.

On the way, we chatted about recent events.

"A lot of refugees really like it here. Some are even starting to work in the city," Helena said.

Things had quickly evolved since our arrival a few weeks ago. Poles were settling in at a rapid pace. Most of them had been part of the upper middle-class and bourgeoisie in Poland, and were eager to reconstruct their wealth and social status. As a result, they started leaving their mark in the capital of Iran and building their name. Many left the camp to settle in the city to find work. Sometimes, they were even more educated than their employers.

We were happy to hear about the successes of our fellow Poles, and were having fun imagining all the possibilities that presented themselves in this foreign land.

Having so many refugees suddenly settle close to or in the city definitely changed the demographics. There were more people but not necessarily more food, which is why some locals perceived us as invaders devouring their resources. Those were probably the locals responsible for recent abductions.

The markets were very, very large where you could buy anything you wanted. There was even an entire marketplace above the streets with another underground!

"Let's try this store."

After walking through the narrow streets of Tehran, we finally stopped at some place to buy notebooks. We entered the small shop, and the clients inside immediately noticed our presence. This sudden attention made us hesitant to look around. Helena nudged my elbow discreetly.

"Go ask them if they have notebooks."

"What? No, you go ask them."

"Aren't you usually the brave one, Hela?"

Jadzia smirked, and since I couldn't let her hurt my pride, I walked in a semblance of confidence toward the counter.

"Um… excuse me. sir?"

The hairy man looked at me, lowering his newspaper. He was a bit intimidating, but I had a point to prove, so I shook away my fear.

"We're looking to buy notebooks for school. Do you have any here?"

He stared at me with a quizzical look, and I quickly figured he didn't understand Russian. The only other language I knew was Polish, which wouldn't have made much of a difference. I tried explaining using hand signs.

"Notebooks. For school." I imitated the gesture of writing, but the man still didn't understand. He said something to another customer in Farsi, then the two men looked at me as I continued my clown show.

"Notebooks. To write." I mimicked the gesture of writing over and over, but they didn't understand. That's when I heard a few snickers, and when I turned around, I noticed Jadzia and Helena were hardly suppressing their giggles. Those girls! However, I didn't have time to scold them because a man came to speak to us.

"*Devuhski!*[11]"

We immediately turned around at the familiar sound of Russian. A man who had just entered the store joined us at the register.

"What is it you need?"

This time, Helena, Jadzia's friend, did the talking.

"We're looking for notebooks for school."

"Ah, notebooks," he said as he scratched his bushy beard. "You won't find any here, but I have some."

"Really?"

"Yes, just follow me."

Jadzia and Helena were glad someone could provide us with what we needed. They naively followed him without a hint of hesitation. On the other hand, I thought the whole thing was very strange. We didn't know

---

11   "Girls!"

this man, and there had been recent abductions. We couldn't simply trust him. I was shaking as we followed him through narrow winding streets, not having a clue where we were going, so it was very difficult to keep up with him.

"Jadzia. Jadzia, I don't think this is a good idea," I whispered in Polish.

"What do you mean?"

"We can't just follow a stranger. It could be dangerous."

She smirked the same smirk from earlier. "What happened to all your bravery?"

Jadzia didn't like her question and frowned.

"Being brave doesn't mean being careless, you know?"

She simply shrugged and said that if anything happened, we'd be three against one, so I didn't have to worry. That didn't help ease my doubts, but I didn't say anything and painfully swallowed the tears itching my eyes.

Eventually, we arrived at our destination. A big house guarded by a tall brick fence and steel gate emerged before us.

"Alright, we're here, girls! Let me just unlock the gate."

A huge lock was on the fence, and the man fussed around with his keys. I glanced at the home and how strongly guarded it was. For some reason, something didn't sit well with me. Why did this man decide to bring us all the way to his house when he didn't even know us? And if something happened, would we even be able to escape? At that moment, it hit me.

"This is a harem."

"What?" Helena turned to look at me and noticed the fear and unease on my face. I whispered once again.

"This is a harem. You know, where they keep girls locked up? He must be one of the locals kidnapping girls!"

We slowly turned to look at the man one last time; he was still unlocking the gate. Suddenly, he looked less friendly. The smile on his lips seemed more like a twisted smirk, and the glare in his eyes showed hidden malice. We all ran away as fast as we could without a second thought.

"What? Girls! Where are you going? Girls!"

We didn't bother listening to him and simply focused on putting as much distance as possible between us. After a while, we were exhausted and parched. Wheezing and puffing, we rested by one of the crowded streets.

"That... was very... scary."

"I told you... we shouldn't have trusted that man!"

Jadzia rolled her eyes at my comment, more preoccupied with catching her breath. Once she was able to breathe properly again, she decided we should call it a day and head back to camp. I didn't complain.

One would've thought that after that incident, I would have learned my lesson. However, despite the fact that I had been scared out of my mind by our misadventure, I still went back to the city to buy notebooks; Alone. Jadzia was too scared to come with me, Helena's mother forbade her to go into town without an adult, and Mother was helping the nurses again. That being said, I decided to conquer my fears and venture into the city without anyone by my side. After all, Polish people were slowly establishing themselves in Tehran, so maybe the locals wouldn't try to harm me.

This time, I was able to find a store with notebooks and quickly made my purchase. On the way back, I kept praying to God for protection and safe arrival. As I walked, I noticed a man who seemed to be European. I decided to stay close to him so that people might think we're together and therefore wouldn't attack me, the same as I did in Uzbekistan; far enough yet close enough. When he sped up, I sped up, and when he slowed down, I did the same. Unfortunately, he eventually noticed my little maneuver.

"Why are you here by yourself?" he asked me in Polish.

I was happier to hear my mother tongue than frightened to have been discovered.

"I went into the city to buy notebooks for class," I answered in the same language.

"Don't you know it's dangerous to go out alone?"

"Yes, but I had to go."

He shook his head in disappointment and then stared at me for a while. "What's your name?" he finally asked.

"Helena."

"Last name?"

"Fąfara."

Unlike the man with the big house, this fellow Pole didn't seem suspicious to me, so I dropped my guard and answered his questions without hesitation. As he heard my answer, a large smile spread across his face. "Oh! Was your Father a professor?"

"Professor? No."

His shoulders slumped, and his smile froze.

"Really?" He seemed to doubt my answer and rubbed his naked chin. "I had a friend in Lwów who used to be a professor. His surname was also Fąfara, and his name was Artur."

"Oh. Well, Tata's name is Ludwig, and we're from Osada Miratycze, Wojewodztwo Nowogródek."

He was clearly disappointed; Maybe he hadn't received any news from that friend in a while. A grim look clouded his face momentarily before he shook it away.

"Anyway, you should be careful. Haven't you heard of recent abductions?"

I nodded, and he continued.

"You shouldn't go anywhere by yourself. Make sure to always have someone to accompany you, even if it's for a short trip. I'll bring you back to camp, OK?"

The man smiled, and we chatted along the way. I learned that he was an ex-military and had been sent to one of the many labor camps in Siberia. I didn't dare ask him how it was. We all wanted to bury and forget our war stories and quickly move on to the next thing. As I waved goodbye, I briefly saw Father's figure in that man. He was also a military man sent to a labor camp in Siberia, and Mother had tried to discover his whereabouts, but all in vain. We didn't have any news of him, and at this point, I didn't know if it was better to stay ignorant or learn the truth. I simply hoped he was alive, somewhere, and enjoying peaceful times like we were.

Part 4

India

Akwaz-Bombay

CHAPTER 9

Transfer

Many months went by, and in the meantime, Iran was bliss. The flesh that had rotted and dried off slowly rebuilt itself back on our scrawny bones. Bigger people regained their lost plumpness, and children grew with rosy and smiling cheeks. Everything was going for the better, and finally, we didn't have to live in fear. The only downside was that our family wasn't all together. We could only pray for each member's safety.

We received news one Saturday afternoon; our time in this country was changing.

"We have to leave?" Jadzia clearly showed her displeasure at the sudden news.

"Yes. More Polish people are still coming from Russia, and the Red Cross has to make room for them. Our stay here is only temporary."

"But what about us? We also need a place to stay!"

"We're simply going to be relocated, so we'll still have a place to stay."

"And where is that going to be?"

"I don't know."

Despite her uncertainty, Mother didn't seem worried about what would happen to us. She trusted the authorities and believed their priority was our well-being, so she didn't oppose their decisions. My sister, on the other hand, was skeptical. I could understand her not wanting to leave such a nice place. It was true that there wasn't enough space, and accepting more people would create massive cramping, but we had a roof over our heads and food in our bellies. There was an unspoken fear that our departure meant returning us to the hellish conditions we endured before arriving in Iran.

"I'm sorry, but we're leaving. I know some refugees decided to stay here, but that's not my intention. You've had a great time here, so think about those still suffering and needing such a refuge. Don't you think we should allow them to taste the same freedom we've experienced, especially since we know where they're coming from?"

We didn't answer, knowing she made a valid point. Mother wasn't trying to ruin our fun but genuinely cared about the other refugees. Truly, I had almost forgotten that not everyone had yet escaped the clutches of Russia, and since we were still in the year 1942, the war was far from over. Of course, I couldn't have known that at the time.

With that, we prepared for departure and left the camp which provided us with such comfort and peace. Near the end of the year, we boarded trains to be shipped to...

"To Ahwaz?"

"That's what Mama just said."

Jadzia rolled her eyes and exaggeratedly sighed to compliment her annoyance with my question. I decided to ignore her and simply bring my attention back to Mother.

"But why there?"

"The soldiers said it's to get us used to the tropical heat weather, so it's just a temporary stop. I believe after that, we'll be going to India."

"To India?"

This time Jadzia was the one who was surprised.

"That's what she *just* said," I exclaimed with a smirk, which was answered by a glare.

Mother didn't address our petty bickering and simply continued her explanations.

"We'll stay in Ahwaz for about two to three weeks, and after that, we'll move on to India. That's pretty much all I know for now."

"And where will we stay?"

"I think in a camp similar to the one in Iran."

We kept quiet for a while, and I looked out the window, gazing at the vast fields passing by. It had been almost three years now since we were transferred from place to place, following orders and clinging to our memories as our only luggage. I wondered if we'd ever have a home of our own again.

"Our house in Poland was really big, wasn't it?"

"It sure was," answered Mama, who had closed her eyes to rest.

"We had all that space just for us and all those orchards."

"I remember, Hela. I was there."

"You said someone gave that property to Tata, right?"

She slowly opened her eyes, realizing I unfortunately wouldn't let her sleep, but she didn't look annoyed. She pondered for a bit before answering, and I knew I was in for a story.

"Yes. Your Father fought in the first war back in 1914. He was barely 16 when he joined the army, but he was a valiant soldier who fought for Poland's liberation. I told you about that, didn't I?'

"About Poland being under siege for over 100 years? Yes, I remember."

"Good. You need to know your history. Indeed, our country was controlled by Russia, Germany and Austria. There were other countries, but those three were the main ones. The war of 1914 was therefore an opportunity for us to be freed from our rulers, and we won! The General, Józef Piłsudski, who had led the Polish army, decided to reward all the young men who volunteered to serve Poland, and so he gave them land. Your Father was one of those men."

Mama paused with an indescribable look on her face. I know she was thinking of her husband, and I also couldn't help but remember my Tata. Where was he? How was he?

Ignorance and worry were slowly killing us, and it was becoming more and more difficult to pray for his safety since I couldn't help but imagine that the worst had happened to him. Without thinking, I placed my hand on Mama's. She smiled at me, and I smiled back.

"Maybe Tata will be rewarded again, and our next house will be even bigger."

Mama forced a smile, but I could see behind her façade. She didn't believe we'd one day return to Poland and receive more than we used to own. Actually, she probably feared going back to our country, just like I did. With that, we kept quiet for most of the journey.

After a long train ride, we finally arrived at our destination: Ahwaz. The climate was completely different from the one in Tehran, and thick drops of sweat already gathered on our foreheads. We were preparing for the hottest climate in the world, the equator in Africa.

"Alright, everyone, this is where you'll stay for the next couple of weeks. It's just so you get used to the climate. We'll provide you with sheets and food. There will also be a medical wing."

The soldiers led us into a big brick building and showed us where we'd stay. The walls were painted white, and vast, empty rooms served as our quarters, where we'd sleep on the flat cement floor. Once again, we were packed like sardines since there was no space. Plus, the hot weather only made our body temperature rise. There wasn't much to do, so we had to stay within the limits of the army camp. People tried to occupy themselves by singing or playing games, but it was so hot that we usually didn't feel like doing anything anyway.

It was now the second night, and the refugees were having quite a hard time accommodating themselves with the weather.

"I can't sleep here. I feel like I'm suffocating!"

"Yeah, me too!"

One by one, they started complaining to the soldiers and members of the Red Cross. There was no cool air inside, making our nights rough. The best solution the soldiers found was that we sleep outside. We had no better option and simply acquiesced, dragging our thin sheets and hot bodies with us.

"You can sleep on the sidewalk here, but make sure you stay within the limits of the camp!" The soldiers stood guard to protect us from animals and locals who were up to no good. We were tired and only wanted to sleep, even if it was on the sidewalks; if that's all there is, so be it.

"What if we wet the sheets? That should help us cool down."

"Oh, good idea!"

Mothers began pouring water on their sheets and squeezing out the excess. They then laid them on their children, who seemed much more comfortable now. Mother followed their example (this is how Mama learned her survival skills, by observing the locals and those around her) and Jadzia and I were covered by damp sheets. It indeed helped cool us down, and I was able to sleep much better.

One of the friends I made in Iran also came with us to Ahwaz. Her name was Regina.

"Hi, Helena! Did you sleep well?"

"Ah, you know."

"Have you gotten used to the weather yet?"

"Only a little bit; the nights aren't as rough as before."

I rubbed my eyes and stretched my back. A week had gone by, but I still wasn't used to sleeping on a sidewalk. Regina was 17 at the time, so four years older than me. Despite our age difference, she still treated me as an equal.

We went to get our breakfast, just like the thousands of other refugees. In the canteen, there were dozens of grey tables, dusty tile flooring and a long line of hungry Poles where the food was being served. Being so many people in the same place certainly had a lot of disadvantages, but after going through hell in Siberia, I wasn't complaining much.

We sat down as we ate our bread, talking about recent events.

"You know," Regina started, "I heard Hitler is doing a lot of harm to the Jews. He's massively exterminating them in concentration camps."

She had big eyes and they widened even more as she shared the news.

"Who told you that?"

"I heard it from one of the soldiers."

Regina was a pretty young lady with curly brown hair and hazel eyes, so I wouldn't be surprised if she had caught the attention of a man or two who decided to give her a bit of intel.

"It's crazy, isn't it? Trying to get rid of a whole race! And then we have to take in all the collateral damage."

We were the collateral damage. We were the ones suffering from the twisted ideologies of a wicked man, to say the least. I thought my situation was bad, but some had it way worse. Then again, there's always someone who has it way worse.

"You're right, Regina. It is crazy. War itself is crazy, and those who enjoy it are even crazier! We just need to look around to see it definitely causes more harm than good."

I tried picturing all those Jews dying in concentration camps, and then I remembered all the Poles who died in Siberia or on the way in or out of there. All those who perished just as we reached Pahlavi, their weak bodies finally giving in to disease and starvation. At thirteen, I had already witnessed so much death that I nearly became numb to it.

"You know, I don't think only those who die are the victims. Those who live have it pretty rough as well."

My friend looked at me with wide eyes, pressing me to continue.

"When you die, you no longer have to worry about anything. It even seems like the perfect escape from our harsh reality. Don't get me wrong; I'm not trying to belittle the horrible conditions in which so many have perished since the beginning of the war. I just think they're better off than us. We're the ones who have to live with the memories, with the pain. We're the ones who have to bear witness to all the blood that's being shed, the children that are killed, and all the wounded soldiers. We have to carry that heavy weight on our shoulders, in our minds. And we have no way to escape it because even when we sleep, it comes to haunt us in our nightmares."

"I understand what you're saying, and that's why it doesn't surprise me when so many choose suicide after having gone through barbaric situations. However, it's a privilege to be alive; we didn't do anything to deserve it. We could have died like so many others, forgotten under the heaps of snow in Siberia or the sandy beaches in Iran. God gave us life, so the best way to thank Him is to live it fully. I think it's our duty to keep hoping for a better tomorrow, or else we won't make it through today."

Her point really hit home, and I pondered her words. Even though I was still young, it was hard to envision the future. There were so many deaths around me I couldn't help but wonder if I'd be next. However, a life of fear isn't a life well lived, and it sure wasn't the life I wanted to pursue.

Regina placed her hand on my shoulder and smiled an empathetic smile.

"I know it's hard, Helena. I know because I'm going through the same thing, so you should know you're not the only one carrying the burden of our past. We're all shouldering it together, and making it through somehow. Just look around you."

I obeyed and turned to see the faces of the other refugees enjoying their breakfast. The atmosphere was completely different than when we were trapped in Russia. Here, people smiled and laughed. And when some cried, others wept with them. We weren't at the epitome of happiness, far from it, but we had hope that strengthened us and empowered us to make it through the day. It was already more than enough, and with this thought, a smile forced its way across my face.

"AAAAH!!"

We jolted up at the sound of the scream and simultaneously turned in the direction of the noise. A woman was yelling and pointing at a soldier making a run for it.

"What's going on? What happened?"

Everyone was worried and searched for answers. It took a certain time for the woman to calm down before she was able to speak again.

"I woke up in the middle of the night and noticed a soldier laying down between my sister and myself! I got so scared that I screamed."

"Did he do anything to you?"

She shook her head, but the fact that a stranger came to sleep next to her was traumatizing enough. We looked up and realized the soldier was long gone. The lady remembered his face, so he wasn't going to show up for a while. Other women tried to comfort her, and we looked at soldiers with caution from that moment. Thankfully, our stay there was almost over, and we'd be leaving the following week.

Two nights before our departure, I was woken up by Regina's voice. She was sleep-talking, which amazed me because I had never witnessed it before. I then remembered hearing somewhere that if we squeeze the pinky finger of someone who is sleep-talking, we can ask them anything, and they'll admit the truth. Eager to verify that theory, I squeezed my friend's pinky finger. Unfortunately, the desired effect didn't occur.

"AAAAAAH!!"

Regina sat up as she screamed for the guards in fear, waking up all the other girls and ladies around us. Scared to get in trouble, I quickly pretended to be deep asleep and pulled my sheet right up to my ears.

"What is it? What happened?"

"Something... something pinched me!"

"Did one of the soldiers come here again? This time I won't let them off the hook!" One lady was already glaring at the surrounding soldiers, trying to find the attacker. They all looked away or shrugged in innocence.

"I think it was something small," Regina added. "It bit my finger."

"Is there a mark?"

She checked, but there was nothing. I continued to pretend to sleep, listening to the conversation.

"Maybe you're just imagining it," said one lady. "You probably had a bad dream."

"But… I'm sure I felt something." Regina was confused, but the other ladies were tired and a bit irritated to have been woken up in the middle of the night. They went back to sleep, and my friend followed suit.

My family got on another train before taking a boat to arrive in Karachi, India - though now the city belongs to the Republic of Pakistan. The British naval units escorted us, and during the trip, we were excited and apprehensive about our new environment. The adults, mainly mothers, were mostly the ones that were worried, but we children decided to simply enjoy the ride, take in each new sight, and appreciate each new experience. The mood of the group improved at every stop, as it meant being further and further away from Russia and all the nightmares it held. We finally reached Karachi near the end of 1942. Our lodgings were tents on the sand, and we also had cooking facilities.

I gazed around in astonishment, looking at the vast blue sky contrasting with the tall green palm trees. Other refugees had already been brought to India, especially children. Actually, the state of Nawanagar, India, had taken in 500 orphaned children to protect them from having to go back to Poland. Life here wasn't exactly the same as in Iran since there weren't business opportunities, and no one really had the intention to stay in the country. Nonetheless, it was still better than other places we had experienced.

"What's that noise?"

Jadzia didn't answer or even budge from her sleeping position. A suspicious sound caught my attention once again. Was it like crying children or laughing? "Did you hear that?"

"Hear what?" she angrily mumbled.

"The noise. It's coming from outside."

She didn't reply, and I knew her silence was a way of telling me to leave her alone. Mother woke up at the sound of my voice.

"What's going on?"

She was only half awake, bed hair sticking out like a sore thumb.

"I think there's something outside our tent. I've been hearing weird sounds."

"Just go to bed, and it'll go away."

Jadzia was becoming increasingly displeased by the fact that I disturbed her night. I ignored her comment and poked my head outside the tent to see what was going on. As I did so, I immediately regretted my act. My whole body froze, and I was afraid to make the slightest movement.

"Well? I bet there's nothing there."

I slowly pulled my head back in and closed the entrance of the tent before fleeing to one corner.

"What's wrong?"

I looked at Mama and managed to utter a single sentence.

"There's a hyena."

She paused, and her eyes widened. Jadzia was now fully awake and looked at me in disbelief.

"You're kidding, right? There can't be hyenas here."

"We're in the wilderness, not the city, remember?"

Her smug expression froze, and she finally took me seriously.

"*Tsk!* I'd rather see for myself."

She opened the tent, and I had just enough time to see the beast's muzzle before my sister closed the entrance. She quickly joined me in my corner.

"There's a hyena out there!" she whisper-shouted.

"Yeah, that's what I told you!"

"Stay calm, both of you. Maybe if we don't bother it, it won't bother us."

We decided to trust Mama and not move from our spot. Eventually, we got tired and passed out. The sun was already seeping through the fabric of our lodging when I opened my eyes. We told the other refugees about the hyena; surprisingly, we weren't the only ones who saw it.

"It came close to my tent too!" Regina told us, her eyes widening. "I was so scared it would attack us!"

"The best thing to do is to stay calm. They won't trouble us if we don't trouble them."

We tried forgetting about the hyena incident, but it kept recurring. The animals would come very close to our tents, and I was always so scared. Those nights, I curled up against Jadzia or Mama, hoping they could protect me if the beasts finally decided to act. Thankfully, they never did, but the fear they ignited in me was just as troublesome.

We stayed in India for a few months, not knowing what would happen next. We weren't aware that our stay there was only to give time to the soldiers to prepare for the next camp in which we'd sojourn. This time, it was located in none other than Tengeru, Tanzania.

"So now we're going to Africa?"

"Seems like it. I just hope they don't have hyenas over there."

My sister and I were tired of moving from place to place, but it seemed we'd be in Africa for a while since a whole village had been built for us. We took a train to Bombay - which is now called Mumbai - before riding a boat all the way to Dar es Salaam, the east Africa sea port of Tanzania. I wasn't pleased to take another boat, especially since we spent a long time crossing the Arabian Sea.

On the way to Tanzania, we befriended a Czechoslovakian man named Imrich. He was middle-aged and pretty scrawny-looking, with a constant melancholy look on his face. We quickly learned why.

"I lost my daughter in Siberia. We had been deported separately, and when I arrived in Iran, I found out she died of typhus fever."

He was very sentimental, so Mother and I tried to comfort him.

"I'm terribly sorry for your loss. I can only imagine how difficult it must be."

"You sure are blessed to have both your daughters, Anna. I would give just about anything to have mine back." He didn't talk much but often smiled at me.

"You remind me a lot of my daughter," he said. "She had that same spark in her eyes."

I didn't know how to feel about being compared to a dead person, so I simply smiled in response. Imrich stayed with us during most of the boat ride and cared for me when I was feeling seasick. He was a kind man, but something seemed off.

Not long after we arrived in Dar es Salaam, I found out what was bugging me about him. I overheard him talking with Mother near our tent one day as my sister and I were coming back after getting some provisions.

"Would you let me adopt your daughter?"

"What?"

"Please, hear me out. I can't bear the fact that I lost Natalia. Helena is so much like her, and she would fill the void my daughter left. Besides, you'll still have Jadwiga."

"That's quite the request, you know?"

"Yes, but please try to understand. Losing a child... it's like losing a part of yourself. Didn't you say your two boys went to war?"

"But they aren't dead!"

"True. However, isn't it painful to be unable to be with them? Or to not know how they're doing?"

Mother didn't reply, which made me worry. I wanted to hear the rest, but Jadzia was tired of waiting.

"Hi Mama, we're back!"

Both adults turned to my sister, and I followed her. Imrich looked at me, but I avoided his gaze. He was nice and all, but I wasn't going to leave my family to replace his daughter.

"How are you doing, Helena?"

"I'm fine," I replied coldly.

He picked up that I had overheard their conversation but didn't mention it. "Well then, I'll see you later."

With that, he left. Once I made sure he was out of ear range, I turned to Mother.

"Mama please don't give me away! Please!"

As a response, she caressed my hair and smiled.

"Don't worry, Hela. I'd never do that."

Reassured, I sat down to eat.

Imrich soon started pestering me, and I liked him less and less.

"Oh Helena! Let me help you with that!"

Without waiting for my consent, he grabbed the bag of bread I was holding.

"It's rather nice today, isn't it?"

"Yeah, I guess so."

"I didn't know Tanzania was such a beautiful country!"

I wasn't in the mood for small talk and only offered him silence. He picked up on the hint and decided to cut the chase.

"Say Helena, would you like to become my daughter?"

I stopped in my tracks and turned to look at him, furious. "No, I already have a Father."

"But he isn't here."

I was taken aback by his remark. However, I didn't want to admit defeat.

"Not yet, but soon we'll all be reunited."

Seeing my stubbornness, he decided to switch tactics.

"Well, isn't that nice, being reunited with your whole family? Some of us can't hope for that to happen in this world anymore."

He tried to make me feel guilty and pity him. I will admit I was almost falling for his tricks.

"You're catholic too, aren't you? Don't you know the Bible tells us to love our neighbours, to help those in need? There's something you can do to help me, to show me love. I'm in desperate need of a daughter, and you'd be the perfect fit. Don't you care about being able to make someone else happy?"

Disgusted, I didn't know how to answer as a subtle triumphant smirk curved his lips. I simply ran away, not knowing what else to do, leaving him with our provisions.

During the next few days, we stayed in Dar es Salaam. Imrich continued to pester me to become his daughter. I was more than annoyed by his insistence and lost it.

"I said, 'Leave me alone!'" I grabbed a couple of rocks on the ground and threw them as hard as I could at him. Imrich covered his face, cowering in fear.

"Whoa... Helena?" He didn't have time to add anything else because I was gone.

Later, I once again overheard him talking with Mother.

"She threw stones at me Anna! Stones! She could have seriously hurt me."

I started regretting my actions and feared Mother would scold me for what I did. However, her response wasn't the one I expected.

"I guess that means you should never come near her again."

Imrich didn't respond, probably surprised by her answer. He then stormed out of our tent, noticing me on his way out. I gratified him with a triumphant smirk, and he clicked his tongue before disappearing. It was the end of that story.

From Dar es Salaam, we took the train through Arusha. It was going to be a temporary stop on the way to the village of Tengeru. We had been told that the jungle was now cleared, and the place was ready to receive us. All the children were fantasizing about the wonders of Africa, and were always amazed every time they saw Black people out the window. They marveled at the exotic fauna and flora, asking a thousand questions to the adults in order to know the name of each plant and each animal. They also asked many questions about the customs of this foreign land, and I, too, carefully paid attention to the few answers we were provided with. As we got closer to our destination, I turned to look out the window, excited to see our new environment. Immediately, I froze in horror.

Outside the train, the hungry wildfire burned our new city of Arusha and screams of the inhabitants.

Part 5

Africa

Arusha-Tengeru-Camp 22E-Tanzania

CHAPTER 10

The protective land

I couldn't believe it. Flames were everywhere, spreading far and fast before losing themselves in the dark night sky. Everyone was glued to the window, frozen and mystified by the destructive power of the fire.

"What... What's going on?" someone finally asked.

We turned to some of the authorities, hoping they could provide an answer. They discussed a bit among themselves before turning back to us.

"We're not too sure what caused the fire, but we heard it didn't touch your camp, so don't worry..."

Obviously, we couldn't help but do just that. We continued to watch the heavy smoke engulf the poor-looking houses. Even if we tried to look away, we were constantly reminded of the devastation happening outside due to the loud screams that could be heard from miles away. The train had stopped to ensure the rest of the tracks were safe for us to ride. As a result, we were stuck in front of this horror show.

A few children cried and cuddled with their mothers, who tried to reassure them. Seeing all those houses burn reminded me how I myself had lost everything. Our house hadn't burned, but it might as well have. In about only half an hour, all our possessions were gone; Seized rather. We only brought back a few curtains and clothes from our big and beautiful home; And even those were gone now. Thus, I was able to sympathize with the citizens being unable to do anything but watch as everything was taken from them.

We left Arusha in the morning to continue our journey. Everyone was tired and grim. We were pretty shaken from yesterday's incident. The timing seemed a bit too perfect to me. Was it really just a coincidence or a sign that coming to this country meant we'd suffer the same fate? I couldn't tell.

"Alright everyone! We've arrived!"

Heavy bodies pulled themselves from their seats before exiting the train. As always, our group was composed of thousands of refugees, anxious and eager to know what awaited them. A group of members of the Red Cross came to speak to us.

"Hi, everyone, I hope you're doing well. We have prepared houses where you'll be staying for a while. Each house has a number and can take a maximum of four people. You can decide who you will share your lodging with. Once you have your groups, come to see us so we can assign you a number. Welcome to Tengeru!"

Clamour rose, and people shuffled around, creating groups or getting their numbers. Since Mama, my sister, and I was only three, Mama decided to also take in Zoszia, a friend she made in Tehran. We got the number 22E, and made our way through the camp to find the clay house which now belonged to us.

I admired my new environment; it was just like a village. The houses were organized as community blocks, divided by rows. At the very end of a road were a set of twin houses. Then behind the twin houses was a small buffer-type clearing before the genuine African forest jungle began. Each house was about two meters apart. There wasn't an actual roof, instead a round clay building covered with banana leaves as a semblance of a roof - I soon found out many snakes slithered through the holes between the leaves. There was only one window and one door. Inside, everything was in one room. Four chairs were placed around a table, and we had burnable lamps running on kerosene since there was no electricity. We also had four beds surrounded by a large mosquito net, and there was an exterior outhouse for the block.

"Well ladies, it seems we'll be staying here for a while."

Mama glanced around at the small room in which we stood. There wasn't much, but it was the first time we had a home since we left Poland. We finally had our own space.

The camp was composed of approximately 6,500 refugees, mostly women and children. Quickly, the place was arranged just like a Polish village. Over some time, we eventually developed primary and mechanical schools, churches, hospitals, and theatres. It was like a little town. A little Polish town in Africa.

The authorities delivered dry foods, such as flour and bread. Children were given eggs and milk - a real luxury, but once they were 16, they weren't considered children anymore, and didn't receive any extra food. Instead, they were given 10 shillings a month to serve as pocket money. We had common kitchens for each block.

A few days after our arrival, we went out to explore the region and came across the small city that had burned just recently. The people were cleaning up the debris, desolate expressions hanging on their faces. The parts of the walls that had managed to stay up were burnt black, contrasting with the white ash on the ground. I felt compassion for these people, knowing all too well the pain of losing everything. It was so hot and dry there, and everything was flammable. At least they were still in their homeland and would be able to build their houses back. In that sense, they still had hope.

There had been other nights when we noticed heavy smoke rising in the dark sky. Was everything always burning in this jungle? Apprehension kept us awake most of the night, until we finally found out what was going on. Turns out the Maasai tribe burned elephant grass for long days and nights, since it was the only way for them to create a living space for the people, and at the same time get rid of the venomous reptiles. It was reassuring to know the fire was purposely caused, which meant it was somewhat controlled.

The first few months were meant for us to settle in, but once we got used to the place, certain activities resumed. Namely: school.

"So tomorrow's your first day, Helena?" Zoszia asked.

"Yes. I still have a few months left before I finish the fourth grade. Though it feels weird to still be in grade school when I'm already a teenager."

"It's still better than nothing. The authorities are doing all they can so that you don't waste time and finish your studies. We all lost a lot of time while we were in Siberia."

"I guess so."

We were getting ready for bed and there was still one lamp that was on.

"You finished school a long time ago, so what are you going to do now?"

Zoszia took a few seconds to ponder my question before answering. "I'll try to find work. I want to become independent as soon as possible to stop moving from refugee camp to refugee camp."

Mama nodded in agreement before turning off the last lamp.

A weird noise woke me up at dawn, and I had trouble identifying it since I was half awake.

"*Hsssss!*"

I rubbed my eyes and looked around to see where the noise came from.

"*Hssssss!*"

Something on the floor caught my attention, and as my vision cleared up, my eyes immediately opened wide, and I couldn't help but scream: "SNAKE!"

The other three woke up right away, and soon enough, it was a calamity of shrieks and panic! At the sound of our voices, the snake quickly slithered away, bothered - and probably scared by all the noise. Even after it was gone, though, we were still pretty shaken.

"No one told us there were snakes over here!" Jadzia said, alarmed.

"We're in the jungle. Of course, there will be snakes," Mother replied calmly.

I knew she was right, but it still freaked me out to be sleeping with venomous reptiles. I hoped they wouldn't be back anytime soon, but, of course, it wasn't the case. I eventually learned that the physical place where our village was built, in the jungle forest, was an 'animal highway'. Many wild animals came through at first, but humans and animals had to get used to each other.

Mama kissed me goodnight, "Dobranoc Helena. Please tuck in your net well tonight."

I hated the net. I always felt like I had no air to breathe. I felt trapped like a bug. The nets were held up by a post on each corner of the bed and were to be tucked neatly under the mattress. They were meant to protect you from flying mosquitos or crawling critters at night; I didn't care though. I sometimes kept a small opening by my face so I could have fresh air.

That night I fell asleep soundly until there was an annoying itch on my side. I had scratched it, but I was still uncomfortable no matter how much I tossed and turned. I finally had enough and sat up from my bed to scratch myself all over.

I tried to focus my sight on my arm in the moonlight. There were little spots! I tried to wipe my arm, but soon, the dots came back. Then I realized these dots were ants! I screamed, "AHHHHHHH!!!"

My Mother ran towards me and lit a candle

"Helena! What happened?"

I can see a mixture of fear and anger in her eyes. I knew I did wrong; She told me earlier in the night to fix my net under my mattress, and now I'm suffering the consequences. Now with all the commotion, light, and movement, the ants were biting me.

"Get up! Now! Gather your things and go outside."

Mama was so mad. I did as she said without hesitation; I was so embarrassed.

"Hold your blanket out."

She had a broom in her hand. First, she brushed me up and down, and smacked the blanket. When we finished, Mama was silent.

"Mama, I'm sorry. I…."

"Ah! Ryby i dzieci nie mają głosu! (This is a popular Polish saying that says, "Fish and children don't have voices," or in other words, "Be quiet.")

Mama would say this when anyone was acting out of line -even if they weren't a child. Soon we went back into our hut. Mama gave me the broom.

"Sweep your bed."

Then she went to our storage chest. I was thinking to myself. How are there so many ants? We must be living on an ant highway. I swept the ants out of the hut. My sister and Zosia were staring at me in silence from the safety of their nets.

Mama handed me some new bedding and a net and said, "I'm sure you've learned your lesson, Dobranoc Dziecko" and went back to sleep in her bed.

Our hut was numbered 22E. It was along the border of the jungle towards the back of the camp. Often there were locals who walked the path, and some stopped to take a rest. This place was appealing to the locals probably because it was away from the main crowd of the village.

I could tell that it made Mama anxious. She was known to be extra vigilant because mischief could occur wherever crowds collected with curious onlookers, or there were secret hideouts.

I was about 12 years old at the time; This meant that I was eligible to receive toys and extra food with our rations. One day, I was given a toy snake. The toy was made with little painted blocks of wood fastened together by a leather thread. So when you wiggle the head or the tail, the rest of the body would wiggle too!

"SSsssssSSsss!" I was playing. I guided the snake up and around my friend's shoulders and along the ground.

"Wow, Helen! He looks so real?! Did you give him a name?" said a classmate.

"Ssssstefan isss my namesss."I replied.

One day Mama came to me with an idea.

"Helena. Can you go play outside by the path behind our home? Bring your snake friend."

I thought it was an odd request, but -oh well, more time to play! Soon I realized it was for those lingering locals. I went along with the gig and played with Stefan, the snake as if he were real.

After some time, just as Mama predicted, two of the local men approached me on the path. They were speaking in their own language, so I kept playing; slithered Stefan around the ground and up my arm. Soon the tone of the conversation changed, and they were concerned. Stefan and I must have looked very convincing because the two men left in a hurry.

Later when I returned home, I narrated the incident to Mama.

"Mama, guess what happened! Those men saw me playing with Stefan, they ran and told all the other nearby locals, and everyone ran away!"

"Oh, really? Maybe they all thought you were a snake charmer." Mama started to dance and wiggle her body like a snake.

Stefan and I joined in the wiggling, then we all laughed.

I know I'm not a snake charmer. I would probably run and scream if I had an encounter with a real snake. Though that doesn't matter. Few people spent their time by those walking paths, which made Mama and I happy.

No one was forced to work in the camp, but there were many jobs available. We weren't allowed to find work outside of campgrounds, so the authorities made sure to provide enough opportunities for us in Tengeru. People could work on farms, in stores or workshops, in hospitals, etc. As for me, my main "job" was attending school; We had three elementary schools, a secondary school with a general education program, as well as special schools for teaching agriculture, fashion, commercial arts, mechanics, and music. Communication was done very efficiently as we were able to correspond with both Janek and Andrzej. My brothers were doing well, still in Italy and Egypt with the army and cadets.

We could receive letters as we had an actual permanent mailing address now. That was when Mother's brother, the one who had visited us just before the war started, wrote to us. He said he returned to our destroyed village and shared that our home had been transformed into a school. Almost all our orchards were dug out; probably by villagers. Hearing that only reinforced what I feared; we wouldn't be able to call that place home anymore.

Though the local authorities tried their best to help us settle in and restart a somewhat normal life by providing education to the thousands of children in the camp, there were still many difficulties. For starters, we had a shortage of teachers. Almost all the male teachers were at war, and there weren't many female teachers. That's why the position had to be given to some people without proper certification or training. Because of that, not many knew how to run a class or teach properly.

Another problem was textbooks. We didn't have enough for everyone, so we often shared with three or four people. However, with time we eventually received more school material. The curriculum was exactly the same as in Poland, and the teachers didn't hide the reason why.

"Soon, Poland will be freed, and you will all be able to return home. That's why it is important that we teach you what you would've learned there."

"But how do you know we'll return?" a boy asked. "Isn't the war still ongoing?"

"It is, but not for long. We must have faith in the Lord and in the strength of our strong, valiant soldiers defending our lives, heritage, and country on the battlefield for our liberation.

"You'll see; soon enough, Poland will be freed."

Unfortunately, even the teacher only half-believed her words. We had a hard time imagining our country being free anytime soon. Actually, we had a hard time imagining it being our country anymore since the Soviets invaded us and changed everything. What was once beautiful Poland was now a communist wasteland. No one wanted to go back to that.

That day, I walked home with my friend, Irena Trybuwski, who sat next to me in class, and we chatted about recent events. We met in Siberia and stayed friends all the way to Africa.

"I still can't believe we're in Africa. Africa! I never thought I would end up here."

"Me neither, but we've moved around so much that I wouldn't be surprised if they brought us to Mexico next!"

"Ha! Ha! You're right! Even though this country is completely different from our own, I really like it. And the Red Cross has arranged things so well. It's as if we're in our own little town. Our own little Poland in Africa."

We looked around the camp as we walked, taking in all the different buildings. There was the church, and over there, the orphanage with its beautiful playground. There was also the theatre that had recently been built. People walked to and fro, speedily with large strides, or simply enjoying the view. After all, there were so many sights to take in that our eyes didn't know where to land.

"I heard some people at other camps already saw lions!"

"Lions?" My eyes grew wide in fear and astonishment.

"Yes! One of my friends who's in a camp in Uganda told me they saw a lion last week. Can you imagine?"

"Hardly."

Indeed, we were a small town in the middle of the jungle, which meant all sorts of wild animals surrounded us. However, I still found it unsettling to know that I could meet one of them, especially if it was the king of the jungle.

Our heads bobbed around, turning towards a bird, flower, or a tree. Everything was fascinating, colourful, and alive! Though some aspects were also terrifying, such as certain insects and reptiles. We dropped our school bags at our respective houses before meeting again with a group of friends to do one of our favorite recent activities: exploring. Almost every child wanted to discover our new surroundings. Having the jungle right next to us was too tempting, so many of us would head out together to see and observe all the wonders this land held. Suddenly, I remembered the news I wanted to tell my friend.

"By the way, I got a job!"

"Really? What is it?"

"I heard there is a scouting program that started for both boys and girls. So as a member, I was assigned with a responsibility. I'll be escorting newcomers to their huts. Whenever a new group arrives at the train station, I'll go pick them up."

I puffed out my growing chest, proud of my new responsibility. I had decided to get involved in the camp, happy to be part of a community, especially one that had just started building itself back up.

"Wow, that's really nice, Hela! I was also thinking of doing something on camp since I have a lot of free time apart from school."

"Well, you can maybe join the scouting program too?"

"Yes, you're right."

We would be out for hours, fascinated by every new species we found. Boys always tried to show off by slaying a snake or climbing a tree. Most girls were impressed, but I didn't bat an eye. Show-offs were definitely not the type to catch my attention!

Once the sun started to set, we quickly made our way back home, as night always came in a flash, engulfing the jungle in a thick darkness prohibiting us from seeing properly. I returned home and told the others about what I had discovered. Jadzia pretended not to care, but I knew she paid attention to my every word.

"…and then we saw monkeys! Actual monkeys!"

"That's nice, Hela, but you should still be careful out there. I heard in Uganda they saw a lion!"

Mama worried as always, but I reassured her that we (kind of) made sure to stay safe.

"I also have something to share tonight."

We all turned towards Zoszia with a perplexed look, since this news seemed pretty unusual. She tucked away a few light brown hair strands behind her ear before continuing.

"I found a job in Nairobi, so I'll be moving there."

"What?"

Mother was the most surprised. Zoszia and Mama were very close to the point where people thought they were sisters. They even thought Jadzia was Mother's only daughter and I was Zoszia's daughter, which would make my sister and I, cousins.

"I know this is sudden, but I've been wanting to become independent as soon as possible. As you already know, my husband fled to Hungary when the war began, and we've been separated ever since. After I was deported to Siberia, I really regretted not following him. *Opportunity doesn't always knock twice, and that's why it's important to seize it when you can.*"

She paused for a moment, looking at us before continuing.

"I have a chance to make a living and become independent. This war won't last forever, so I want to be able to have a life again once it's over."

"But I thought you couldn't get a job outside the camp," I said.

"If you're still living here, you can't. I'm moving, so it doesn't matter."

"Well, it seems you pretty much made up your mind, right?"

The young lady nodded, and Mother smiled a sad smile.

"Then I won't stop you. I simply hope you'll be better off there."

"Don't worry, I'll be fine. Besides, Nairobi (capital city of Kenya) isn't that far, so I can always visit during my days off."

With that, she gave us the details of her departure, which was scheduled for the following week. We were sad to see her go but relieved to know it was for a good reason.

"I guess it's back to the three of us."

Mama looked at Jadzia and I, and I looked back at her. She had started to change; Physically; Her face glowed, and her health improved. Also, the white patch on her hair had almost completely disappeared. It seemed she was slowly regaining the beauty that was stripped from her in the cold shackles of Siberia. Slowly, she came back to life.

"Yeah, just the three of us," I said.

Little did I know that was about to change soon.

With all the activities and institutions organized in Tengeru, there were many in which I took part. I was quite happy and proud to have joined the scouts' program, and I was having a great time with the other girls. Finally, it felt like I was doing something productive. One day, while also participating in the task of bringing newcomers to their designated houses from the station, something caught my eye. There was still a suitcase left behind in one of the wagons.

I retrieved it to bring it to the lost and found, but I paused as soon as I saw the name on it. *Ludwig Fąfara.* Everything froze, time stopped, and the world came to a halt.

What?

I read and re-read the name, which was slowly disappearing behind my teary vision. After staring at it for a few seconds, I ran to one of the authorities.

"Excuse me sir!"

"Yes, Helena, what is it?"

"This!" I shoved the suitcase in front of his eyes, and he stepped back.

He blinked, confused. I was having trouble arranging my words but somehow managed to pronounce an intelligible sentence.

"This suitcase belongs to my father. It has his name!" I lowered the object and stared right into the man's eyes. "Where is he? Where is my Father?"

"Well, who is your Father?" he asked, most likely not having read the inscription.

"Ludwig Fąfara."

"Ah! Ludwig!" He smiled broadly, and my heart skipped a beat. "Yes, I know Ludwig. We are good friends, you know?"

I didn't care about his relation to Father. I simply wanted to know where he was and repeated my question. The man scratched his head and looked around in confusion.

"Isn't he here?"

"Well, I haven't seen him."

He went to check the passenger list for the new batch of newcomers. After a few minutes - that seemed a bit too long to my liking - he returned to update me on the situation.

"I don't know why Ludwig isn't here. He was supposed to come, but it seems there has been a mistake, and he went to Uganda, Nairobi instead. He'll probably return and come back on the next train, so for now, you can keep his suitcase until he arrives."

With that, I went back home. Actually, I ran back home, tears flying from the corners of my eye. As soon as I saw the number 22E, I barged inside.

"Mama!"

Mother nearly spilled her tea and looked at me in confusion.

"What is it, Helena? Did something happen?"

"Look!"

It was all I was able to say as I brought the suitcase to the table, my hands trembling. Mother read the name and immediately let a gasp escape her lips. She then turned towards me.

"Where is he?"

I explained what the man at the station told me. She listened to every word, clinging to them as if they were the salvation she needed all along. At the end of my tale, she let out a long sigh before tears ran down her cheeks.

"He's alive."

A faint smile crept up her lips as she repeated herself.

"Oh, thank God he's alive!"

It was only then that reality hit me, and I realized Father wasn't dead. We hadn't seen him since September 1939. We hadn't received any news or letters. All we had was hope and prayers, and finally, God rewarded us for our faith. I could relate to all the broken families that one day discovered the existence of members they hadn't heard of or thought were dead. The reunions were always emotional, as if reconciling with a part of oneself. Wartime taught me the value of family bonds. I tried to wipe the tears from my face, but there were too many. Not only was Father alive, but he was also coming HOME. I was finally going to see him again!

"What's going on?"

Engulfed in our crying party, Mama and I hadn't heard Jadzia come in. She looked at us with concern, probably scared of discovering the reason behind our tears. Mama ran to her and hugged her tight.

"Ludwig! He's alive, Jadzia! He's alive!"

"What?"

More tears!

We spent so much time crying about him being alive that we didn't bother opening the suitcase until my sister pointed it out.

"Don't you think we should see what's inside?"

"Oh yeah, you're right!"

We hurried to the table and Mother did the honors. Three faces bent over the open suitcase, eager to see what it contained and somewhat confused when it was finally opened. Inside were...

"A pillow?"

"And two hairpins?"

"Is that it?"

There were also a pair of pants and a shirt. We kept searching the empty suitcase for more clues, but nothing else was inside.

"Why did Tata have a big pillow and two hairpins?"

"No idea."

I kept staring at the accessory, thinking it looked nice. It was blue and pink and had a purple flower on it, probably for his two daughters; Tata was still with us.

"You know, he was taken from the streets, so he only had the clothes on his back. Someone must have given him these things."

Mother made a point, and we were less surprised by the light luggage. From that day, we clung to the suitcase almost as if it were Tata himself. We told everyone who came by, and showed them the clothes, the pillow, and the pins. Everyone was happy for us. Joy was contagious in the camp, so when one person was reunited with a family member, all the others rejoiced. It meant there was one more life Russia couldn't terminate. There was one more life that was saved.

A few days later, we received a letter.

"Uganda?"

"Yes, but he'll come back here. It says he'll come by bus."

We finally found out what happened to Tata. It seemed he had been sent to Nairobi by mistake and was now making his way to Tengeru. Such news only revived the excitement in our hearts. We would soon see him, and the thought of that kept our spirits high during the few days separating us from his arrival.

It was one afternoon in June 1943, when the African sun was high in the sky, and clouds were scarce. I returned home from school and paused at the door.

He was there. Sitting at one of the chairs, talking joyfully with Mama; the scene was all familiar. Just as they noticed my presence, I ran towards him and hugged him as tightly as I could. Tears flooded my cheeks as if they were only waiting for their cue. Father wrapped his arms around me, and my body instantly recognized his warmth.

Four years! Four years had gone by since I last saw him. Four years had passed since he was stripped from our family and me, taken from the streets like a worthless thief. The emotion rose up my throat, preventing me from speaking. No words needed to be exchanged anyway. He was here, alive and somewhat well, and that's what mattered. Our hearts communicated in a way our mouths couldn't. The silence that filled the room told the other everything we couldn't utter; Our tears did all the talking.

Tata stroked my hair for a bit before turning to Mother. He finally spoke, and the sentence that escaped his lips almost made my heart stop.

"By the way, where is Helena?"

What? Why was he asking that? I looked up at him, thinking he was probably joking, but he was serious. Didn't he remember me? His eyes caught mine, but I could tell he didn't recognize me. I wanted to cry; out of sadness this time.

"Yes, where is Helena?"

Mama pretended not to recognize me as well, and I was lost for words. Had I waited four years to meet Tata again only for him not to remember my face? As I was about to finally say something since I arrived home, Mama beat me to it. She pretended to be looking around, and then had an "Aha!" moment as her eyes locked on me.

"Well, there she is! On your lap!"

Tata looked at me again. Really looked, and then his eyes grew wide.

"Helena!"

He hugged me again, tighter this time. It was the type of hug you give to someone from whom you've been separated for a long time. It was the type of hug a father gives his daughter.

"I can't believe it! I thought you were Jadwiga! How could I not have recognized you?" He pulled back to look at me once again, smiling from ear to ear. "You've grown so much! How old are you now? Thirteen?"

"Yes. I'll be fourteen in a few months."

"Fourteen…" He whispered it.

I was his favorite; my change was unbelievable and clear in his tone. I also took the time to notice how much he'd changed. He kept his small mustache, though there was also a bit of a goatee growing on his chin. His blue eyes lost their shine, and his dark brown hair had many grey spots. His face looked much older, and his body was skinnier. Nonetheless, he still detained the traits that made him my Tata. Later on, Jadzia came home, and the emotional reunion continued. We were all so joyous, laughing as if there was no tomorrow. Happiness filled our hut that night, and we were not willing to go to bed.

The atmosphere was merry, but something didn't seem quite right. I could tell Tata was perturbed by something, and finally, he told us what weighed on his mind.

"So where are, uh… where are the boys?"

Worry was clear in his wrinkled face and he seemed to fear asking the question just as much as hearing the answer.

"They're in the army now," Mom said casually.

"The army?"

"Yes. Well, technically, only Janek is in the army. Andrzej joined the cadets."

Tata let out a long sigh of relief and released all the tension that built up in his shoulders.

"Thank God. Oh, thank God."

He covered his face with his hands as he muttered the words. We all understood how he felt. Wartime brought separation and uncertainty, to the point where we couldn't know any more if our family members were safe or not. Unlike us, he had been deported all alone, travelled all the way here on his own from Russia. He didn't have the support he desperately needed during this harsh period.

"You know," he finally said, "when I arrived in Persia, I heard that the names of all the Poles that escaped from Russia were registered in these big books. Immediately, I went to go see if your names were there. I was very happy when I saw Anna, Jadwiga, and Helena Fąfara. But…" He paused and sighed again before continuing. "I didn't see the boys, and because of that, I thought… well, I feared they might be…"

The words stayed stuck in his throat, but he didn't need to say them for us to understand. Mother placed her hand on his shoulder and smiled at him.

"They're alive. We're all alive, thanks to God."

Father smiled, and I saw a glint in his left eye that vanished in the span of an instant. That being said, we finally went to get some shut-eye.

CHAPTER 11

Prelude to problems

In the following days, Father told us his story, gradually, in bits and pieces, since it was still fresh and too frightening.

"I was taken from the streets because I was an ex-military from WW1. I joined the military as a volunteer when I was 16 years old and later became a soldier. The police were taking anyone with military history, education, wealth, or power. After I got arrested from Poland, I was brought to a prison in the Ural Mountains in Siberia and worked in a mine. They focused mainly on wiping out the people who had the power or ability to fight back. Most of us were wealthy, established people or had been in the military at some point, so they believed this was a threat. … the living conditions were inhuman, but I'll spare you the details, partly because I don't want to relive them."

He looked very grim saying that, and even though he didn't tell us everything that happened to him in prison, we could just imagine, since we endured something similar. I had a hard time believing Tata had been in the same frozen hell as us, only a couple hundred miles away. We had prayed for him each night, not knowing that the distance separating us was much shorter than we thought, also in Siberia, just a different place. Normally, he would have enrolled in the army after he was released, like most men, but the mine had weakened him too much to fight.

"I wasn't able to receive letters from my family because they lived close to the German border, where everything was restricted. Because of that,

I was completely cut off from the outside; no news whatsoever. In prison, they didn't tell us much either. That's why we were always excited when new prisoners arrived, because they informed us on what was happening outside our four walls."

We also didn't have much news of the outside during our stay in Siberia, so I could empathize with Tata.

"No one told us about the amnesty we received. I don't like that word, 'amnesty.' It's not like we did anything we needed forgiveness for. Anyway, that's a political debate for another time. We were released much later, so I arrived in Persia after you."

Once again, the thought that Tata had been in the same country as us without me knowing was unbelievable. It made the world seem a bit smaller than I imagined.

"I think we just missed each other, which isn't too surprising since we were so many. Plus, you all left before I did. After leaving Persia, I was supposed to come here, but as you know, there was a mistake, and I was sent to Kenya instead. Anyway, long story short, I'm here now and more than happy to be reunited with you three beautiful women."

I embraced him in a tight hug, also delighted to have him with us once again. It was truly a blessing for us to see him. Countless families had lost their father, husband, and brother. Many Polish men died either on the battlefield, in the harsh Siberian camps and prisons, or on their way to freedom. But God favoured us and allowed me to see my Tata again. I couldn't be more grateful.

Tata wrote to his family in Poland to let them know we were alive and well once he was reunited in Africa. They replied, saying they were surprised and relieved at the news since they thought we had all been murdered. We understood their fear since such an outcome was unfortunately not uncommon. Hundreds of thousands of us had been murdered, directly or indirectly. Our people had been killed by starvation and cold and disease and misery. All caused by the same enemy, Russia.

On a more positive note, we were getting used to our new environment, and things were going quite well after a few months - and a new family situation.

Then Jadzia announced her departure.

"To England? Why?"

"You also heard the news, Tata. They need people to help in the air force."

"So you're joining the army?"

"No, Mama. Well, not exactly. I'll be volunteering to help bring supplies to the soldiers at the front. I'll be packing and cleaning bullets; stuff like that. It won't be anything dangerous."

My parents were still weary of letting her go, but she had made her decision. Mother was the first to protest.

"Wouldn't you rather stay here with us? I know the snakes and insects can be unpleasant, but at least we have everything we need. And your Father is finally back. I think you should stay instead of going there by yourself."

"Wait dear. I want to believe Jadzia put some thought into this."

Father turned towards my sister, who explained herself.

"You remember when Zoszia said she wanted to seize opportunities to become independent? I feel the same way. This war has been going on for so long, and because of it I, my life, haven't moved forward. If I go to England, I'll finally be doing something with my life, and that could open up new doors for me as well. I'm already 17 now. It's about time I became an adult, don't you think?"

My parents kept quiet for a bit, and then Mama turned towards her husband, waiting for his judgement. He let out a loud sigh before shrugging.

"If it's what you want, then it's fine by me. Just make sure you won't regret it."

"I promise I won't, Tata. thank you!"

With that, Jadzia left for England, and I was now alone with Mother and Father.

Even though Tengeru was great because it allowed us to live again, there were a lot of inconveniences. The first one was the jigger fleas. They were parasites that lodged themselves in softer parts of the human body, most often under the toenails. Then they laid eggs, which would cause acute inflammations. Our skin got very itchy and hurt, and if not treated could become infected and develop into a tropical ulcer. My sister had this, and she had to go to the doctor, where they applied a blue stone (antiseptic germicide copper sulfate)

The whole sack of eggs had to be removed with a needle to prevent infection. The locals were used to removing them, but for us, it took a bit of practice before we got the hang of it. My duty was to check my parents' legs and feet each night before bedtime. Whenever I saw black dots, I knew these pesky fleas had laid their eggs, so I carefully removed them with a sewing needle and dabbled their feet with some topical iodine to prevent infections.

Apart from the jigger fleas, there were also these small worms that would pester us. One girl, three houses down, told her mother one day that she could feel something moving around in her shoulder and was itchy, to which her Mother didn't pay much attention to it. Then a boil developed and grew on her shoulder, so her mother finally brought her to the doctor. The doctor wasn't certain either, so they decided to pop the boil, and a tiny worm came out!!

The snakes and insects were quite troublesome, but at least there were also some good perks about the camp, like the cinema. Mother sometimes gave me a bit of money, fifty cents each month for doing chores, to watch a movie so that I could be with my friends.

"Were you able to understand something today, Helena?"

"More than last time. Though there are still too many words in English that I don't know."

"I wish they could play movies in Polish. It's nice to see something entertaining, but I would enjoy it much more if it was in a language I understood."

I nodded in agreement with my friend Irena. I had gone to see a few movies already, but I couldn't figure out much since they were all in English. (I remember some of the movies were about Shirley Temple and other movies for children and youth)

"So what's the story you're going to tell your Mother this time?"

I took a few moments to think before answering.

"I'll say the movie was about a soldier who ran away from the army and decided to pursue his dream of becoming a musician."

Irena laughed as I elaborated my plot.

"He only joined the army to please his Father, but deep down, he always knew he was an artist."

"And your Mama will believe that?"

"Of course! I can't tell her I didn't actually understand the movie, or else she'll worry I still don't understand English. I know that means I'll be lying, but at least she'll have one less thing to worry about."

We continued to talk about my make-believe story when someone called out to me.

"Excuse me, are you Helena Fąfara?"

I turned around to see a woman I didn't know. "Yes, why?"

Her face twisted in a nasty grimace, and she stepped back as if facing a monster. I didn't understand her behaviour or have time to ask her about it.

"So you're his sister. You're the sister of that Janek Fąfara, aren't you?"

"How do you know my brother?"

The grimace intensified, making her look more hideous by the minute.

"Do you know all the trouble he caused us? Do you?"

"I don't understand what you're talking about. Who are you?"

She kept glaring at me. "My husband is Jakub Kaminsky. He was arrested because of the wood incident back in Siberia."

It took me a little while to finally understand what she was talking about.

"You mean your husband was the one who cheated on the amount of wood?"

"That's not important. Your brother caused him a lot of trouble with his supervisors!"

Even though I had a better idea of what was going on, I still didn't comprehend this lady's behaviour. Why was she mad at us because of something her husband brought on himself?

"So what are you saying? My brother should've quietly taken the blame for something he didn't do so that your husband could get away with it?"

"Don't try to act smart with me. You don't know all the problems his arrest brought on the rest of the family. We'll remember this!"

With that, she sashayed away. Janka and I kept quiet for a bit until my friend finally said something.

"Um... What just happened?"

"That's what I'd like to know."

As I arrived home, I found my parents bent over a letter they just received.

"Welcome back Helena! We just got news from your Uncle, Wujek Sowa."

"Wujek Sowa?"

"Yes. He's my cousin who lives in Canada, remember?"

I tried recalling Tata talking of the said cousin, but the memory seemed too distant and vague.

"What did he say?"

"He told me my family shared with him the news that we're all alive. He's so happy that he wants to bring us straight from Africa to Canada, sponsoring us fully for the whole trip."

"Really?"

I grabbed the letter lying on the table and quickly read through it. Indeed, our Uncle wanted to sponsor us and offer us a new life in North America. He was boasting about his country, saying there were beautiful blue skies and lots of land. As I neared the end of the letter, I hadn't noticed the large smile creeping up my lips during my reading.

"Does this mean we'll be going to Canada?"

I hadn't heard much of the country, but it seemed quite appealing. I was thus excited to discover yet another place, another land. Plus, unlike in Africa, I could imagine establishing myself and living in Canada.

Tata scratched his head and didn't seem to share my enthusiasm about this opportunity for a possible new beginning.

"Well... not right now at least."

The smile on my face froze and then dropped.

"Why not? Wujek Sowa will even pay for the trip and our stay there!"

"I know. He could really help us start over, but I don't think now is the right moment for that."

I didn't understand, and he explained himself further.

"I'm very glad I was able to find you, my girls, but this situation still isn't ideal. The three of us are here, Andrzej is in Egypt, Janek is in Italy, and Jadwiga is now in England. I want all of us to start over together, so I'll wait for our family to be reunited before I take up his offer."

Mama didn't oppose it, and I felt I shouldn't either. I would've liked to go to Canada right away, especially since they most likely didn't have as many dangerous insects as in Tengeru, but I also believed we should wait until the full family was together again. I had to keep hoping that such a day would come.

"Alright then."

With that, Tata went to write his reply. I grabbed a mango and started peeling it before remembering what had happened on the way home.

"By the way, you'll never guess who I met!" I told my story, and both my parents were surprised.

"What is that woman mad about? It's her husband's fault for not being honest with his work," Mama said.

"Exactly what I thought! But she didn't seem like the kind of person to listen to reason."

"You should stay on your guard Helena. We don't know what that woman or her family plan on doing."

The worse they did, however, was to simply ignore us.

One day as I made my way back from school (1943, grade 5), a certain commotion caught my attention.

"What did you say, you punk?"

"You heard me!"

I got closer and noticed two boys fighting. One of them was shorter than the other, but much stronger. He was landing solid hits in his opponent's face, making him bleed each time. I recognized the tall one as being Alex, and the short one was Karol, our neighbour; both of them were my classmates. Even though most of the young boys were well behaved and focused either on their studies or on exploring the area, some had practiced hooliganism, mainly by starting fights. Many reasons explained their misbehaviours, such as coping mechanisms for their trauma or bad influences. Whatever the case, I couldn't stay idle while someone was being disfigured before my eyes. Alex switched from punching to kicking. Without thinking, my legs jumped forward.

"Hey! Hey, you guys, stop!" I came in between them right at the moment when Karol wasn't able to defend himself anymore. Alex had geared up for his next blow to send a kick to his adversary. Unfortunately for me, I'm the one who inherited the next kick, the steel enforced toe of his shoe, straight in my leg, right above the ankle.

"Ow! Owww!"

"What the… Helena? What are you doing here?"

The boys seemed more perplexed by my sudden appearance than worried about my injury.

"Isn't it obvious? I was trying to stop you guys!"

I yelled in pain, but that didn't make them pity me either. Instead, it aggravated their anger.

"Why'd you come here? Nobody asked you to interfere!"

I didn't have the strength to argue since I was too absorbed by the growing pain in my leg. I was crying and screaming, which only irritated them more.

"Be quiet! Hey, I'm serious!"

Alex shot me an evil glare, making me pipe down instantly. I wanted to shout, but tried my best to restrain myself, not wanting to receive another kick in the leg. Karol got close, with his menacing eyes.

"You better not tell the teachers about this. Do you hear me? Or else we'll do much worse than that!"

He pointed at my injured leg and didn't need to say more for me to get the picture. Quietly, I nodded in submission. They glared at me a bit longer before walking away.

For about two weeks, the pain was agonizing. I tried my best to keep quiet about it and simply wait for it to go away, but it never did. Each day, I suffered more than the previous, limping to and from school. Karol and Alex always sent me side glances to keep me in check. I was so mad at them, especially Alex. Didn't he realize how hard he hit me, and how much pain he caused? He never apologized for what he did, and it had heavy repercussions. Even through my whole life, I will always remember.

One afternoon, I simply couldn't take it anymore.

"AAAAAH!"

"Helena, what is it?" Mother abandoned the potatoes she was peeling and rushed to me, alarmed. Fat tears rolled down my cheeks as I held my leg in pain.

"It hurts so much, Mama! Too much!"

"A doctor! We have to bring you to the doctor!"

There was a newly built hospital up the hill, and I knew that's where she wanted us to go, but I was in no condition to walk, especially not such a distance. However, it was clear that my leg needed to be treated by a professional. So instead of walking to the hospital, I was brought there on a stretcher made of blankets and sticks, and I couldn't make it up the hill alone. Despite the agony, I was relieved to know something would finally be done about it. The doctor made his examination and scratched his thick black beard.

"Hmm… Nothing is showing on the outside, so I can't say for sure what the problem is."

I was utterly disappointed to hear these words. Surely, I wasn't screaming in pain for nothing, which meant that there was clearly a problem. I was about to give up hope when he took something out of a cabinet.

"For now, I can apply this medicine on the leg, and we'll see what happens."

He opened the little container, and inside was this iffy-looking smelly black paste. He spread some on my leg before sending me back home.

A few days later, a big swollen red spot emerged where the paste had been rubbed, and I was brought back to the hospital.

"It's an infection."

The doctor was sure this time. He opened up the red spot, then puss and other liquids flowed out, confirming an infection. However, this also made us more worried about my condition. I was getting tired of doctors not being able to locate the problem, and that's why I was happy to hear they finally figured out what was going on and what to do about it.

"Your tibia has been fractured, which explains why you've been feeling so much pain. There also seems to be a lot of puss in there. How long ago was it that you got injured?"

"About two weeks."

The doctor's eyes widened.

"Well, frankly, I'm surprised you were able to move with that injury. We'll need to do a minor procedure in order to fix it. It will thoroughly clean the infected area so that the bone and infected area can heal properly."

Tata and I looked at each other and smiled in relief. Unfortunately, our joy didn't last long as the doctor continued to speak.

"There is one problem, though."

His expression looked grave, which alarmed us. What was it this time?

"The hospital doesn't have any anesthesia."

"What?" Tata got up from his seat, his face angry. "How come? How are you going to perform surgery, then?"

The doctor's silence confirmed what we feared. After a long pause, he finally answered. "She'll have to be awake during the surgery. It's the only option."

"Aren't you going to get a shipment of anesthesia or something?"

"We placed an order, but it won't be arriving anytime soon. Also, I don't think we should risk waiting any longer to clean out the infection. There could be permanent consequences if we don't act now."

Tata crumbled back down into his chair and sighed heavily as he rubbed his eyes. I was still trying to process the conversation. Were they really going to... going to cut me open while I'm awake? I turned towards Tata, who didn't look straight at me.

"Helena."

His voice was shaking and he bit his lower lip before continuing.

"Do you think... do you think you could...?"

"Tata..."

He let out another long sigh. The doctor stayed quiet and patient the whole time, letting us agonize over the fact that I'd have to undergo a major procedure without anesthesia.

"There isn't another option, you see…"

He turned towards me, but didn't look me in the eyes. I knew I didn't have a choice and should have this surgery right away, but it still frightened me. Somehow, though, I was able to find enough courage to accept my fate. I placed my hand over Tata's and smiled at him.

"I'll do it."

He looked at me, and I saw the fear and doubt in his eyes. He paused for a bit before forcing a smile. It seemed all his strength was required to perform such a simple task.

"Alright."

A few hours later, I was lying down on a hospital bed with nurses and doctors around me. There was a bright light on the ceiling, blinding me and forcing me to turn my head to the side. Tata held my hand and tried to uphold his forced smile.

"It'll be alright, Helena. I promise it'll be alright," he kept repeating.

I wanted to believe him, but I was very scared. My heart rate went up rapidly, and heavy sweat drops gathered on my forehead and my palms. The nurses and doctors spoke in their jargon, getting all their medical tools ready. Each one seemed more frightening and painful than the previous. I had trouble controlling my breathing, and my thoughts were a mess. *Was I really about to do this? Was I really going to let them cut me open while I'm still conscious?*

I didn't have the time to answer my questions as several pairs of hands held me down. I wanted to say something but didn't get the chance as the scalpel pierced my skin.

"Aaah!"

I let out my first scream, and definitely not my last. The doctor continued to cut, and I saw the blood and pus coming out of the red spot.

"It's alright Zuzulka (my darling bird). It's alright."

But it wasn't alright! The pain only grew, and soon enough I could feel tiny tools moving around in my leg.

"AAAAAH!!"

I kept screaming, and the nurses tried their best to keep me in place for the doctor to do his job. I cried and cried, unable to withstand the agony. Tata kept trying to reassure me, but I could only hear myself yelling at that point. My face was soaked in tears and my leg was soaked in blood and puss. I wanted to be anywhere but there, squirming on that hospital bed.

"We're almost done, Helena. Just hold on tight, you're doing great!"

How could that nurse simply ask me to "hold on tight?" Did she know what I was going through? They were all trying to reassure me, but none of them could fully understand the profound torment I was undergoing. I kept praying and praying for all this to be over and for the pain to go away. I can't remember how much time I spent on that hospital bed. I simply hoped to make it out of there alive.

CHAPTER 12

Confined

"How are you feeling, Hela?"

I turned my head towards Mama as she entered my hospital room. Since my surgery, she came over as often as possible to take care of me. I was glad she kept me company because there was absolutely nothing to do during my recovery.

"Not too bad."

She sat on the chair nearby and extended her hand towards me.

"Here you go, Tata picked them yesterday."

She held two beautifully ripened mangoes. She peeled and cut them into small slices before serving them to me.

"It looks like you lost weight. Are you eating properly?"

I shrugged in response. Maybe I was going through a rebellious phase, or my brutal disinfection procedure had left my spirit numb. I didn't want to eat and refused almost everything that was brought to me. I simply nibbled something here and there. Mama quickly caught on and tried to get me to nourish myself properly, mainly by bringing me food.

"It's important you eat well if you want to get better faster."

Her advice didn't affect me, so she quickly changed the subject. She spent the afternoon in my room, chatting about local news and the likes. Our theatre ensemble was doing quite well with its performances and had been invited to play in the capital, Dar es Salaam.

"I'm so glad they perform plays about our history. When I watch them act, I feel like I'm transported back to the times before the war. It's truly beautiful."

Mother wiped away a secret tear as she reminisced about a time belonging to another era. Oftentimes, I also thought of how things were before the war. I remembered our big house by the lake and the many orchards decorating our yard. I remembered our barn, our horses, and our hens. I remembered Mama's beautiful garden and our wide veranda. Peaceful summer days when we played outside to our heart's content, not ever wanting anything because all our needs were met. Mama interrupted my reverie as she got up from her seat.

"Well, I should go now before it gets dark."

I was sad she had to leave. As much as I loved her visits, I disliked her departures. During the night, I felt terribly lonely, even though all these sick people surrounded me. I quietly watched as Mama closed the door, leaving me behind.

Weeks passed, and my body kept weakening because I didn't eat. I had a cast on my leg, and there was a hole where the blood and pus came out. Because of that, my bandages had to be changed daily. Everything had been going well until one inexperienced nurse arrived.

"You're Helena, right?"

There was something in the way she spoke and looked at me that I didn't like.

"Yes."

"I'm a new nurse here. My name is Hellen, and I'll be changing your bandages today."

I wanted to point out that I found it funny we had the same name, but she didn't seem like the type to joke around. I simply nodded and let her do her work. She began by removing the old bandages and throwing them out. I didn't pay much attention to her procedures, until I noticed it was taking longer than usual. She stared at the new bandages with confusion, as if she didn't know how to put it. After a short deliberation, she decided to stuff them in the hole and keep the bandage inside the hole where the blood and pus were supposed to come out.

"Um…Excuse me, Mm 'am, that's not how you do it."

"What are you talking about? Are you the nurse?"

Her reply scared me, and I didn't dare answer back.

"You don't know anything, so you should just stay quiet." She snapped.

I nodded, and she walked out of the room. I looked at my plugged cast, wondering if I should have said something or not. Thinking back now, I definitely should have.

"Who did that?"

A different nurse came the next day to change my bandages and was undignified at how my cast looked.

"Where is the sonda (the bandage)?"

"Well… it was that new nurse. The one called Hellen. She put the sonda right inside!"

"Hellen?"

She looked at me with disbelief before shaking her head, making her ponytail jump in all directions.

"No, she should never do that. She had a three-month training, so she'd know what she's doing."

"But she DID! It's left inside my leg!"

Three-month training? No wonder she seemed so confused! As if she could know most of what she should do in such a short amount of time. The nurse cleaned up the mess her colleague had created and kept sighing all the while, clearly displeased by such poor work. She directed her irritation towards me though.

"You must be stupid to think Hellen would ever do something like this."

She clicked her tongue and properly changed my bandages before leaving. I was surprised and sad she didn't believe me, but didn't have the courage to tell anyone else the truth, so I kept quiet.

Time passed, and I spent it in my hospital room. I could see children playing out of my windows and couldn't help but envy them. It was so unfair that I spent months in the hospital because of some stupid boy who was now running free without a care.

"Hi, Helena! How are you feeling today?"

"Homesick."

Mama looked at me with worry, and I made her understand I was tired of this place. She let out a sigh and sat on the only chair in the room.

"Well, I brought something that might cheer you up."

She pulled a beautiful dress she had made. The pattern was just as exotic as our new environment, and the cloth radiated with colour. I looked at it, amazed, but soon a frown twisted my face.

"What's wrong? You don't like it?"

"It's not that."

I put the dress down and looked out the window where children from the orphanage were having fun playing with the small toys they had made. Mama instantly understood what concerned me and placed her warm hand on mine.

"I know it's tough to stay here all the time, but it's for the best. Once you're completely healed, you'll be able to run and play as much as you want."

For a young teenager who had spent weeks cooped in a hospital room, a future where I was completely healed was hard to fathom. I wanted my life back now, not later.

"Can't I come home just for a little bit? You and Tata have been visiting often, and I'm very thankful for that, but it's not the same as me being physically home."

"I understand. It's just that the doctor said…"

"Please?" I cut her off. "I just want to go back for a little bit."

I played all the cards I had in order to earn her pity. My tactic worked as she finally gave in and agreed to speak with the doctor.

Tata came to bring me home.

"Alright," the doctor said. "She can go back for the weekend, but she needs to be careful! No running, no jumping, and no climbing!"

He looked at me sternly, and I smiled with the biggest grin I could make, trying my best to convince him that I wouldn't try something so reckless. He kept giving us warnings and instructions until I was finally able to leave that dreaded hospital. Walking was a bit difficult, but I was ready to overcome any pain if it meant returning to my little hut home.

"I hope you'll respect the doctor's instructions, Hela."

"Yes, Tata."

It was hard not to roll my eyes. I wasn't a child anymore; I knew how to be careful!

"By the way, I have something special waiting for you at home."

"Really? What is it?"

"You remember the small garden I started a while back? Well, I just picked some fresh tomatoes the other day. They aren't fully ripe yet, but they seem promising."

"So when will we be able to eat them?"

I was licking my lips as I imagined biting into the nice, juicy tomatoes.

"Hmm… Probably another day or two. I put them in the little ventilation spot just outside the door, under the roof so they can ripen."

The thought of having to wait once again didn't excite me. Wasn't there anything I could have right now?

"Oh, OK then."

I forced myself to hide the disappointment in my voice. However, my mood switched when we approached our destination. As the number 22E emerged in my line of sight, a broad smile stretched my lips.

"We're home! Finally!"

I was tempted to run - not that I was in any condition to - but remembered the doctor's instructions.

"Welcome back, Hela!"

Mama and Zoszia were both at the table, working on a new tapestry. Mom had gotten rather good at it and made beautiful designs.

"Zoszia! I didn't know you'd be here today!"

"I had a day off, and since you were coming home, I wanted to see you."

I was glad we could meet again; Her job in Nairobi kept her pretty busy. I sat down and we chatted for a bit. She had been working very hard and got the position of head chef. I was glad things were working out for Zosia so well. Later on, Irena dropped by and updated me on recent events.

"And at the safari, we saw real zebras! They were right there in front of us, only a few meters away!"

Hearing all the fun activities our class was doing reminded me of the fun things I couldn't do. I couldn't help but be envious of the other students going on excursions and visits to local villages; It was a new form of torture.

Zoszia ended up spending the night, and we were going to bring her back in the morning. Every now and then, I looked up at the tomatoes Tata put on the roof to ripen. There was a small ventilation space between the end of the wall and the beginning of the roof, and he had managed to place the fruits there. They seemed fine to me, so I wondered why I couldn't eat them yet, but I didn't ask.

"Alright, Helena, I'll drop off Zoszia at the station, as she's returning to her job in Nairobi. Then I'll also stop by the post office to send our reply to Bolek. Tata is out working on repairing roofs in the village."

My older brother had recently been badly wounded in the battle of Monte Casino, Italy. His friend, Bolek informed us of his condition as he took care of him. Like Mama, I couldn't help but worry. After all, Janek was in the army; He was on the battlefield risking his life just like everyone else, so the thought of us losing him crossed my mind multiple times. It certainly was God protecting him, because he could have died just like many other soldiers.

"We shouldn't be too long."

"See you next time Helena!"

I waved goodbye at Zoszia as she left with Mama. At first, I didn't know what to do since I didn't have many options. Irena said she would stop by later, which meant I had to occupy myself in the meantime. Once again, my eyes drifted towards the tomatoes. The tomatoes looked back at me, taunting.

"Maybe..."

I looked outside to make sure no one was in sight, then climbed up a chair to reach the tomatoes. I extended my hand as far as I could.

"Just a little more..."

My fingers barely touched the fruit's soft skin before I crashed down.

"AAAH!"

My body collapsed hard against the ground, and I felt pain all over. Blood and pus came out of the hole in my cast, and a piece of rotten bandage; It was the piece that had been stuffed by that nurse Hellen. I cried and screamed until Mother returned because she had forgotten something. Although, now I think it was a good thing that I fell because they would have never discovered the rotten bandage.

"What happened? I heard screaming!"

It didn't take her long to understand what was going on. Quickly, she picked up the bandage and placed it in a dish, then she grabbed me by the hand and rushed me to the doctor's office, which was only three doors down. I sensed panic in her eyes and her abrupt and speedy movements. I tried to hold back tears as I explained what happened to the doctor.

"I told you not to climb, didn't I?"

"I know, but...it's a good thing that the bandage came out!"

"This is what happens when you don't listen to instructions. Now things got worse! You better pray for no bones to be broken."

"We'll need to do an X-ray to know exactly what's going on. Though the problem is that we don't have that sort of equipment here." Said the doctor.

"So what do you suggest we do?"

"They have x-ray equipment in Moshi[12], so we can transfer your daughter there."

That being said, I was taken to the hospital in Moshi and finally did the X-ray.

I was instantly placed in a lora (truck), and the doctor drove me immediately to the hospital. We drove all the way to Moshi, where my leg was once again examined. Mother and I sat in the uncomfortable hospital chairs, on standby for the verdict. After waiting for quite some time, a doctor with photographs in his hand called us into his office.

"Alright, Helena, I'll show you what's going on with your leg."

He placed the black and white pictures in front of me. It seemed like abstract art; Painful abstract art.

"So this is your tibia bone, and there's a part of it that started rotting. Right here." He pointed at a part that seemed kind of blurry in the photograph. "It was caused by a bad bandage that's been in your leg for months. I'm not too sure how that happened."

I had a very good idea of how a rotten piece of bandage made its way there.

"Anyway, the point is we'll need to stop the rot from spreading, and to do that, we'll have to scrape it off."

"Scrape it off? How?"

I was scared to hear his answer. He didn't sugar-coat it and bluntly said: "We'll need to operate."

---

12   Capital of the Kilimanjaro region

At the sound of the word, I was triggered. Images of my previous operation flashed through my mind, and I instantly remembered the painful instruments cutting me open as I lay awake.

"No. No way!"

The doctor was surprised by my immediate opposition.

"Well, it's the only way, Helena. If we don't do that, your whole tibia bone could end up rotting, and you don't want to know the loads of problems that'll bring."

I was still opposed, even though I knew that I had to proceed with this operation.

"Doctor, my daughter had to undergo surgery a little while back. And, well, it was conducted without anesthesia, so I'm sure she doesn't want to relive that painful experience."

I was glad Mother was there to explain what I had trouble saying.

"Oh, don't worry about that," the man said, waving his hand nonchalantly." We're much more equipped now, so she'll be asleep during the surgery."

"Really?"

"Yes, you'll receive anesthesia; no problem!"

Relief brought my heart beat back to normal, and I looked at Mother.

"Alright then. Let's do it."

CHAPTER 13

A trip to the hospital

The doctor in the Moshi hospital didn't speak much English. He always come to visit me once in a week

"Home?"

"No Home."

Next week again, "Home?" I'd ask.

"No Home." The doctor would say.

I couldn't help but pout. My leg was healing properly, and like any teenager, I became impatient and wanted to leave the hospital as soon as possible. Unfortunately, my doctor's answer was always negative. Waiting and doing my rehabilitation exercises were all I could do.

Then FINALLY, I asked, "Home?"

"Yes!"

Back at our hut home, Mama and Tata were really worried because it was too expensive to travel to Moshi and visit me. They could only rely on the doctors, nurses, or people travelling and passing by from Moshi to give information. They all said that I looked really unwell for many days, so my parents thought I was dying. I had developed jaundice; my whole body was yellow, shiny, and lethargic. People had begun to spread rumours that I had died.

I was finally sent home by truck again to continue my rehabilitation. From the Moshi hospital and all the way back to the hospital in Tengeru, we had to pass through a beautiful safari sanctuary. Our convoys had to stop often, so we saw lions, zebras, gazelles, and all sorts of incredible African wildlife at the roadside. The giraffes would completely block off the road as they wanted to inspect what was driving by; They would come to our trucks, peer their heads through the roof, and once satisfied, the magnificent long-legged and long-necked beasts stepped aside and let us through."

We arrived at the hospital which was closer to my home, then the nurses gave me a bath, changed my dressings, and settled me in my new hospital bed. Well, the same one, but different location.

It was at that moment Mother barged in like a storm.

"HELENA!"

She was crying, which immediately alarmed me.

"Mama, what's going on? What happened?"

"Helena! Oh, Helena!" She avoided my gaze and wiped her eyes frantically, trying to hide her distress. Eventually, she finally told me the reason for her panic.

"I heard on the news that an English ship was blown up by the Germans. And since your sister doesn't write us any letters, well, I thought... you know..."

I understood she would be worried if Jadzia was on an English ship, but it wasn't the case. Her story didn't make sense, and I was about to inquire further when Father burst into the room.

"HELENA!"

I noticed tears in his eyes, which accentuated my worry. "What is it, Tata? Why are you crying?"

He stared at me in disbelief for a moment before quickly looking away, with a blush on his cheeks and ears, then cleared his throat before speaking.

"What are you talking about? I'm not crying, this is just sweat. You know this hospital is on a hill, right? It can be pretty tiring to walk all the way up."

It was obvious he was lying, just like Mom, which only confused me more. "What's going on? Really?"

My parents looked at each other before letting out a sigh. Mother spoke first.

"The truth is someone told us they saw how skinny you became and that your nutrition was so bad that... well..."

"They said you were dead," Father admitted, "so we heard the truck was coming from the Moshi hospital, and we rushed here since we were worried. But I guess we feel embarrassed now to have believed such a tale right away."

Mama and Tata were really worried because it was too expensive to travel to Moshi and visit me. They could only rely on the doctors or people passing by from Moshi to give information. They all said that I looked really unwell for many days, so my parents thought I was dying.

"Thank you for worrying about me, but I promise I'm fine. I'll make sure to eat well too."

They smiled, and I saw a tear slide down Father's cheek; He didn't wipe it away.

It's true they looked embarrassed, but the relief was the main expression on their faces. I realized at that moment how bad my health had become. I had developed jaundice, and my whole body was yellow, shiny, and lethargic. People had begun to spread rumours that I had died. What had gotten into me? After starving in Siberia, I purposely refused to eat when I had food at my disposal? And I had made my parents worry so much. I felt a lot of shame and guilt, and decided I would properly nourish myself from now on. After all, I wasn't going to rot on this hospital bed, not after everything I went through. I had to get better as soon as possible to enjoy the life and youth I still had.

"Your rehabilitation is going well, Helena. You're making good progress!"

"Really? So I'll be able to go home?"

"Not yet, not yet."

"But sir! I've been doing quite well lately, and…"

I was interrupted by someone opening the door of my room. Father emerged, and I heard the doctor let out a short sigh of relief.

"Well, it looks like you have a visitor! I'll leave you two alone."

Without a moment to spare, he quickly exited the room. I was astonished because I almost never had visitors, especially family.

"Hi, Hela! How are you feeling?"

"Same as always. Mama isn't with you?"

"No. She had a few errands and said she'll drop by tomorrow instead."

He sat down, and we chatted a bit. He told me about the stove he built with one of our neighbours, which his wife and Mother used to bake bread.

"We also built a gazebo; it's rather nice! Some nights, we go there and play cards. I'll show you when you come out."

"A stove and then a gazebo? What's next, a house?"

"That's not a bad idea. Anna does sometimes complain about our hut being too small."

Soon, it was dark outside, and Father got up to leave. Unconsciously, I grabbed the hem of his shirt, and he turned to look at me. "What is it?"

"Um… well…"

Lately, I'd been thinking about how I had not attended school because of my injury. I missed my whole sixth grade and wasn't in the mood to repeat it since I was already pretty behind due to the war. However, the words didn't come out at that moment and I simply let go of his shirt.

"Nothing. I just can't wait to finally get out of here."

He nodded before leaving the room.

I thought the day would never come; The day I would be free from the squeaky rusty bed, the poorly painted walls, and the smelly antiseptics. On that day, both my parents came to pick me up the day I got discharged, and I walked away from the hospital with a broad smile on my face, hoping I would never have to set foot back in there again.

Even though I was finally back home, my leg hadn't completely recovered. I could walk and run but didn't have my full mobility back, so sometimes I got tired or felt pain from covering a long distance.

My friend, Irena came to visit me the day after I left the hospital.

"Welcome back, Helena!"

"Thanks! It's good to be back!"

"Now that you're discharged, you'll finally be able to take part in our excursions and safaris. They're so much fun! We get to see all sorts of wild animals in their natural habitat. At first, I was a bit scared, but not anymore. And..."

Irena rambled about all the fun I'd finally be able to have until she stopped suddenly.

"What is it?"

"Well... I just thought that you've been in the hospital for a long time and missed all of sixth grade. We're moving on to secondary school, but I don't know if that'll be the case for you."

She touched on the subject I had been avoiding to address with my parents, but since Tata was in the room, I could no longer keep it under wraps.

"It's true, Helena. What are we going to do about your schooling?" It was as if he only realized the predicament I was in at that moment.

"I don't know, but what I do know is that I don't want to repeat sixth grade. I'm already so behind!"

"Hmm... you're right."

Thankfully, he didn't oppose it but instead decided we'd think about it before making any decision. I simply wanted to move on to secondary school like the rest of my friends.

"Don't worry! I'm sure we'll find a solution!" Irena said to me with a smile.

Actually, the solution did come, and sooner than expected, too.

One evening, Tata returned with great news.

"Helena, you won't have to repeat your sixth grade!"

"Really? How come?"

"Well, you know that Irena's mother is the principal of one of the trade schools in camp, right?"

I had completely forgotten about that detail.

"I bumped into her today, and she told me she was talking about you with her daughter. Irena told her you were out of the hospital and didn't want to return to sixth grade in elementary school, so she said she'd be happy to take you into her sewing college since she knows you're a bright girl. Isn't that great?"

He almost seemed more excited than I was. A proud smile stretched my lips and I was overjoyed at the news.

"That's perfect! I'm so glad I get to advance like the others!"

I had feared I wouldn't be progressing in life yet again, but things were turning out quite well. All that was left was to do the paperwork for me to register, and soon enough, I became a fully-fledged senior student in trade school.

Later in life, I realized that attending this sewing college would have been the best gift. I excelled so well and later became very popular and skilled in this trade. Irena went to regular high-school, however, we met and talked after our classes all the time despite being in different schools.

Irena and I made our way down the road after school, chatting as always.

"Ugh, my project is giving me so much trouble! I always mess up the sewing and have to restart!"

"You have to do the technique the teacher showed you, remember?"

"I tried, but it's pretty hard. Do you think you could help me, Hela? You seem to be doing just fine with your lessons."

"Sure, I'll help."

I attended the dress-making and designing school her Mama ran. I really enjoyed it and always learned a lot. My friend, on the other hand, sometimes struggled with her assignments. As we walked, we heard the sound of voices, which intrigued us. We got closer to the noise and discovered the members of the theatre ensemble rehearsing.

"Oh! Let's go take a look!"

"Why?"

"What do you mean, 'why'? It's not every day we get to watch them rehearse. And with how popular the troupe has become, it'll be like watching celebrities."

Her argument didn't convince me since I knew from the direction her eyes were pointed at; there was an actor in particular - and not the whole troupe - that interested her. Nonetheless, I followed my friend to have a seat on the benches in front of the stage. The theatre was open to the sky, having no more than a few leaves as its roof. The stage was simply a platform and had curtains as well. The audience area gradually inclined towards the slope, which allowed for great acoustics. Vegetation was all around us, creating a beautiful and organic setting.

Irena and I sat on the furthest benches, trying to stay quiet and hidden from the actors. My friend was getting an eyeful of the one she came to see, but I, on the other hand, simply enjoyed the beauty of their play. Oftentimes, the ensemble performed religious plays, native plays, or some literary creations adapted for a stage representation. I could sense the passion and enjoyment in their performance; Acting was a great way to get the youth involved in creating and working hard on a common project.

It was evening, and the sun was setting on this beautiful stage. Shades of orange invaded the green plants as the melting sun poured itself on the land. Golden highlights lit up the eyes of the actors, interpreting the excitement they felt each time they took on the role of a given character. I looked at Irena; she was beaming. Her blond hair glimmered, and the same light was in her gaze. But for her, I knew why.

All was going well until I was spotted.

"There is Fąfara up there!"

Somehow, one of the actors noticed my presence. Instantly, I turned to my friend.

"We need to run away."

"What? Why?"

"I heard them shout my name. They know I'm up here!" Without waiting for her reply, I quickly got up and left, dashing up the hill as fast as I could.

"Wait! It isn't like that!"

Irena tried her best to catch up and get me to come back, but I wasn't listening. I was scared the actors would get mad at us for spying on their rehearsal, and I had had my share of boys getting mad at me! I kept running and running until I made it up the hill. Once I arrived at the top, I finally stopped and rested. A throbbing pain spread throughout my leg, and I regretted pushing myself so far. A few moments later, I saw Irena panting and puffing as she walked up and joined me.

"Geez, Helena! Why'd you have to… sprint up this huge mountain?" She leaned on a tree to catch her breath, fanning herself with her hand.

"I told you it's because they spotted me and called out my name."

Irena glared at me, clearly mad that I interrupted her admiration but also annoyed about having had to run up this hill.

"OMG, for GOODNESS sake!" She had finally caught her breath and stood up straight. "They didn't say 'Fạfara,' they said *kotara*[13]!' One of them said they had to close the curtain."

"*Kotara?* Are you sure?"

"Yes! I can't believe you made me run for this." She dusted off her hands and started walking again. I joined her.

"I'm sorry, I was sure they called my name!"

She shook her head as a reply, and I decided to quickly change the subject.

"By the way, I can help you tonight with your project if you want."

---

13   Curtain

She didn't answer for a bit, before muttering a "fine" between her teeth. As we kept walking, the road was getting worse. It had rained hard the previous night, so there was mud everywhere. At some point, we reached a large puddle that blocked our way.

"Hmm… Maybe we should try going somewhere else," I suggested, but Irena shook her head.

"No need. We can just jump over the puddle."

"Yeah, you're right." I decided to go first. I bent my knees before leaping as far as I could. Unfortunately, I couldn't jump too far and landed right in the middle of the puddle. *Splash!*

"Helena!"

I was all wet and muddy, and the feeling was disgusting as everything splashed under my skirt. I turned to look at Irena, who stared at me with round eyes.

"Why'd you suggest we jump?"

"I said to jump *over* the puddle. Not right into it, silly!"

Once again, she shook her head, clearly disappointed by my behaviour.

"Look. *This* is how it's done." She took a few steps back, then ran and leaped right over the puddle. She turned around, and I noticed the smug look on her face.

"Make sure you do better next time!"

"Yeah, yeah."

I was mad that my friend was trying to 'one up' me. With that, I returned home, covered in muddy water.

<hr />

That night as I was getting ready for bed, I realized I had left my school books in the gazebo when I went to study there during the evening. Janek had shipped them to me since they had better resources in Egypt, so I knew they were very valuable and irreplaceable.

"Tata, could you get my books for me, please? They're in the gazebo."

It was already nighttime, and I didn't want to go out, especially since I was only in my nightgown. Unfortunately, Father also didn't seem too keen on going out at this hour.

"It's a bit late. Can't you just go tomorrow?"

"Someone might steal them! You know how precious textbooks are."

"I'm sure no one will take them."

"But there are also snakes out there!"

"Don't worry, snakes don't read."

Seeing I wasn't getting anywhere, I sighed and simply went out myself. I reached the gazebo and opened the green fence, quickly spotting the two books I had left on the table. However, there was something on them.

"A rope? Who left it here?"

As I came close and extended my hand to grab the object, I noticed the long green rope was actually a boa constrictor! It popped its head towards me, fangs out and eyes menacing.

"AAAAAH!" I took several steps back before deciding it was safer to run straight home. I sprinted as fast as I could and closed the door behind me.

"What is it, Hela?"

"Snake! There's a snake out there! It's in the gazebo!"

Father immediately knew what to do and grabbed the small axe he kept for emergencies. He left the hut only to return about ten or fifteen minutes later with my books in one hand, and his bloody ax in the other.

"Here."

He handed me what I went out for before going to clean his weapon.

"Did you get him?"

He looked at me, a smirk on his face.

"Chopped his head right off!"

"Eww!"

Mama and I were disgusted, but also relieved. Not that killing one snake would change much. Even if one died tonight, we'd find another ten in the morning. Since that incident, I hardly ever went to the gazebo alone.

A little while after I got discharged from the hospital, Mama was admitted as a patient.

"So the doctors still aren't sure about what she has?"

"Yes. Dr. Nowak said there seems to be abdominal swelling and is trying to understand what's causing it. For now, they'll make her run some tests and watch how she reacts to certain treatments."

Tata seemed just as unsure as I was about Mama's condition. It was hard to come back to the hospital all the time to visit her because it reminded me of my own convalescence period. We waited until we finally received the verdict.

"She has excessive gas build-up. I haven't been able to identify the exact cause, but it might be linked to a lack of fiber in her diet or, if the cause is more severe, a large bowel obstruction. That means there's a blockage in her large intestine that is preventing her from passing gas or stool from the body. It would also explain the abdominal bloating she's been suffering from."

None of these medical terms sounded reassuring. Father was also getting worried and asked what we both needed to know.

"Please, Doctor, Can you help my wife?"

"Well, unfortunately, we don't have the technology to do anything fancy. The best I can recommend is that she drinks more water and eats more fruits and vegetables. She should also try to do more exercise if she can. We'll keep her in the hospital to monitor her in case any complications arise."

Hearing that wasn't encouraging in the least. Father and I couldn't do much but hope and pray that the doctor's recommendations would suffice. We kept going to the hospital to visit Mama, and it pained me each time.

"How are you feeling today, Mama?"

"Ah, same. I did everything Dr. Nowak advised me, but it doesn't seem to be helping much. Maybe I just need to wait a bit longer."

"And have you tried exercising?"

"I take walks now and then, but the bloating really hurts. Sometimes I feel nauseous or have very bad stomach aches, which makes it hard to move."

I was saddened because I had to see Mama in such a state. Back in Siberia, I saw how stress had ruined her physically. During the two years we spent there, it seemed as if she had aged by ten or fifteen years. I still remember the large white patch growing on the side of her head. However, since we came to Africa, she had regained her former beauty and joie de vivre; at least until now.

"Well, we'll keep praying, and hopefully, you'll be out of here soon. Don't forget you told me to be patient when I was in the hospital."

A forced smile crept up her lips. I knew her situation was different from mine. In my case, all I had to do was do my physiotherapy and wait for my leg to heal. However, it was different for Mama because the doctors weren't sure how to help her, and even if they gave a few suggestions, they didn't believe it would heal her.

"By the way, Ludwig isn't here again today?"

I sadly shook my head. Tata hadn't been feeling well for a bit, so it was just me visiting Mama.

"He said he'll try to drop by tomorrow."

"That's what he said yesterday too. Are you sure he's OK?"

I wanted to answer her, but honestly, I couldn't. Somehow, my Father hadn't been doing so well lately. Tata tried to convince me that he had a small fever, but a week had passed, and there were no signs of his health improving.

"Maybe he just needs some rest. I'm sure it's nothing serious."

Mama looked at me dubiously, and I began to doubt my own words. Tata couldn't possibly get sick now, not when his wife needed him by her side. Not when I needed him to reassure me everything would turn out OK.

It was a real summer day. The sun burned our tanned skin, and the cicadas sang louder than ever. Heat waves emerged from the earth, and thick sweat drops pearled on our foreheads. Once again, I was in the hospital visiting Mama. Her condition wasn't improving, and the doctors feared she might have complications.

"And Ludwig? How is he?"

I lowered my head. Tata wasn't necessarily in a critical condition but wasn't doing well. Actually, he was now spending his third day in the hospital due to a heart problem, so when I finished visiting Mama, I went to see him.

"Well… the doctors are doing all they can, but he's still feeling very weak."

"I'll go see him." Mother made tremendous efforts to extract herself from her bed, and I tried to stop her.

"Are you sure you should be moving? Your stomach has been getting bigger because of the gas, so maybe you should lie down."

She nagged me like a pregnant woman, demanding that she's fine.

"Don't worry. Besides, I was told to exercise. This is a great excuse!"

She got up and trudged to the door without listening to what I had to say. I stayed close to her in case she needed some assistance. It took us a while, but eventually, we made it to Father's room down the hall.

"Ludwig!"

He turned at the sound of his name, and a smile spread his lips.

"What are you doing here? You should be in bed."

She ignored his comment and nearly collapsed in the chair next to him, letting out a sigh of relief.

"How are you feeling?"

That seemed to be the only question we'd been asking each other lately, and I was slowly growing tired of it. My parents chatted a bit until they were interrupted by a loud noise.

"AAAAH!!"

I poked my head out of the room to check who was screaming and saw two nurses trying to calm down a lady who seemed familiar.

"AAAAH!"

"Please, calm down, Mrs. Jankowski!"

She didn't listen and kept screaming until they forced her into a room and shut the door. We could still hear her yelling, but at least it was muffled now. I went back to my parents and explained what had happened.

After that incident, I stayed a little longer before heading back home. Zoszia had come once again, and I was glad I wasn't alone. However, she was heading back to Nairobi the next day. She didn't come to the hospital with me because she had gone to see a few friends, but she promised to visit my parents before she left.

"How are they?" she asked as I arrived home that evening.

"So, so." I sat down and let out a long sigh.

She must have noticed my fatigue because she asked: "And you? How are you?"

I looked at her and noticed worry on her face. It was nice to know she was concerned about me.

"I'm just trying to stay strong. It's not easy to have both my parents in the hospital and no siblings around. Plus, I also need to keep up with my studies."

For the past few days, I'd been feeling exhausted, having to do shuttles from home to school, to the hospital, and back home. Zoszia sat in front of me and smiled.

"You're doing great, Helena, and I admire your resilience. But don't forget you're human too, and still a teenager. I'm sure your parents won't be mad if you take some time for yourself."

Her reassuring words were just what I needed to hear, instantly relieving me of my pressuring stress. I guess you're right; I am doing a good job!

A little over two weeks had gone by, and my parents were still hospitalized. In fact, Mama was getting worse by the day. Her stomach kept getting bigger due to all the gas pent up inside. Because of that, she felt awful pain. Tata, on the other hand, was getting better.

"I'm sorry, but there's nothing more we can do for her."

"But doctor! My wife is slowly dying on that bed! Isn't there some medicine that can help her?"

"I'm really sorry."

Dr. Nowak was of no use, which only upset us more. Father especially had a hard time dealing with this situation.

"I will not let her die there! I will not!"

Tears pricked his eyes, but he didn't have the chance to shed them because we were disturbed by the same loud noise.

"AAAAH!"

"Ugh, Dear Lord! Not again!"

As always, the screaming lady made her way down the hall, bothering everyone with her shrieks. I finally remembered where I knew her from. She had been one of the teachers at the elementary school I went to before my injury. It seemed like one day, she simply lost her mind and started yelling and cursing all the time. Some doctors suggested it might have been caused by the trauma she went through in Siberia and decided to let her "express herself" in order to let out all her "negative emotions." I didn't know how much of that was true, but I did know that she was quite noisy and getting on everyone's nerves.

"You know what? Enough is enough!" Father marched straight towards her, more determined than ever. I recognized the stern look in his eyes, meaning he wasn't playing anymore.

"Hey you! Jankowski!"

"AAAAH!!"

"Mrs. Jankowski!"

The lady turned around, surprised to hear Father call her name. He kept coming closer until they were only about 50 centimeters apart. Many doctors and nurses paused in the hallway and turned to watch the scene.

A few patients also came out of their room, curious of how things would unfold.

"Do you know my wife is ill and lying on a hospital bed?"

"Um... I..." she stammered.

"Do you?"

"No! I didn't know!" She was clearly startled by how serious he was.

"Well, even if you didn't know, you do know there are other patients in this hospital, don't you?"

Her loud voice had disappeared, and she simply nodded.

"So why do you scream? Don't you know people come here for rest and proper care? Why is it that you have to bother everyone?"

"Well... I...."

"I don't want to hear it!"

Father was really giving her a lecture now. Not minding her trauma! He was more than fed up with her behaviour. He pointed a menacing finger toward the window and said: "Do you see that lake?"

Mrs. Jankowski slowly turned in the direction he pointed at. From where they were, they could see Lake Duluti. It was bottomless and surrounded by red stones. Everyone was afraid to swim there.

"Yes," the former teacher shyly answered.

"If you continue screaming like that, I promise I will tie you up in a potato sack and throw you in that lake! Then you can have fun bothering the fish with your annoying yelling. I'll be watching you, understand?"

She quickly nodded, and I could see her hands shaking. No one talked and instead had their eyes opened wide after hearing Father's threat. He stared at her sternly for a few more seconds, making sure she knew he wasn't joking, then made his way back to his room. Slowly, the small crowd dispersed and returned to their own business. I followed Tata.

"I can't believe you just told her that!"

"Someone had to. Trauma or no trauma, she can't penalize everyone for what she went through. And Anna..."

He didn't finish his sentence and just let out a sigh. I understood his feelings. We were very worried for her, and it seemed like even the doctors had given up hope.

"You know, Helena…"

Father looked at me, and there was a sadness in his eyes that immediately alarmed me.

"What is it?"

He stayed quiet for a bit. Actually, it seemed like the words he wanted to say didn't come out. Or couldn't?

"Never mind."

He laid down in his hospital bed and pulled the blanket up to his ears. I wanted to ask what he was about to say, but for me too, the words were stuck in my throat.

"I really want Anna to live."

"Yes, me too."

A silent tear slid down my cheek as I exited the room.

I was making my way toward Mama's room as usual. As I approached the door, I heard voices coming from inside. One was Mama's, and it took me a little while to recognize the other.

"Through this Holy anointing, may the Lord in His love and mercy help you with the grace of the Holy Spirit. May the Lord who frees you from sin save you and raise you up."

A shiver went down my spine as I heard all the familiar prayers; the one recited for the anointing of the sick.

It was the last blessing where we asked God to receive Anna in Heaven. Memories are shared, grudges are resolved, and Anna was coming to terms with her own death.

I listened in a bit longer, not wanting to believe my suspicions. There was a bit of muffled noise, but I had no trouble imagining what was going on. It was time for the final prayer.

"This is the Lamb of God who takes away the sins of the world. Happy are those who are called to His supper."

Not being able to bear it any longer, I opened the door, finding Mother extending her hands to receive her last Eucharist. She was surprised to see me, just like Father and the priest.

"Helena?"

"So it's true?"

My parents seemed confused, and the priest didn't know what to do. Uncontrollable tears streamed down my cheeks. "Mama's… dying?"

CHAPTER 14

Return of peace

It took me a good 15 minutes to calm down. I didn't want to admit Mama was dying, but I knew that if the priest came to perform the last rites, she wouldn't have much time left.

"You can't go now, Mama! Not after everything we went through! You didn't die in the first war or when we were in Siberia, so you can't die here!"

"Zuzulka. (My darling bird)."

Her voice was calm and resolute. She caressed my straight hair and smiled.

"I don't get to choose when I die, only God does, and it seems He's made His decision. At least I can go peacefully, knowing my children aren't in danger anymore."

I shook my head, refusing to accept her words. Stubbornly, I kept clinging to the possibility of her making it through this disease. After all, she was one of the strongest people I knew. Somehow, she had taken care of four young children all by herself during a time of war. Even if we were undernourished, she always provided just enough for us to survive. She always placed other people's interests before her own. Mama was my angel, and I selfishly didn't want to give her back to her Creator.

Tata extended his hand to give me yet another tissue. For 15 minutes, I hadn't stopped crying. The situation was heartbreaking to bear. During that time, Tata's condition also worsened, most likely due to stress, so he still wasn't out of the hospital.

"I don't know what I'm going to do, Helena. Without your Mama, I…"

Even though the last rites had been performed, neither of us was ready to have Mom pass away. Thinking back, Tata had only been reunited with us for about two years. He feared having to part from his wife again, but this time forever.

Painful weeks sauntered by, filled with anguish and agony. I cried myself to sleep nearly every night. When I thought my tears had dried up and I had nothing left to shed, more emerged, soaking my damp pillow. Honestly, I thought I might even die of grief. I couldn't concentrate much in school and spent a lot of time in the hospital visiting my parents. Smiles were scarce, though we all tried to keep our morale high. I fervently prayed for a miracle or anything that would allow Mama to live a little longer. The good news did arrive, though they weren't what I expected.

"The war is over! The war is over!"

Shouts resounded from every corner of the camp. People ran in the streets with broad smiles and thick tears. Joy beamed on the faces of the inhabitants. All the radios had their volume cranked up to the maximum as we tried our best to receive whatever additional announcements we could.

"That coward Hitler couldn't face justice and preferred to commit suicide! Well, he better knows nothing but hell is waiting for him now!"

"Down with the Nazis! Down with Hitler!"

Everywhere was ecstasy. Everyone heard the broadcasts and talked about the same thing: the end of an all-too-long war. It was May 10, 1945, only a few days after the Reich surrendered, only a little over a week after Hitler's suicide. The Allied forces, namely the United States, England, France, and the U.S.S.R. took over, dividing Germany among these four parties and bringing an end to their reign of tyranny. Saying we were happy about the Reich's fall is an understatement. We were jubilant!

Celebrations exploded left and right; as some danced, others sang, and others feasted. Still, there was a melancholic undertone in the air, as we couldn't help but think of all those who perished in the deadly claws of the war, soldiers and civilians alike. We couldn't help but wonder if it was really worth the huge human sacrifice.

"Mama, did you hear? The war is over!"

I also had mixed feelings because of Mama. I couldn't rejoice now, thinking of all the innocents who would be spared when she was on the verge of death.

"Don't worry, Helena. I'm happy to hear this mess is over. I am now assured that there is hope for the future."

"But what about your future?"

She didn't answer, so once again, I couldn't stop myself from crying. What was the point of being free if she wouldn't enjoy that freedom with us? She fought too! Even if it wasn't with guns and tanks, she fought for our safety and survival. Didn't she also deserve to reap what we all sowed: peace?

One day, I got to the hospital with my heavy body and puffy eyes. I always feared going to the hospital because I never knew if I'd find Mama alive or not. I'd pause for a few seconds before knocking on her door and entering, unprepared for whatever I'd find inside. Thankfully, that day she was still alive.

"Hi, Helena."

"Hi, Mama."

I didn't say much lately. Not because there wasn't much to be said but because some words were too hard to pronounce. So we sat there in silence, simply enjoying the other's presence, ignorant of how long it would last. Sometimes, I would randomly start crying, and sometimes my eyes were too dry. My mood didn't change much; I simply moved back and forth from a depressing state to a slightly less depressing one. I was growing numb.

"You know, Helena... for the funeral..."

My head turned, and my eyes widened. My senses were on alert, and my heart started pounding. My throat felt awfully dry, and I wanted to say something to stop her from continuing, but the words were stuck.

"I'd like it if you wore that dress I made you. You know the dark one with the flowers on the bottom?"

I didn't answer because I was unable to. Mama probably interpreted my silence as an encouragement for her to continue.

"And you should wear the black shoes Zosia gave you. They look very nice. Your hair can be in a bun, but make sure it's neat. And..."

"Stop." Finally, I said something. Mama obeyed. I saw the tears crashing on my lap, soaking my skirt. We both stayed quiet, and an awkward silence filled the room. I had my head down but could tell from my peripheral vision that Mama's shoulders were shaking, meaning she was trying to control her sobs. I couldn't move. There was an immense pain in my chest, so vivid and acute that I thought I might die. And then my savior came.

"Hi, Anna!"

"Oh, Ludwig."

Tata entered, followed by the priest. I saw the servant of God as an angel of death, remembering the last rites he performed on Mama not too long ago. Without thinking, I got up and glared at him.

"Why are you here? Didn't you already do your job?" I knew it wasn't his fault Mama was dying, but it felt like he had confirmed it, and since I was full of pain, I had to direct my negative feelings towards someone. Unfortunately for him, he was the victim I chose.

"A priest from another camp came to visit the other day and brought me this medicine. He says it's quite effective, so I thought it might help."

He showed us a small container full of yellow pills.

"It's our last option," Tata said. "I thought we might as well try it."

He looked at me, then looked at Mama. She didn't say anything and simply stared at the container before nodding slowly. The priest gave us the medicine and left. Father explained the dosage to Mother, who kept nodding. He also spoke with the nurses and doctor taking care of her.

"Now, all we can do is pray." Tata placed his hand on my shoulder, and I nodded in response.

Miracles happen in the most unexpected ways, which is probably what defines them as miracles. I didn't expect those pills to do much for Mama, but they did! They did more than enough.

"It seems the gas is leaving, which is a good sign. Her bowel movement is also becoming more frequent."

For once, Dr. Nowak's words were reassuring. Mama had been doing much better in the past week and a half, and hope was suddenly in sight again.

"If this keeps up, she might make it out of here on her own two feet!"

Just as Mother was getting better, Father's health improved as well. His stress level decreased, allowing him to focus on his recovery. Mama never spoke of her funeral again, so I forced myself to believe it was because it wouldn't be happening anytime soon.

"How are you feeling today, Anna?"

"A lot better. I don't have those stomach aches anymore, and I've been getting a lot of rest."

"I'm glad to hear!"

"You know, ever since you threatened Mrs. Jankowski, she never bothered me or any other patient again."

"It's because she understood that she shouldn't mess with me!"

Tata winked at me as he flexed his biceps to show how tough he was, which made me laugh. Finally, genuine smiles appeared on our faces, and the atmosphere in the room wasn't as heavy. We also informed my siblings of the situation, and they were happy to hear Mama was doing better. It was good to know we had their support even if they were in different parts of the world. Actually, it seemed they would soon all meet up in England. The Polish army planned to go there, meaning Janek would be with Jadzia.

The cadets were also on their way to England. This meant half my family would be there and the other half here.

As time passed, our prayers were indeed answered. Mama's gases were gone, and we couldn't thank the priest enough. He himself was surprised to learn the medicine he brought actually worked. Soon enough, both my parents and I were back in our little hut; our home.

Joy filled our hut again, and peaceful times were upon us. A few months passed, and Mama's condition was finally back to normal. A few changes in her diet and routine helped prevent constipation, and everything worked fine. It felt good to see my parents so happy. The war was over, and everyone was healthy and safe. Our only regret was that the family still needed to be fully united.

"There has been a lot of talk about what to do with all the Polish citizens that have been displaced. Most of us don't want to go back to Poland, so we need to find a country that'll welcome us."

Tata took a sip of his tea, pondering. Even though we were happy in Africa, we knew we couldn't stay here forever, so we needed to figure out our next steps.

Mama sat down with her own cup in hand.

"I heard the authorities are considering bringing the orphans back, but I'm worried about their safety. The war might be over in the world, but not in Poland."

Indeed, the Russians were still present in our motherland. Our country didn't belong to us anymore. Communism had taken over, bringing us back under siege after only a few decades of independence.

"Poor things. It's not because they don't have parents that they don't have any say in this. I doubt any child would want to go back to Poland after everything they've been through."

Tata took another sip, and I stared blankly at my empty mug. I was more than blessed to have both my parents with me, and knew it wasn't the case for everyone. I had become friends with many orphans, and even though they laughed and smiled here, sometimes they would have breakdowns and crumble because those who brought them to this world were no longer alive. Many witnessed their parents' deaths, while others simply heard of it. In all cases, it was never pleasant, and I was happy to have been spared from such anguish.

"I really hope they don't have to go back. At least, here they have opportunities, they can play and fool around, and you know, do kid stuff! Too many of us were robbed of the chance to simply be kids."

Mama placed her hand over mine. She knew it had been hard for me to deal with our circumstances at such a young age. Thankfully, I could still cling to the beautiful memories of my happy childhood before the war, and that's what helped me remember that there was a time when I too, had the chance to experience peace.

"Some of these kids were four, five, six years old when the war started. They barely remember a time before that, and now they only have bad memories of Poland. It would be too traumatizing for them to go back. Even I wouldn't want to."

***

"Don't worry, Hela. We're most likely going to stay here a little while longer."

I was about to reply but was interrupted by a knock on the door.

"Oh! That must be Regina."

I found my friend waiting for me in front of our hut.

"Hi, Helena! Are you ready?"

"Yes, let me just grab my bag."

I waved goodbye to my parents before exiting our home. Regina wanted to go to Arusha, the next town, to buy sewing material, and since

I also needed a tape measure, I decided to accompany her. We took the bus, and about 30 minutes later, we arrived at a store selling what we were looking for.

We walked to the counter where an Indian clerk, or perhaps the owner, welcomed us.

"Hi, sir. We're looking for some fabric and a tape measure."

The man didn't answer Regina and instead stared at me, which made me rather uncomfortable.

"Um... sir?" my friend asked.

He stayed quiet and kept staring at me. I considered leaving the shop, but then he finally spoke. "Is your family royalty?"

"Excuse me?"

"You must be royalty, right? Because of your mark."

He pointed between his eyes, and I understood he was referring to my birthmark in that spot. However, I still didn't see the link between my appearance and his assumption.

"Is your Father a King?"

At the time, I didn't know that apparently in India, only royals had a small dot on their forehead. I was becoming weary of this middle-aged man and thought of leaving, but then he spoke again.

"Since you're royalty, I'll give you whatever you want!"

"Whatever she wants?"

All of a sudden, Regina was very interested in the conversation, but I wasn't. I tugged the hem of her shirt to make her understand I wanted to leave. Unfortunately, she didn't - or wouldn't - get my message.

"He'll give you whatever you want, Helena!" she repeated with a smile.

"What if he's dangerous?" I whispered in Polish.

My friend scoffed and waved her hand nonchalantly. She was 20 now and believed she was the mature one between the two of us.

"Don't be ridiculous! He isn't going to hurt you," she whispered.

I was about to retort, but she turned to the shop owner.

"Her highness would like to see your best fabric, please!"

"Yes, right away!"

The man went to get what Regina asked for. While he was busy, she turned to me and winked, a triumphant smile stretching her lips. Oh boy!

"I can't believe we got all these sewing materials. For free!"

Regina wouldn't stop talking about what happened in the store during our whole trip back.

"I'll have to tell everyone about this. And from now on, I'm always taking you shopping with me!"

"So you can cheat shop owners?"

"It isn't cheating. Your Father *is* a King. The King of kings!"

"I don't think he meant my Heavenly Father."

She didn't care about my remark. Eventually, she calmed down and promised she wouldn't do such a trick again.

"We'll just let it slide for today. And besides, you did need the tape measure."

"Yeah, yeah."

"What is it again that your class has to make?"

"We'll be helping out the theatre troupe by making their costumes. I'll be taking the actors' measurements tomorrow."

"That's nice. And how's school going?"

"Pretty well. I like the projects we're given. It's just that..."

"That..?"

In Tengeru, I went to an all-girls school, and we learned about different fashion trends from different eras. Even though we were a trade school, we also studied basic school subjects such as history and math.

"Well, we have to write an essay in history class titled 'The Situation of Poland in Present Time.' It's pretty self-explanatory, but basically, we need to write about Poland's current situation. The problem is we don't have many resources, so I don't know how I'll be able to do this project."

I was a very competent student and didn't have trouble getting good grades, but this assignment was giving me issues. I had brainstormed ideas, though they weren't great.

"I'm sure you'll do fine. Don't forget you're someone *really* special!"

I looked at her, confused. A large smile stretched her lips.

"You're royalty!" She burst out laughing before I had the chance to say anything.

The deadline for my essay was fast approaching. I still didn't know what to write and was prepared to receive a bad grade; At least, until we received a letter from Janek.

"What? He wants to go to Brazil?" I asked.

"Yes, to live with his girlfriend and her family."

Father put down the sheet of paper and rubbed his blue eyes as he let out an exasperated sigh. Now that the war was over, soldiers were told to choose a country to immigrate to and establish themselves in. They were given the option of countries willing to accept them, and all the expenses of the trip would be paid for. I took the letter and read it myself. Not only did my brother want to go to Brazil to follow his girlfriend, but he also wanted us to go with him!

"There's no way I'm going there," Father said. "What are we even going to do in Brazil?"

"Maybe there'll be new opportunities for us there? We never know."

"Opportunities for what, Anna? I'm not saying it's a bad country, but I don't think it's the one for us."

"Then tell your son that."

I agreed with Father and wasn't too keen on going to South America. For the past few years, I had been moved around from place to place without much choice. Now that we got the chance to make our decision, I thought we should choose wisely and not naively pursue someone we loved.

"I got it!"

Tata suddenly rose to grab a pen and paper. We asked what was going on, but he didn't answer. Instead, he started writing. He continued for a few minutes and then, satisfied, proudly showed us his work. I took the letter and read it aloud:

"Dear Janek, I am happy to hear you are doing well. I understand your desire to want to live with the person you love. You are an adult now, which means you are old enough to make your own decisions, so if you want to go to Brazil, I won't stop you. However, the rest of the family won't be following you. Instead, we will go back to Poland. Now that the war is over, we should do our part and help rebuild the country. I look forward to hearing from you again. Sincerely, Your Father, Ludwig Fąfara."

"You want us to go back to Poland?" Mama asked, alarmed.

"Of course not. It's just to scare him a little. I want all of us to be reunited, but not in Brazil.

Mama smiled as she understood her husband's little trick.

"You little sneak!"

"Let's see if Janek will pick his family or his girlfriend."

With that, he left right away to send the letter.

The reply arrived about ten days later, and we were surprised to receive two thick envelopes. Father's trick worked perfectly, as my brother was alarmed to hear we'd return to Poland. Obviously, no one wanted to go back since it was still too dangerous, but he fell for Tata's trap. He fervently advised us against it. In his letter, he explained how Poland used to be, and how it is now. His goal was evidently to dissuade us from going back to our home country. He meticulously detailed the sociopolitical state of our country before and after the war, naming major actors and using complicated terms that would even put some scholars to shame. He concluded by saying we'd be making a huge mistake if we went back.

"Wow, I didn't expect this much of a reply."

It had taken Tata about 10 minutes to read the whole thing. Mama only skimmed through it after he told her the gist of it. I also read the letter and was quite impressed. This material was conveniently perfect for my essay!

"I don't want him to think this is going to convince us to follow him. I'll just plainly say that if he goes to Brazil, we're going to Poland. He knows how bad it is there, so if he cares about us, he'll cancel his trip."

As Tata began writing his reply, I began working on my assignment. There was so much useful information in Janek's letter that I decided to use it all, tweaking a few parts here and there. Late in the night, I looked at my finished product, exhausted and proud. My school project was complete.

My heart started beating a bit faster as I made my way to the principal's office. I didn't know why I had been called; I wasn't the type of girl to get in trouble. Shyly, I knocked on the door and only entered the room after I heard a voice say, "Come in." The principal looked at me and gestured for me to take a seat in front of her. I tried my best to relax and keep my composure. Even though Mrs. Trybuwski was the school principal, she was also Irena's Mama, and I had known them both since we were in Siberia, making this situation a bit awkward, however, I believed we had a bond.

"Do you know why I called you here, Helena?"

"No, Ma'am."

"It's about this."

She opened a drawer in her desk and pulled out two sheets of paper. After looking at them for a few seconds, I recognized my handwriting and knew this was my essay. Oh no! Had she figured out these weren't my ideas? I was becoming more and more nervous; suddenly, she smiled, revealing a dimple on her left cheek.

"I must say, I was quite impressed by your work. It's so detailed! Even I learned a few things while reading it." She gazed at it and kept nodding. "Your teacher insisted that I read it, and I'm glad I did. You are a smart student, Helena!"

"Thank you, Ma'am." I felt bad taking credit for my brother's work but didn't know how to tell the truth. The principal kept admiring my essay as if she couldn't get over it. After a few seconds of awe, she turned and stared at me straight in the eyes.

"I have one question, though. Did your Father help you write it?"

"No, Ma'am."

I wasn't lying since Tata had nothing to do with this assignment.

"So you wrote it yourself? All of it?"

My guilt amplified, and my palms became sweaty. I was too scared to tell the truth at this point.

"Yes, Ma'am."

You see, the thing is that I wasn't lying, but I wasn't telling the whole truth either. I DID write it by myself, but nobody asked if the essay was my own idea!

She raised a thin eyebrow, dubious, but then suddenly, her expression relaxed, and a large smile beamed on her face.

"Wow! I knew you were a great student, but this is fantastic! I'm very impressed you did this all by yourself!"

My heart was beating faster, and I tried my best to look normal. Inwardly, I kept begging God to forgive me for this lie. Mrs. Trybuwski got up and paced back and forth as she rubbed her chin with her long fingers.

"You know, I was thinking of having this published."

"Published?"

"Yes!"

Her eyes were full of enthusiasm, which only made me feel guiltier.

"I want other schools to read this and have it in the paper too, so that the other Polish public can read your work. It will be a good way to show one of our students' talent and educate the population. I think we should also keep it as a model when we teach students how to write essays."

She went on and on, but I barely listened. After rambling for about twenty minutes, she let me return to class, saying she'd be looking forward to reading my next essays. I only hoped Janek would start writing to us more often.

My Father, Ludwig Fąfara, in his WWI Soldier Uniform.

My Father's portrait, Ludwig Fąfara.

Recovering from my leg injury at the hospital with my patient mates. I am front row, first from the left.

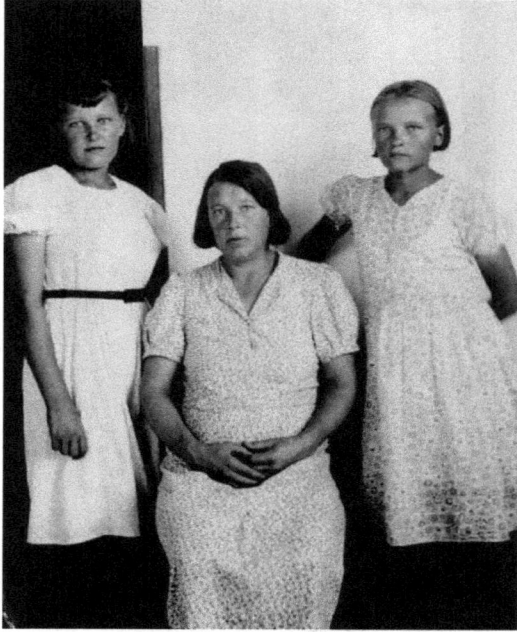

From the left, my older sister Jadzia, My Mother Anna, and
myself Helena to the right, Tengeru, Africa.

My family at our home in the Tengeru village. Front row on the left, our
neighbour, Mama, Tata, and myself, sanding right behind my Tata.

My parents Anna & Ludwig and I, Helena at our home 22E, Tengeru, Africa.

Gathering of my family and our neighbours from our settlement in Tengeru,
Africa. My Father Ludwig is sitting in the middle of the group with a
blazer and a tie. My Mother is standing on the right in a white dress with
dark buttons and I am kneeling with my white teacher's uniform.

One of my classes. I am the first person standing from the left and my supervisor fourth from the left is overseeing my successful instructions and the students.

**Myself and my colleague posing together before teaching sewing
classes. I am first from the left, Tengeru, Africa.**

My sewing school students proudly wearing their own designs and
creations of our Polish national costumes, Tengeru, Africa.

My senior students and I as their sewing teacher, Tengeru, Africa.

One of the many beautiful embroidery pieces I taught my students, which eventually became part of the exhibitions celebrating our Polish national culture. From the left, me and my student, Tengeru, Africa.

Myself and my students from sewing school, Tengeru, Africa. I am second from the left.

The teachers and senior administrators responsible for organizing and running our community in Tengeru, Africa and then later in England.

I am wearing a white dress right at the middle of the tree, top row, 12th from the left. Class photo, Tengeru, Africa.

School staff, administrators and teachers at our settlement in Tengeru, Africa. I am in the middle row, 6th from the left.

My photo Helena Fąfara, Tengeru, Africa.

My classmates and teachers, Tengeru, Africa. I am kneeling, right side, at very front.

My classmates and our beloved priest Fr. Krulikowski (who wrote about his experiece titled *Stolen Childhood*), who saved us all from Siberia and organized the African settlement in Tengeru. I am second row standing, first from the right.

My future husband, same age as me when I was in Africa. Zbyszek as a cadet, Egypt, WWII.

**MV Winchester Castle Union-Castle Mail Steamship Company Ltd. sailed from Mombasa
with 790 Polish displaced persons arriving in Southampton on the 15th of August 1948.
My name as well as the names of Mama and Tata were listed on the actual manifest below.**

	NAME	M	F	OCCUPATION
123	FAFARA Ludwik	49		
124	FAFARA Anna		43	Housewife
125	FAFARA Helena		18	

Part 6

England

MV Winchester Castle Union

Dar es Salaam–Arabian Sea–Red Sea–
Mediterranean Sea–Atlantic Ocean–English
Channel–Port of South Hampton

Air Force Base in East Moor

Yorkshire

CHAPTER 15

Opportunities

I was taking notes in class as usual when the teacher interrupted her lesson.

"Helena, go to the bathroom to wash your face. You have mud on your forehead."

"Mud?"

"Yes, right here." She pointed at the space between my eyes, and I knew she referred to my birthmark. I was so embarrassed. No one had mentioned it before, but lately, I'd been scratching it a lot, which somehow made it grow and become much more noticeable.

"Actually, Ma'am, that's not mud."

"Of course it is. I can tell."

"But it's…"

"Helena, I know what I'm seeing." She snapped.

Unfortunately, she didn't want to listen, and I was feeling more and more embarrassed since all the attention was on me and my huge birthmark. Thankfully, the girl sitting next to me intervened.

"Excuse me, Ma'am, but that's how her face actually is."

"Nonsense. I would have noticed such a mark before. Is this supposed to be some joke? How dare you?"

She was becoming irritated, her thin brown brows furrowed. I didn't want things to worsen, so I tried one last time to convince her.

"I've always had this mark on my face. I can't remove it."

I rubbed my forehead to show I wasn't lying. The lady inched closer and examined me attentively, her green eyes zooming in on my forehead. Then she took a step back.

"I guess you're right, it isn't mud, but you should probably get that checked out by a doctor."

I was already fed up with doctors and hospitals but simply nodded in response. With the interruption over, she continued her lesson.

"So, as I was telling you girls, it's very important that you master these skills. You are now in your last year, and after that, you enter real life. I know some of you think school is boring or like a prison, and you can't wait to be out, but trust me: *this* is the time in your life when your entire future is founded from. Once school is over, that's when you have the opportunity to build the life you wish for."

We had been receiving many similar speeches lately since the end of our school year was nearing. Like many of the girls here, I was excited to finally enter adulthood. All the knowledge learned in class only became useful when we could put it into practice, so we were eager to do just that.

"The war is over, and the world is slowly going back to normal. Eventually, you too will be going off somewhere to start a life. That's why you need to learn some skills to find work. The Bible also tells us that 'the one who is unwilling to work shall not eat.'[14] God doesn't condone laziness, and this world doesn't either."

My teacher approached me as I gathered my notebook and pencil case at the end of class.

"Helena, please follow me to the principal's office."

She didn't give me time to respond and simply turned towards the door. I feared this was about the "mud" incident and thought of justifying myself.

"You know, I didn't mean to be disrespectful in class. It's just that my birthmark..."

---

14   2 Thessalonians 3:10

"It's not about that," she cut me off. She didn't add anything, and I didn't inquire. We arrived at the familiar office, and I felt uneasy being here again. I hadn't written any new essays, so hopefully, this wasn't about any work I plagiarized. The principal smiled at me, and even my teacher's expression seemed more welcoming.

"You're probably wondering why we brought you here, so I'll get right to the point. Your teachers have told me how wonderful a student you are. You've mastered all the techniques they taught you and created beautiful designs. Since you're graduating next month, I wanted to offer you the opportunity to teach young girls how to sew."

"You want me to teach? Me?"

"Yes!"

"But... aren't I too young? I *am* barely seventeen."

"Don't worry about that. I value skill over age. You're the first one in school to whom I've asked this, and I'm sure you'll do well."

I was honoured to have been chosen for such a task. However, even if Mrs. Trybuwski had faith in me, I still had doubts.

"But... what if the students don't respect me because of my age?"

"Well, it's true that you would be teaching some girls you attended elementary school with, so they might have a hard time seeing you as their teacher, but it doesn't mean they shouldn't respect you. Make sure they call you Miss and aren't too informal. Also, if you ever make a mistake while teaching, don't say it or else they'll think you don't know what you're doing. Just do or say the correct thing next time."

She gave me more teaching advice as if I'd already accepted the job, and I carefully listened to everything she had to say. At the end of our meeting, I was still somewhat uncertain but enthusiastic about this new opportunity and decided to accept the offer.

"I'm sure you won't regret it!" were the principal's parting words as I exited her office.

The day finally came; at last, I graduated from college. I was ready for the next step at seventeen years old with my diploma in hand. Mrs. Trybuchowski and a few other teachers helped me prepare for my new job, and in September, I began teaching in a trade school with girls almost my age whom I knew from grade school. It was a bit awkward on the first day as I walked to the front of the class and saw many of my former classmates staring at me, wondering why I was up there and not sitting among them.

"Well, good morning, everyone. My name is Miss Helena, and I'll be your new sewing teacher."

Right away, the surprise was evident on the faces of those who already knew me.

"Since when are you a teacher?" one girl asked.

"This is my first day, but I received the offer a little while back."

"Why were you chosen?"

"Yeah. Aren't you too young?"

Questions fused left and right, and what I feared happened. I didn't have control over the class and didn't know what to do. I tried my best to remember all the advice I had received and attempted one tactic.

I tapped my ruler on my desk and said, "Everyone, quiet down, please. If you have a question, raise your hand."

I made sure my tone was firm and showed I wasn't intimidated by them. It took a few tries, but eventually, the girls calmed down. After that, there were a couple of other instances when I slightly lost control, but my first day wasn't too bad.

Later that evening, I played cards with my parents and our neighbours at the gazebo.

"So? How was it 'Miss Helena'?"

Tata nudged my elbow and wiggled his eyebrows. Everyone turned towards me, awaiting my answer. I did a run-through of my first day on the job, and each time I mentioned a moment when the students weren't listening, Tata laughed.

"Don't worry," he said. "I'd also have a hard time listening to a small girl like you. Especially if you were my age."

"Ludwig!"

Father ignored my Mother's scowl and took a bite of papaya.

"But what you're doing is good, Hela," my neighbour said. "Young people need to be able to make a life for themselves because the world won't be pitying us forever. It's great that you were given this opportunity and that you'll be helping other girls learn the skills that will open doors for them too."

"Well, you may not be the greatest at teaching yet, but if it reassures you, you're also not the greatest at playing cards."

"Tata, please!"

He smirked as he shuffled the deck. We spent the next two hours playing and laughing, merry as carefree children.

I soon became comfortable with my teaching job and gradually earned my students' respect. In Arusha, Tanzania, the big city which was previously burnt down was now rebuilt. The government made a program for young adults to make a living for themselves now that the war was over. I was chosen to teach one of the courses, much like Home Economics today. It was pure luck! I didn't do anything special to get this. All these girls were forever and endlessly thanking me, even to this day, for giving them the skills to live and provide them with a sense of normalcy after the war.

Things were going well, and people talked of soon going to England. Since the Polish Armies had moved there to be demobilized, scattered families might reunite there as well. Because of that, those who had family members in the army were among the first to leave Africa. But before we left, I received another job offer.

"You want me to teach older women?"

"Yes! I've heard of the wonderful work you've done for young girls. I would also like you to help older women learn to sew so that they can get jobs later on."

One of the priests approached me at the end of my shift, saying he wanted to speak to me. However, I wasn't expecting this request.

"I would love to help, but…"

Frankly, I was feeling intimidated by having to teach someone older than me. After all, I had barely overcome my uneasiness at teaching those my age, so this was too much for me. "I'm sorry, maybe someone else would be better suited for this."

"But Helena, these women really need some training! The war already took everything away from them, so how about we give them an opportunity for a change?"

I knew he wasn't wrong and that these ladies, just like us, would have to build themselves up again. After thinking it over for a few moments, I realized I had to do my part too. "Alright then. I'll teach them."

"Perfect! The other priests and I will finish organizing the logistics of the program and let you know when you'll start."

He left a skip in his step. I kept wondering if this was the right decision and if I was up for the task. All I had to do was wait; only time would tell.

It turns out I had been worried for nothing. The women didn't treat me differently because I was younger and quite eager to learn. I also had great moments with them, and it was rewarding to see the beaming expression on their faces when they proudly showed me their work. They welcomed my criticism and appreciated my praise all the more.

"How was your day, 'Miss Helena?"

She liked to call me like that outside of class with a wink. I rolled my eyes at Irena's usual joke. It was already bad enough when I was only teaching young girls, but after I told her I'd also be teaching older women, she always addressed me as "Miss Helena."

"It was great. All my students were very attentive, unlike some."

I gave her a knowing look, and she feigned ignorance. Irena was done with school but still unsure about what to do next.

"You know, I heard the priests are trying to protect the orphans and prevent them from being sent back to Poland."

"That's good news. No one wants to go back there," I replied. There were 1.5 Million people in the camp. Obviously, not all of them could go to England.

"I think they'll try to bring the children to a different country. My mother was saying they might go to Italy, but it's supposed to be secret."

I looked at Irena, knowing she wasn't the best at keeping secrets, but didn't say anything.

"Apparently, Poles are choosing between countries like New Zealand, Australia, and Canada. Soon enough, everyone is going to leave."

I sensed the melancholy in her tone and placed my hand on her shoulder.

"It is sad that we'll soon part ways. I quite enjoyed the time I spent here and the friends I made, but eventually, we have to move on. Our lives have been on pause for too long, so it's time for us to finally move forward."

"Yeah, you're right."

With that, we returned home. As I entered my hut, I was shocked by the state in which I found Mother. "Mama?"

Tata held back her hair as she threw up in a bucket. This was the second time this had happened. I quickly fetched a glass of water in an attempt to help. When Mama finished vomiting whatever had upset her stomach, Tata handed her a towel to wipe her mouth, and I gave her the cup I held.

"She was feeling nauseous again today. We're not sure what's causing it."

"Shouldn't she just go to the doctor's?"

"Don't worry, I'm going tomorrow."

Mama tried to get up, and Tata supported her because she had trouble staying straight. It always hurt to see her like this. I couldn't help but remember when she was hospitalized because of her constipation. Was her immune system simply that bad, to the point where she always got sick? Whatever the case, I hoped she would soon get better because I knew I couldn't handle seeing her on the brink of death once again.

"By the way, Helena, there's something we wanted to tell you." Tata helped his wife sit down, and then he himself took a seat. I did the same.

"We're going to England!"

"Really? It's been confirmed?"

"Yes! The Red Cross is now organizing trips by boat to bring us all to Europe, and the military families will be going first."

I was happy to hear we'd be leaving, though I was less excited about our means of transportation. I remembered how seasick I was when we crossed the Caspian Sea to come to Persia - Iran. As I recalled the horrible ride, I couldn't help but also worry about my Mother.

"But what about Mama? Will she be able to ride a boat in her condition?"

We turned to look at her. Her face was pale, but she tried to smile to reassure us.

"Don't worry. I'm built strong, remember? I can handle the trip."

I wanted to believe her, but it was hard when she was on her knees only moments ago, vomiting in a bucket.

"Going to England will allow us to see the rest of our family, so I'm getting on that boat no matter what."

It was only then that it hit me. Our family was about to be reunited. We had been scattered for almost a decade, but now we'd finally get the chance to be together again. A tear escaped my eye as the thought crossed my mind.

That night, I could barely sleep. I only thought of how ecstatic I would be once I saw everyone again. I wondered if Janek grew facial hair, if Andrzej was taller than me now, if Jadzia looked the same. I imagined each member's reaction as they met. I knew Mama would cry. Tata would probably try to hold back tears but let a few escape. I would definitely get emotional. A smile crept up my face as I plunged into the land of dreams.

A few weeks went by, and our departure was finally at hand. We had the greatest time packing our belongings, since, for the first time, we actually had something to bring with us instead of ragged clothes and morsels of food. Andrzej had told us he was also going to England, though he didn't know where. Tata wrote back, saying we'd find each other somehow. Mama went to see the doctor twice, but to no avail. They couldn't identify what was wrong with her, so she continued to suffer, feeling nauseous quite often, with pain in her stomach. Sometimes, she felt horrible cramps and wasn't able to move. I seriously wondered if she'd survive the trip.

We were thousands of families getting on boats to travel to Europe. With mixed feelings, we left the tropical African land which welcomed us for over six years. We were sad to leave behind the wonders of the jungle and multiple beauties of Africa, but at the same time, we were eager to be reunited with our loved ones, for those who still had some.

As we boarded the enormous *MV Winchester Castle Union* and sailed away, we all waved goodbye to those who stayed behind, to the many wild animals we never thought we'd meet in their natural habitat, to the pesky mosquitoes, flies and parasites bringing us nothing more than discomfort and diseases, to the venomous snakes that sneaked up on us in the night and surprised us in the morning under our blankets. To the beautiful songs of the exotic birds, to the warm welcome of the locals, to the authorities and clergy that watched over us, to the scorching heat and burning bright sun, melting the sky and sending out its rays to each corner of this land. To all of it, we waved goodbye with heavy hearts and teary eyes.

Mother was placed in a nursing cabin because of her condition. I visited her a few times a day whenever I wasn't feeling too seasick.

"How are you today, Mama?"

"Ah, same as always."

Unwillingly, we had fallen back into the routine of regularly asking her how she felt. She had trouble walking because of the acute cramps in her stomach.

"Could you wash my hair, Helena? I tried to ask one of the nurses, but she didn't understand me."

Mother didn't speak English, so she often had trouble communicating with the nurses. I went to get a bucket of water and a comb, then got to work. After a short while, the door opened, and a nurse appeared.

"Oh! You're washing her hair?"

I was about to answer, but suddenly Mother got up, and I saw panic in her eyes.

"My hair is clean! Tell her my hair is clean!"

She spoke to me in Polish, so the lady didn't understand.

"Why are you reacting this way, Mama?"

"I know what she said. She thinks I have lice. I heard her say *wash*."

It took me a few seconds to understand. In Russian, the word *vshi*, which sounds like *wash*, means lice.

"Don't let her cut my hair, Hela!"

I couldn't take her seriously and burst out laughing. I didn't know to whom I should explain first. Once I calmed down, I turned to Mama and explained what the nurse actually meant.

"Are you sure she won't cut my hair?"

"Mama, she doesn't even have scissors!"

Then I turned to the nurse. "Mama thought you said she had lice and that you'd cut her hair."

The nurses and I laughed, and mama also joined in full relief

Since that episode, every time the nurse came to her cabin, she teasingly asked, "Ma'am, no wash today?"

Unfortunately though, the whole ride wasn't just fun and games. Mother's case worsened, and we couldn't wait to arrive at our destination to provide her with proper care.

Three weeks passed on that boat, going up the Red Sea, across the Mediterranean Sea, and north around Spain, through the English Chanel and then we finally set foot on English soil, at the port of South Hampton. However, we didn't spend much time celebrating our arrival because Mama was our top priority. She was rushed to the hospital, and Tata and I waited for the doctor's verdict. He conducted a series of tests before explaining what was happening.

"We found a gastric polyp, which is the most common form of non-cancerous tumour, pressing against a nerve in her abdomen. That is what has been making it hard for her to walk. If the polyp had stayed small, your wife might not have felt any symptoms. However, since it grew very large, it also caused nausea and vomiting."

Hearing Mama had a tumour growing in her stomach only increased my concern. That's why Tata asked what we both absolutely needed to know.

"Can you help her?"

"Fortunately, we can. The standard treatment for this type of tumour is surgery, so we will perform a gastrectomy to remove the tumour."

He went on to explain the procedures of the surgery, but we were simply relieved something could be done. After talking with Mother a little longer, Father and I finally left for our new lodgings. Some of the refugees had been placed in an ex-Canadian military base in Yorkshire: the Royal Air Force in East Moor. Since the war was over and the Canadians returned home, the place was vacant, and we stayed there.

The authorities were well organized and sorted out all the refugees so each family had a place to stay. Tata and I inherited a room separated in two by a curtain. Even though we only had a semblance of a wall to give us privacy, we were happy.

"Well, Helena. Looks like this will be our new home for a little while."

"Yes, Tata."

That being said, just like we hadn't stopped doing for the past decade, we settled into our new environment.

We never had to pay for doctors or medicine because nobody had any money. When the war began in 1949, the Polish government transferred all their money and gold to London, England for safekeeping (anticipating an invasion from both Russia and Germany). Some of the money was used to support the Polish people in Africa, India, and so on, for food, transit, housing, and the sort. Then when London was bombed, some money was moved to Montreal, and Canada because they were not directly involved in the war; Although Canada was still under England's reign. This is why the Polish people immigrated to Canada. Some of their money was already there, and there was empty land that needed to be filled, under England's name, via the Red Cross.

CHAPTER 16

Fated reunion

Not long after our arrival, Father got a malaria attack. Since malaria symptoms usually manifest a few weeks after being bitten by an infected mosquito, he had mostly been bitten just as we left Africa and now suffered the consequences. He often had chills, headaches, and nausea, so he spent most of his time in bed. Therefore, I brought him his meals from the cafeteria.

"Once again, both Anna and I are sick. I'm beginning to think our health is linked."

"I wouldn't be surprised if it was the case."

Father sat up as I placed on his lap his meal consisting of rice, vegetables, and meat stew. He didn't have much appetite because of his sickness, but still made an effort to eat.

"So, my child," he said between bites, "have you started getting used to this place?"

"Yes, I no longer get lost on my way to the cafeteria. It's also nice that I met a new friend, Stefa, so we spend a lot of time together exploring the area."

"Beautiful! That's good."

I saw by the look on his face that he was already getting full. I pressed him to finish his meal, and he took a few more bites of rice before pushing away the plate.

"I'm sorry, I just don't feel very well."

"I know."

We were a step closer to getting a normal life back, but there was always something in the way. My parents were both sick, and my siblings were still dispersed. Nothing had really changed. I tried to ignore the negative and focus on the positive, and that's when I remembered something.

"Oh! I forgot to tell you I got a job!"

"Already?"

"Yes! I'll be teaching girls how to sew again."

"That's great! How did it happen?"

"Well, you know how Stefa usually knows everything that's going on. So she told me the priests organized schools to teach ladies over 16 how to work. She then told them about how I used to teach in Tengeru, and they offered me the job!"

"I'm so happy to hear that, Hela! You're becoming more and more of an independent, strong woman."

A faded smile floated above his lips, and his eyes were filled with melancholy. I don't know how Tata felt, witnessing my growth but not his other children's. Bedridden and knowing very little English, there wasn't much he could do. It was at times like these I tried to reassure him and show support. During the war, Mama had always been by my side, and though Tata hadn't been physically present until we met in Tengeru, he never forgot us. It was now my time to be there for them.

"Well, I'm off to go see Mama now."

"Alright. Be careful."

With that, I left and made my way to the hospital.

We received news from my sister, Jadzia. Since the war was over, she was now working as a housekeeper in Leeds. We were happy to know she was doing well and hoped to see her again soon. In the meantime, I started teaching, and my group was very nice. All the girls were eager to learn and produced wonderful results.

"One of my students is always messing up and keeps pricking herself with the needle. No matter the advice I give her, the outcome is always the same: terrible!"

"I think you just need patience. Not everyone is good with their fingers."

I walked to the cafeteria with my girlfriend, Stefa. Even though she often complained about a few of her students, I knew she liked her job and enjoyed teaching. She talked with her hands and did all sorts of gestures when she told me about her day. As we entered the crowded cafeteria, I headed towards the lunch ladies and placed my usual order.

"I'm here to pick up Tata's meal."

"Yes, yes. Have a seat; we'll make it soon."

The cafeteria was full of Polish people since we all ate at the same time. Shoes clicked and clanked on the grey tile flooring, and the brick walls were painted white and blue. On the high ceilings were rectangular blocks of blinding white light bulbs. Savory smells tickled our noses, and lively chatter prickled our ears. Stefa and I sat down on the metal benches and continued our conversation, but at some point, I noticed she wasn't paying attention.

"Are you listening?"

"Huh? Oh, yes. It's just that there's a new man over there. He's been staring at you for a while now."

"At me?"

"Yes. I don't recognize him. He's with a bunch of other senior officers, and they are also staring at you and laughing."

I didn't know how to react. At the time, I was quite shy, so decided to simply do a quick but casual glance at the man. I didn't dare look at him too long and only saw his face in the span of an instant. However, in that short moment, I was able to recognize some of his traits.

"He looks familiar."

"Do you know who he is?"

"I didn't see him long enough to tell."

"Then maybe you should look again."

"No way! I don't want him to think I'm staring!" I blushed and tried to remember where I had seen the man before, attempting to match the vague traits with all the male faces in my memory.

"Maybe he's someone you knew from Poland?"

"Maybe…"

I still couldn't place the face, which bothered me. A few minutes passed, and I asked Stefa if he was still staring.

"He sure is, and his friends are still laughing. I think you should just go see him."

She urged me on, and her persistence gave me the courage to turn around and properly look at this man finally. At the same time I turned around, he got up and walked towards me. It didn't take me another second to finally recognize him.

"Janek." My voice was barely a whisper, but he heard it and replied:

"Helena?"

Without further ado, I shot up and ran to him. He swung his arms wide and welcomed me in a tight embrace. Before I knew it, tears streamed down both our cheeks. Mixed emotions rushed up my throat, preventing me from speaking. My whole body warmed up at the familiar touch, the familiar aura. My heart was beating fast, and I couldn't believe that before me stood my older brother, whom I hadn't seen since we left the camp in Uzbekistan about seven years ago. Janek was injured when he reunited with the family from his service in Italy.

"What's going on? Who is he?"

I turned around and noticed Stefa staring at me, and then I saw the men who were laughing with Janek. I wiped away a few tears and cleared my throat.

"This is my older brother, Janek. We've been separated for quite a while now since the war started."

I didn't need to add anything more - not that I could, with all the emotion piling up in my chest - and immediately Stefa rejoiced, the other men joined. Quickly, euphoria contaminated the whole room, and the people were all delighted. The lunch ladies hurried out of their kitchen to hug us and celebrate our reunion.

"How beautiful is it that the two of you found each other!"

"Truly, this was God's will to bring you back together after everything you've been through!"

The whole room was merry, as this reunion also symbolized that of many other scattered families. We weren't the only ones who had been dispersed, so coming here, many hoped to regain the bonds they had lost through the war. I suddenly remembered I wouldn't be the only one who would rejoice at Janek's return.

"Come, you have to see Tata!"

I quickly led him out of the cafeteria, nearly forgetting Tata's meal. We hurried through the military base and to the dorms. I didn't bother knocking on the door to our room, swung the door wide open, and barged inside.

"Tata!"

Father jumped in surprise, but then his eyes widened as he saw us. Nothing needed to be said. I simply let the two men enjoy their reunion.

"Janek..?"

"Hello, Tata."

They stared at each other for a few moments, and then Father mustered the strength to extract himself from his bed and welcome his son. Just like my brother did with me moments ago, he hugged Tata tightly. I watched the scene with teary eyes. Though silence befell the room, a lot was said in that hug. Every sentence, every word that wasn't pronounced for almost a decade. Every sentence, every word, the agonies, anecdotes, encouragements, reproach that wasn't pronounced for nearly a decade; Everything a son could have wanted to tell his father for nine and a half years. All the emotions he needed to share; the tears, the cries, the hurt, the joy; All of it was said through that very long embrace.

Finally, they parted to get a good look at each other. Janek had grown so much, now 24 years old. He didn't have a beard or mustache, though his black hair was shorter than the last time I saw him. His blue eyes glittered, not with a child's innocent glee, but with an adult's mature fervor. Father had left him a teenager and found him a man. It must have been quite a shock.

"My son…"

Tata tried to say more, but the words were stuck in his throat. He bent over in pain, and we sat him down on the bed.

"Don't worry, I'm fine. It's just a headache."

He raised his head and tried to gaze at Janek through the tears in his eyes. His son, too, stared straight at him, noticing how the war had weakened Father, who now looked twice his age.

"I'm really happy to see you, Janek."

"Me too, Tata."

Father sighed in relief as if a weight had been lifted from his shoulders. I couldn't imagine the pain and anxiety of a parent who had been forcefully separated from their child for years due to the war. But to see him alive and well was more than he could ever ask for.

"Now tell me, son, how did you find us?"

Janek smiled as he sat down.

"It's quite a story. I had been notified of your arrival and given this address, so I decided to take the day off from work and come to find you. I went to the main office to know where you were, and they told me that since dinner time was approaching, I should just wait for you in the cafeteria because everyone eats at the same time. I went there and found some friends from the army. I sat with them and carefully watched each person coming in and out of the cafeteria. Then Helena came."

He paused and looked at me; I did the same.

"As soon as I saw her, I knew she looked familiar. I told my friends I felt I knew you from somewhere, and they laughed at me, saying I had had so many girlfriends I couldn't remember who was who. Which isn't true, by the way!"

Tata and I laughed, and he continued his story.

"Eventually, I decided to simply go see you, and I guess you had the same idea because you turned around at the same moment. And well, you know the rest."

Tata hadn't touched his meal, as he was too captivated by his son's tale. A large smile had been growing on his lips, and I hadn't seen him this happy in a while.

"I'm so glad you're here Janek, honestly."

My brother was also very glad with the outcome of the situation. However, there was suddenly a change in his expression.

"By the way, where's Mama? I thought she was with you."

The happiness we felt slightly faded, and we explained the situation to him. Thankfully, Mama's health wasn't in any danger. Her surgery had gone well, and she was recovering. We kept talking until late at night, exchanging stories and news we hadn't gotten the chance to tell each other through letters. Slowly but surely, our family was getting back together.

Every now and then, dances were organized on weekends in the cafeteria, and I went with Stefa. I wasn't much of a dancer but I still enjoyed the atmosphere. It was a good way to put our worries aside and simply have a nice time.

"I don't understand how you always get guys to ask you to dance. I barely have two or three talk to me during the night."

"Don't worry, Stefa. Maybe tonight will be better."

As a young adult, I attracted quite a few young men. The birthmark on my forehead had somehow disappeared - one day, I just noticed it was gone - and therefore didn't hinder my appearance. However, I didn't attend those dances for the men. I went to have fun, and also to get information.

We were happy we found Janek - who told us he worked at the same place as Jadzia - but we still didn't have any news from Andrzej. Communication had stopped between us since we left Africa, and we didn't know where he was. Many soldiers and cadets were coming to these weekend dances, either to see family members or simply to have fun on Friday nights. I tried to find my younger brother or at least someone who knew him.

My friend and I arrived in the big hall, and people were already on the dance floor. We went to sit at our usual corner after getting a drink.

"I think tonight is the night. For some reason, I have a strong feeling I might meet the man of my life!"

"Of course, Stefa."

I didn't add anything and simply took a sip of punch. My friend rearranged her curled bangs for the fifth time now, making sure her hair looked perfect. She was beautiful in her navy-blue wrap dress, bringing out the colour of her eyes. She punctuated her look with silver jewelry. I had opted for a black and white shirtwaist dress with gold earrings. It was nice seeing everyone dressed up with smiles on their faces.

We had all come a long way; A very long and harsh way. No matter how many times my environment changed and my situation improved, I could never completely forget everything that happened in the past. There were still nights when cold sweats ran down my spine as I remembered the brutalities of Siberia, the intimidating Russian uniforms, and the menacing heavy guns. I couldn't forget the long days we spent freezing and hungry, walking desperately to any land ready to welcome us. It contrasted so much with the scene in front of my eyes, where people were merry and carefree, had food in their stomach and nice clothes on their backs. We truly came a long way.

"Excuse me, miss?"

I was pulled out of my reverie by a deep voice. As I raised my head, I noticed a nice young man extending a hand toward me.

"Would you care for a dance?"

He smiled broadly, and I accepted his offer, letting him lead me onto the dance floor. I glanced at Stefa, who wasn't pleased to have been ignored again. Maybe the next one would be hers.

"You look very lovely, Miss."

"Thank you."

I wasn't wooed by sweet talk and soon forgot about his comment. Besides, I hadn't come here for romance. There was a mission I had to carry out.

"You seem to be a soldier. Were you with the army or the cadets?"

Happy to see me make conversation, the man's smile widened.

"Why? Do you have a preference?"

"Not really. I'm just looking for my brother, who was in the cadets."

"Well, I'm sorry, but I don't think I can help you. I was a soldier with the army, not the cadets."

At that point, I wasn't interested in pursuing the conversation and continued dancing in silence. The man kept trying to talk to me, but I only provided short answers. By the end of the dance, he knew his advances were futile and didn't bother staying in my company any longer.

"So? How was it?"

Stefa sipped what could have been her third cup of punch.

"Same as always. And you?"

She rolled her eyes. "Still waiting."

"You'll get someone, I'm sure."

At that moment, another deep voice caught our attention. "Excuse me?"

Stefa turned around excitedly, but her smile vanished as soon as she saw who the man was looking at.

"Would you join me for a dance?"

He seemed a bit nervous, which made it harder for me to turn him down.

"Oh, OK."

He sighed in relief as I grabbed his hand and followed him. I turned around and mouthed, "I'm sorry." Stefa didn't seem to accept my apology.

"How are you feeling today, Mama?"

"Pretty good. I started eating solid food again, though the doctor told me to only have small portions."

After her surgery, Mama had been fed through a tube in a needle until she'd be ready to eat and drink normally. Seeing her hooked up to all these gadgets was strange, but now she looked much better.

"Janek dropped by again yesterday. He brought me those flowers."

I turned in the direction she pointed and noticed beautiful hydrangeas on the bedside table.

"They sure are nice." I went to sit next to her, and we chatted for a bit.

"By the way, any news of Andrzej?"

I shook my head, and Mama's expression saddened. Since she was hospitalized, I wanted her to focus on her recovery, but of course, she couldn't stop worrying about her son.

"I'm sure we'll find him soon. He should be in England too, so that's already great news."

My little brother was the only one missing in action. Jadzia worked in Leeds with Janek; they managed an old lady's household. My sister took care of chores, whereas my brother was in charge of the garden and maintenance. They seldom got the chance to visit us at the same time, so instead would alternate their days off, but at least we could still see them.

"I guess you're right. Also, how was that dance last night? Any prospects?"

Mom wiggled her eyebrows, knowing how popular I had become among young men.

Many young adults just wanted to find somebody; Anybody to marry. Deep down they wanted to fill their empty war-torn hearts.

"Well… there was *one* gentleman…"

We spent the next hour or so talking about who could become my potential boyfriend and who was definitely off the list. We giggled and gossiped like two teenagers. Throughout the years, Mama and I had become very close, and she was now (and still is) my best friend. I would tell her each time I had a date, and she advised me on what to wear and what to do. When I came back, she immediately wanted to know how it went, then gave her opinion on whether that person was the right choice or not. We always had a great time, and I loved confiding in her.

"I should get going now. I don't want to be outside when it gets dark."

"Alright then, thanks for dropping by."

"Soon enough, I won't have to anymore!"

We both smiled, knowing the date of her discharge was approaching and she'd finally be able to stay with Tata and I. Funny enough, just as she was getting better, Tata's condition was also improving; Maybe their health was linked after all.

I watched over the ladies as they worked on their quilts. Oftentimes, we sewed some for refugees who didn't have any to help them out.

"Miss Fąfara? Could you come take a look, please?"

I made my way to the other side of the room to observe the pattern Lena, one student, created on her quilt. She had done white and red stripes to match the Polish flag.

"Is this alright?"

"Yes, it looks very nice."

I took a few more seconds to check her stitching and examine the cloth before smiling at my student.

"Excellent work Lena!"

She smiled back, relieved.

"You know, I've learned quite a lot from you, Miss Helena, and I'm always excited to attend your class."

"I'm glad to hear it."

Another lady turned around to partake in the conversation.

"I feel the same way! It's great to come here and learn something that'll help us get a job one day. We might be building our lives back up sooner than we think!"

"That's a great attitude to have. I know you ladies are much older than me, but I encourage you to understand that there are many opportunities for you out there."

"Who knows? Maybe one day we'll teach other ladies like you do, Miss Helena!"

A few girls laughed, distracted from their work. I thought a break wouldn't hurt and didn't remind them to focus on their task.

"Since you already have a job, what are you going to do next?" Lena asked.

"Well… I haven't thought much about it. Right now, I'm mainly taking care of my parents."

"Are you planning on staying in England?"

"I can't say; we've only been here for two months. But if I had to move, I would probably settle in Canada."

I remembered the letter my Uncle Sowa sent us when we were still in Tengeru. He was already willing to sponsor us and pay for our trip there. I really would have liked to go to Canada right away, but as Tata said, it was better to reunite the whole family first. And since we arrived in Yorkshire, we still had no news of Andrzej, so I knew we weren't leaving anytime soon.

"That's a bit far. Is it because you have someone waiting for you there?"

In a sense, there was someone waiting for me in Canada, though I knew that's not what Lena meant.

"No, it's nothing like that."

"Then do you have someone here? I'm sure a pretty girl like you isn't single. Or at least won't be for long."

At that point, a small circle had formed around me, and many ladies had abandoned their work, clearly more interested in my love life. They all stared in anticipation, waiting for a scoop. Unfortunately for them, they would be quite disappointed.

"I'm not looking for romance. I'd rather get my life on track first."

"That's boring. Isn't there at least someone you're interested in?" Lena inquired.

"No, there isn't. Like I said girls, I'm not looking for romance."

My very short teaching career in Tengeru taught me to be stern with my students when needed, and right now was the right time. I saw by their faces that they realized they shouldn't try too hard to peer into my life. Lena, however, still had a few questions in her.

"I'm sure you'll find someone soon enough, especially if you go to those social dances. There's another one tonight, right?"

"Yes, but…"

"That's perfect! All the young soldiers just want to find a wife now that the war is over, so you're bound to find someone you'll like. You know, last time I went, I…"

"OK, that's enough now. I think you should get back to work. And you other ladies too."

Disappointed mumbles echoed in the room as the students reluctantly returned to work.

In the evening, Stefa and I were on our way to the grand hall again.

"Do you think I look OK?"

She moved around in her blue short-sleeved shirtwaist dress. The small belt accentuated her thin waist, giving her a nice figure. She tied her hair in an elegant low bun resting on her nape.

"You look great."

"Are you sure?"

She couldn't help but worry, and it was evident why. About two weeks ago, she finally got herself a man who was interested in her. They'd gone out a few times, but this was the first dance they would attend together. Naturally, she wanted to look her best.

"Don't worry. If he doesn't like you in this outfit, he's either dumb or blind."

She smiled, and we entered the room. Music filled every corner, and it was the same atmosphere as usual. Stefa quickly spotted her man and half apologized as she left me alone. I didn't mind and went to sit with a few girls I recognized. We had a good time talking until one man asked me to dance.

"Lucky you, Helena! Having such a handsome man come to you!"

I ignored their comments and followed my partner on the dance floor.

"So your name is Helena?" he asked in a baritone voice.

"Yes, and what's yours?"

"Marek."

He had a charming smile; I'll give him that, and his eyes were filled with tenderness. He had short light brown hair and a lean body. I wouldn't have minded getting asked to dance by guys like him. However, I always remembered the question I had to ask.

"Excuse me, but are you a cadet or a full, fledged soldier?"

"I'm a plain cadet, Miss Helena!" he stated proudly.

My heart skipped a beat, but I tried not to get too excited. Each time I finally met a cadet, they didn't know my brother, so I thought it might also be the case with this man. We continued to sway on the dance floor, and I asked my follow-up question.

"Would you happen to know someone named Andrzej Fąfara?"

Marek stopped dancing and looked at me straight in the eyes. We both froze on the dance floor, and a broad smile stretched his lips.

"Of course, I know Andrzej! He's my roommate!"

"What? Really? Is that true?"

"Yes! We also work at the same factory. Wait. Don't tell me you're interested in him?"

He looked panicked, but I didn't care. Tears of joy ran down my cheeks, and my heart beat madly against my chest.

"Miss Helena, are you OK? Is Andrzej your lover?"

I tried to control my emotions and managed to answer.

"No he's not. He's my brother."

"Your brother? Oh good, he's just your brother!"

Suddenly, he shared my joy, and we laughed on the dance floor. Others shot us quizzical side glances, but I couldn't care less. Immediately I calmed down, I asked Marek to give me Andrzej's address and decided to leave right away.

"Wait! Are you going to find him now?"

"No, I just have someone to share this news with. But *then* I'll go find him."

With that, I made my way to my room.

"What?" Tata's eyes widened after he heard what I said. "Are you sure of this, Helena?"

"Yes, Tata! He told me Andrzej is his roommate and that they work together, and he gave me his address. I'll write him a letter to let him know we're here."

I didn't wait for Father's response and looked for pen and paper.

"I can't believe it. This is all so… so…"

"Sudden, I know. But you just wait, Tata. Soon enough, we'll all be together. Finally."

"Yes, finally."

I sat down and got to work.

CHAPTER 17

Holidays and heroes

I read Mother's letter for the third time, still feeling her emotion in each word.

Dear Helena,

You won't believe the surprise I had the other day! Your brother Andrzej came to visit me at the hospital! At first, I didn't think it was him. He was so tall and so handsome! Definitely not the Andrzej from Siberia. I thought maybe he had gotten the wrong room, but when I took a good look at him, I knew he was my son. I can't explain how happy I was! Can you imagine we hadn't seen each other since we were separated in Iran? It's been six years now. He hugged me, and I wouldn't let him go for a long time, crying endless tears of joy. After I calmed down, he sat next to me, and I had to ask how he found me. He said you wrote him a letter, telling him how we were doing and that he should come to visit me at the hospital. I can't thank you enough for this beautiful surprise, Hela! Andrzej and I talked for a very long time, and he stayed until the end of his visiting hours. The next day, I cried all morning because I still couldn't believe what happened. It is so wonderful to be reunited with loved ones! God has blessed our family and spared us during the war. I can't wait for all of us to finally be reunited.

Sincerely,

Your Mama, Anna Fąfara

I wiped away silent tears and at that moment heard a knock on the door. I thought it was Tata, but when I opened it, I was more than surprised to find...

"Andrzej?"

Shock overcame me momentarily, but once I came back to my senses I leaped forward, embracing my brother tightly.

"I can't believe it! It's really you!"

"I missed you, Hela," he whispered.

I cried uncontrollably, sobs shaking my shoulders. So many emotions overflowed within me, and I thought I would burst.

"Helena?"

Another deep voice interrupted my train of thought. It was Father coming down the hall.

"Who is this..?" He didn't finish his sentence because right then, Andrzej turned around.

"My son... you..."

"It's good to see you again, Tata."

Father ran to him and hugged him tight. He let tears run freely down his cheeks. Seeing them together was surreal. Nine and a half years had passed since they last saw each other. Nine and a half years since our family was all together. So much had happened in the last decade that it seemed we had had the time to live a hundred lives before meeting again. We all entered our room, knowing this night would be as long as when Janek had come for the first time.

"Good morning, everyone! Today, I would like us to do something a bit different than usual."

My students stared at me, perplexed.

"You all know how we sometimes make quilts for other refugees, right? Well, today, I would like us to make toys."

"Toys?" Lena asked.

"Yes. As you all know, there are countless children here who didn't enjoy their childhood because of the circumstances we are all aware of. That being said, I would like us to give them a chance to simply be kids. Just like you are getting the chance to enter adulthood and the working world, I want us to help those children regain what they have lost: their childhood!"

The ladies looked at each other, and some nodded in agreement. The holiday season was approaching, and I thought it would be great if each child could wake up to a gift on Christmas day.

"Excuse me, Miss Helena? I think it's a great idea, but how are we going to make toys? I think at most we could make dolls since it involves sewing, but that's about all I know how to do."

A few other ladies acquiesced and didn't seem as keen anymore to follow my idea.

"Don't worry, I thought of that, and we won't be making anything complicated. As you mentioned, dolls should be doable, but they will mainly just please girls. That's why for boys, I thought we could make stuffed animals. They'll probably only be popular with younger boys, but it's still something."

They pondered my suggestion before deciding it was feasible, though it would be quite a challenge. I had already proposed the project to my superiors, and they supplied me with the necessary material. All that was left was for us to get to work.

"Alright. So this is how we're going to make the toys."

We worked hard for the next couple of weeks making dolls and stuffed animals. Since the ladies were enthusiastic about the project, they quickly picked up the techniques. It was also a good experience if they ever worked in a toy factory. As we had our last class and completed our last toys the night before Christmas, we admired our work with pride. Unfortunately, it was too big a task to make something for every single child in the military base. However, we had a good amount of dolls and stuffed animals to please a lot of young boys and girls. The toys were to be distributed the next morning, and I was excited to see the kids' reactions.

Even though I was paid, giving back to others, especially the children, felt great. I still remembered the desolate looks on the faces of three-year-olds, five-year-olds, and seven-year-olds who had just lost a family member, or were battling typhus fever, or held out grubby hands to receive even half a loaf of bread. They were now well-fed and properly taken care of, but that didn't erase the memories. I hoped these toys could at least give them back part of their childhood.

"Well, everyone, I want to congratulate you on your work. Truly, you've done something amazing and overcame quite a challenge. You should all be proud of yourselves."

The ladies smiled; happy their effort hadn't been in vain.

"This was our last class before Christmas. I'm very happy I got such an amazing group, and I hope you all have a wonderful holiday!"

They thanked me in turn, and then we parted. I scurried through the hallways because I had a very important dinner to attend.

"Hi, everyone! Sorry I'm a bit late."

"Don't worry, your sister isn't here yet."

As Mother said that, Jadzia appeared.

"Oh Jadwiga, good to see you!"

"It's nice to see you too, Mama!"

"You don't visit us often enough."

"I'm sorry, Mama. I don't get many days off."

We set the table as we chatted. Our room wasn't too big, but we didn't mind. There was a curtain separating the space into two, in an attempt to create two rooms. We were gathered in the bigger one where my parents slept, because there was a table and chairs.

"Andrzej, it seems you grew again!" I pointed out.

"Yeah, I'm 6"3, almost 6"4."

I saw the pride in his eyes and realized...

"People would hardly believe he was my little brother anymore."

Indeed, Andrzej was now 18, but his height made him seem much older. We kept joking and laughing and then sat down to enjoy our meal.

"I would like to say a few words before we eat." We all turned towards Tata, who clasped his big hands together, beaming with soulful adoration that his entire family was at the table. "Anna, children, I couldn't be happier to have you all around me this evening. When I think back on all we went through, all the separations, the hurt, and the hardships, I can't believe we're now sitting in a warm place with nice clothes and wide smiles. The Lord truly has been good to us."

We nodded in agreement, aware of how blessed we were to have been able to all make it out of the war. Countless families had been ruptured, children left orphans, and women became widows. We all knew someone who had lost a brother, father, mother, or daughter. We'd seen it all. But thankfully, we had been spared. It didn't mean we came out of the war completely unscathed. We still had the psychological scars that would remain forever, but at least we had each other for support.

"As you all know, Christmas is the celebration of the birth of baby Jesus. Just as Mary and Joseph rejoiced that the Savior had been born unto them, I rejoice to have my children around me. Now, let us bow our heads in prayer."

We all obeyed in silence, closing our eyes and bowing our heads.

"Our Father, who art in heaven, hallowed be thy name. Thy kingdom come, thy will be done, on earth, as it is in heaven. Give us this day our daily bread and forgive us our trespasses as we forgive those who trespass against us; and lead us not into temptation, but deliver us from evil. In the name of the Father, and of the Son, and of the Holy Spirit. Amen!"

"Amen!"

We each did the sign of the cross before digging in. Utensils clicked and clanked against serving dishes. Food piled up on our plates and our mouths. Everyone was merry as we enjoyed a tasty meal as a family. There were potatoes, bread, rice, stew, and chicken. Common foods in England. A real feast!

"Do you remember how we used to celebrate Christmas in Poland?" Janek asked.

"Hmm... not really."

Since Andrzej was barely nine when we left our homeland, he didn't have many memories of our traditional celebration.

"Oh, I remember! We used to have supper late, and then right after, we all went to midnight mass, and then after, Mama and Tata sent us to bed", I answered.

"Yes! We had the pieces of the Holy Eucharist and exchanged good wishes around the table. We did the same with all the animals in the barn and the whole farm. We also kept an extra table setting to symbolize those in need and those who didn't have family or were only with us in spirit.

"Yes! And then when we woke up the next day, suddenly there was a Christmas tree and presents in the living room."

My siblings and I were having fun remembering the holidays we spent in what was now a different era.

"Wait. You did all that set up through the night?"

Our parents exchanged a knowing look and didn't answer my question. Not that they needed to, since the evident grin on their faces told me all I needed to know.

"You only figured this out now, Helena? I already knew."

"Yeah, me too."

Janek and Jadzia didn't seem surprised, but I wondered if they weren't just pretending.

We all silently reminisced about the warmth of our family and how life was at their heart and home.

"I only remember eating very good food on Christmas Eve," Andrzej said, taking a bite of his baked potato. (A traditional Christmas menu was fish on Christmas Eve ((no meat for respect of Jesus)), clear barszcz ((beet)) bullion with uszka ((wild mushroom dumplings)), makownic ((poppy seed roll)), pierogis stuffed with kapusta ((sauerkraut)) and wild mushrooms, and ones with potato and cheese with caramelized onions and lots of sour cream!!

"It's true; we had really big meals."

We kept reminiscing and having a good time. There was so much to say that we often talked one on top of the other, telling tales old and new. Everyone had new stories since we spent Christmas in many different countries.

"By the way, I don't think I told you guys, but I'm going to be awarded with a pretty important medal soon." Janek shared.

"Really? What did you do to receive such an honour?"

Jadzia seemed dubious, so Janek told his story.

"It was before we were sent to Monte Casino. I was driving a tank with some of my friends behind. Eventually, we arrived at a field and there were bundles of buckwheat tied up. I told my friends they should have some fun and practice their shooting skills. We all got out and started shooting the bundles. Little did we know...?"

He paused to add suspense, and Jadzia pressed him to continue. ".... there were about five German soldiers hidden behind each bundle, and we killed all of them."

"What?"

"Those Germans were most likely waiting to ambush us, but we foiled their plan."

"By accident!" Jadzia thought it important to add.

Janek frowned, but didn't reply. After all, our sister wasn't wrong.

"So they'll give you a medal for that? Even if it was just an accident?" Mother seemed quite surprised, and I felt the same way.

"Well... we more or less told them it was an accident. But in any case, it doesn't change the fact that we saved our troop from an ambush!"

"Unbelievable."

Tata shook his head, and I noticed a small smile on the corner of his lips. Honestly, I didn't know if I should congratulate my brother or not.

"And when are you going to receive that medal?" I asked.

"The ceremony is supposed to be in January."

"Had I known it was that easy to receive a medal, I also would've lied about my age to join the army," Andrzej commented.

"With how small you used to be, no one would've believed you were over 16."

Janek ruffled our little brother's hair, and we quickly moved on. We talked until late in the night, when our bellies hurt from overeating and laughing too much. Since there wasn't much space in the room, we slept in the sleeping bags on the floor. The lights were off, yet we were still wide awake.

"Do you think tomorrow we'll find a Christmas tree with presents underneath?"

"Andrzej, you're not a kid anymore," Jadzia said.

"Hey, it doesn't hurt to dream!"

We laughed, and then Tata spoke.

"Your Mama and I don't have anything to give you, except our love and support. And besides, I think all of us being here together is big enough a gift, don't you agree?"

We acquiesced, realizing the greatest gifts are those we can't buy. With that, we fell asleep, innocent smiles lingering on our lips.

⁂

Christmas came and went, and the children were very pleased with the gifts they received. My students were even happier to see their reactions, and made me promise they'd get the chance to do another similar project. January arrived and it was time for the military award ceremony in which Janek would receive his medal. The whole family sat together as we watched the many men in uniforms come and go on stage. Then one of the veterans stepped forward to begin his speech and announcement.

"Now, I would like to give a very special medal to a group of young soldiers who protected their troop from a German ambush."

"Oh, it's Janek's turn!" Mama whispered.

"These brave men foresaw the danger and, though they were outnumbered, raised to the challenge of defeating the enemy. One of these men in particular even managed to kill half of their adversaries single-handedly!"

"I don't remember that part in the story."

Jadzia was clearly unimpressed, and I didn't know how to feel as my brother and his friends were being praised for a mere accident. With all this hype, it was probably too late to tell the plain truth. The speech went on, and eventually my brother and his friends made their way on stage to receive their metal. They all looked sharp in their polished uniforms, and seemed like true heroes. Janek's expression was serious and he appeared so grown up. It almost made me forget the brother who chaperoned us as we played by Lake Świtez, parade in our Father's army boots, enrolled in military school right before the war or the one who spent days cutting wood and carved out a realistic gun in Siberia. He may have saved his troop by accident, but it was willingly that he put his life on the line for his country, so he definitely deserved a medal for that.

The soldiers turned towards the audience - more precisely towards the cameramen in front of the audience. A series of flashes highlighted their fixed smiles. Janek looked at us and winked. I couldn't help but smile as well.

Just like every second Friday, I attended the usually organized dances. Now that we had found Andrzej, I went just for fun. It was nice to have an evening where all we had to do was relax and enjoy ourselves. Stefa's relationship with her fellow was getting serious, so she didn't accompany me as much and usually went with him; I didn't mind.

Not long after I entered the room, I was greeted by a familiar voice.

"Ah, Helena!"

I turned and noticed Marek's handsome smile. We had talked a few times, and I was developing an interest in him. We sat together at a table and caught up on recent events.

"How is work at the sugar factory?"

"Not too bad. It's just that we have long shifts so it's pretty draining. That's why I always look forward to these social gatherings because they give me a break. Well, there is also another reason I enjoy coming here."

He looked at me tenderly, and I saw right through him. I decided not to put up any guards and let him flirt. I was about to respond when a loud voice called me out.

"Excuse me? Are you Helena Fąfara?"

I turned around and noticed a big lady - almost six feet tall - staring at me with huge brown eyes. Before I could answer, she exclaimed herself.

"Yes, it is you! I knew I recognized you!"

She embraced me tight, lifting me and throwing me in the air. I was surprised not only by how sudden all this was but also by her incredible strength! I wasn't that heavy, but it was still impressive she could lift me up so effortlessly. Eventually, she put me down and kept staring, with her face beaming.

"I'm so happy to see you again, my dear teacher!"

"Teacher?"

"Oh, don't you remember me? I was in your class in Tengeru."

Her face was vaguely familiar, but I couldn't remember her name. She didn't bother telling me and kept talking.

"I learned so much from you, Miss Helena, and it's thanks to you that I am now an expert in sewing. I even got a job!"

"Is that so?"

"Yes! I work as a supervisor in a factory, and the pay is quite good. It's because of you that I have this great opportunity and a brand new life!"

She was about to add something, but a man placed his hand on her shoulder.

"There you are. I was looking for you."

"Sorry, it's just that I bumped into my dear teacher Miss Helena. You know, the one I told you about?"

"Ah, yes!" The man smiled at me, and I blushed. For a second, I forgot Marek was still there.

"I'm Dana's husband, Filip. Nice to meet you!"

Dana stayed, and we talked for another couple of minutes to catch up with what we had been up to. I didn't know she was also in the military base, but then again, there were so many of us that I could have easily missed her.

"By the way, is he your husband?" She pointed to Marek, who hadn't said much during the conversation. His head sprang up, alert and eager to hear my answer.

"Ah, no, we're just friends."

"Oh, really? Well, I think you two would make a great couple."

I blushed again, not sure how to answer.

"Dana, don't embarrass her."

"What? It's true." She didn't seem to mind her husband's reprimand, and eventually, they left. I was now alone with Marek and didn't know what to say. Thankfully, he took the lead.

"Would you care for a dance?"

"Gladly."

Without adding another word, we made our way to the dance floor.

One evening, Janek and Andrzej came by with a few of their friends. As the small group of men entered the room, I immediately noticed Marek. Janek had written us a letter saying he'd drop by with some friends but hadn't specified who.

"Hi Helena, how are you?" Marek asked with a smile.

"I'm good, and you?"

"I'm feeling much better now."

I was about to respond, but noticed Andrzej sending me a knowing look. His grin discouraged me from saying anything, and I simply let the boys in. They took place at the table and chatted about various subjects. Tata sat with them, and Mama brought them drinks. I didn't know what to do, so I sat in a corner with one of my books. Lately, I'd been reading a lot about Canada and became more and more eager to live there.

At some point, the group decided to play cards, and Father wasn't too interested in their games, so he left them. I kept watching from the corner of my eye, eavesdropping on their conversation. They mostly talked about guns and tanks and people I didn't know and didn't care about. My main concern was Marek, and I noticed him shooting me a couple of subtle side glances every now and then, which always made my heart beat just a little bit faster.

"How about we make this game more interesting?"

Andrzej came up with the *brilliant* idea to start playing with money, which excited his friends. They had already been here for about two hours, and I wanted them to leave. Even though I was happy Marek was there, I was also very nervous. What if I did something embarrassing, and he saw it? Or what if my brothers told him one of my embarrassing tales? I wouldn't be able to attend another social dance after that.

"Tata, don't you think it's late, and they should leave?" I whispered.

"They'll leave when they want to, Helena."

Tata didn't want to disturb his eldest son, to give him space as an adult. Unfortunately, my plan A didn't work, so I decided to go with plan B.

"But they're playing with money. Isn't gambling bad? You should tell them to stop."

He sighed and looked at me.

"Janek is old enough to play responsibly. And as for Andrzej, I also trust he won't do anything reckless."

Clearly, Father wasn't going to say or do anything, which wasn't reassuring. Also, the boys didn't seem to be ready to leave anytime soon. I was still feeling quite nervous and decided to take matters into my own hands.

"Hey Janek, I think it's probably time for you guys to go."

"Not now, Hela, things are getting interesting."

"Yeah. Your brother still has some money in play, so I have to make sure to get all of it," Marek added.

"I'd love to see you try!"

The boys laughed and continued their game. I knew I was getting nowhere, and since plans A, B, and C had all failed, it was time for plan D: destroy everything! Resolute, I walked up to the small table.

Andrzej glanced at me, confused. "What are you doing, Hela?"

Without answering, I completely cleaned the table with one big sweep, sending all the money and cards on the floor.

"What gives Helena? Why'd you do that?"

"It's getting late! You guys have to go!"

I don't know why I thought this would be the solution, but I did what I did. Irritated, the guys picked up their cards reluctantly, taking the opportunity to also stuff their pockets with a few loose bills, nagging me all the while, but I simply wanted them to leave. Marek looked at me with disappointment before shaking his head. It was the end of our "story."

CHAPTER 18

Exhibition

Surprise was evident on my face when one of my supervisors approached me after class, saying he needed to talk to me. I followed the lanky man to his office, where another man was waiting. Thinning brown hair created a crown around his head, and he wore a plaid vest that probably fit him some twenty years ago, but not anymore.

As he saw us enter the room, he got up and smiled. "Ah, you must be Miss Helena Fąfara!"

"Yes, I am."

The man extended a welcoming hand as he replied.

"My name is Marcel Kaminski. Pleased to meet you!"

I shook his hand, and my supervisor invited me to take a seat, and he did the same. "Well, Miss Helena, I'll get right down to business. Mr. Kaminski here is the principal of one of the local elementary schools and had a request for you."

We both turned towards the man who explained his request.

"Yes, I've heard a lot of great things about you, Miss Helena. A friend of my daughter is one of your students, and she told us how good a teacher you are, helping the other refugees by making quilts and toys. I can tell you're a hard-working young lady, and you produce wonderful results."

All the refugees from our camps in Africa could not speak English. This made their employment situation very hard. Through my teaching, I gave women the ability to support their families. Trades were not popular for refugees, however, once they had a skill, they did not need to know English to sew!

I blushed, slightly embarrassed but also honoured to receive such praise.

"You may already be aware, but a Polish holiday is coming soon. I was wondering if you could make traditional Polish costumes for my elementary school's students. We would have an exhibition, traditional dances, and other activities. I believe that fellow Polish people would love to see their culture highlighted, and this could also be very educational for the English folks. What do you think?"

The eagerness in his eyes was evident, and I felt I couldn't turn him down. Besides, I, too, was excited to take on such a project.

"I would be delighted to make those costumes, Mr. Kaminski."

"Wonderful! I'm glad you accepted. I believe this will indeed be a great initiative, Miss Helena."

For the rest of the meeting, we discussed the details of the event. My supervisor told me I'd have to write a letter to our superiors in London to receive permission to take on this project. Thankfully, they were on board with the idea, and even provided a subvention to pay for the material. All the formalities had been taken care of, and it was time to get to work.

"Good morning, ladies! I hope you are all doing well on this fine morning."

I could tell the students were perplexed by my over-excited behaviour. Now that we had everything we needed to start working, I didn't want to waste any time.

"Today, we'll be starting a new project. I was approached by the principal of one of the local elementary schools to make Polish costumes for a holiday that's coming up soon."

I explained to them the details of the request, and they were all enthusiastic about it. With that, I divided the tasks, and everyone got to work. I supervised the ladies as they created colourful patterns and elegant embroidery. Poland has various traditional costumes depending on the region. Since it would have been too much effort to represent all of them, I decided to simply focus on Bronowice from the Krakow region, since they were the most popular. The general format for the women's traditional costume includes an embroidered vest, a white shirt, and a long skirt. The style can vary, but that's the basic formula. The traditional male costumes are quite similar, usually composed of a long-sleeved shirt, a long coat, pants and high leather boots.

Not only did I supervise my students, but I also contributed in making pants and ponchos, shirts, and vests. I wanted to give my very best and diligently created each piece.

"Did you read the newspaper, Helena?"

I answered without raising my head, too focused on my embroidery. "No."

"They're talking about your exhibition."

"Really?"

This time, I put my work down and walked to Mama, who was holding today's newspaper. She showed me a small ad on the last page talking about the upcoming event. "An exhibition of Polish culture, led by Miss Helena Fąfara, will be held in the local elementary school in Yorkshire, England, on Saturday, June 4. All visitors welcomed."

The ad was just that, but I kept reading it over and over. A peculiar feeling filled me at the sight of my name printed in black on the local paper.

"I'm so proud of you, Hela! You're doing something amazing with this project."

"I simply hope I'll be able to pull it off. Our deadline is soon, and I want to ensure everything is done on time. And now that the event has been advertised, I'll have to make sure each piece comes out perfectly."

"I'm sure you'll do great!"

My motivation renewed, and I got back to work.

Finally, the exhibition day arrived. I managed to complete everything with the help of my student. The children loved their costumes and wouldn't stop parading in them. Some even refused to take them off, but ended up removing them after some pleading. Honestly, I was very proud of my work. Being so young, I had doubts and wasn't sure if I'd be up for the task, but thankfully all went well.

When I arrived at the school, I was surprised by the number of people there. It seemed as if entire villages had come to see the exhibit! The advertisement had certainly done its job.

"Miss Helena!"

I turned at the sound of my name and came face to face with the principal.

"Ah, Mr. Kaminski! Nice to see you."

"I'm quite happy to see you too! Look at this crowd! I wasn't expecting these many visitors."

"Me neither, Sir!"

"This event is sure to be a success. Everyone will love your designs!"

His compliment gave me courage, and the slight nervousness I felt earlier slowly dissipated. I strolled around a bit, with Polish music playing from a band ensemble. The event was very festive.

My students also came, so I bumped into many of them.

"Miss Helena, I can't believe this is finally happening!"

"You all worked hard, and now it's time to enjoy and rejoice to see your talents admired."

"I hope the visitors will like our clothes. I think I messed up on a few skirts."

"Don't worry, Lena, I supervised you the whole time, and everything you made was beautiful." She smiled, reassured, before leaving with her friend.

After some time, the main event started.

"Ladies and gentlemen, thank you all for coming here today. Quite frankly, I was *not* expecting such an outcome, but as they say: the more, the merrier!"

The principal was beaming, and everyone seemed thrilled to see the costumes. He talked a bit more and then introduced his students. One by one, they came on stage, just like they had rehearsed. Some were nervous, but others were natural fashion models, flipping their hair and twirling around so everyone could admire them. In the crowd, people were amazed, as "OH's and "AH's fused from every corner. The children danced in their costumes, and the public couldn't get enough of it. They held hands and danced in a circle; in, out, and around, following the beat of the music. Everyone clapped along as the students were showered with praise and camera flashes. The event was clearly a success, and I felt an immense sense of pride.

Towards the end, the principal went up on stage to make his final speech.

"I want to thank you all again for coming. I hope you were able to enjoy this wonderful event highlighting the beautiful Polish culture!"

When I saw those amazing costumes I made, I was also amazed.

"Before we end this event, I wanted to give credit to the young (I was 19 yrs. old then,) Lady who made all this possible. Please welcome Miss Helena Fąfara!"

I was surprised to be called out, and a few of my friends urged me on stage. I walked up at the sound of everyone's applause. Standing in front of so many people, I was a bit uneasy at first, but then I saw my parents in the crowd and was a bit at ease. The principal asked me to say a few words and stepped back. Thankfully, my English had improved from listening to the radio and keeping a dictionary close by to search for new words, so I could better express myself.

"Good afternoon, everyone, my name is Helena Fąfara. I want to thank you all for coming. I'll admit I had a few doubts when I took on this project, but everything turned out so beautifully and I'm quite happy about that. The ladies I teach helped me greatly and did wonderful work, so they deserve some credit. I wish tonight for all of you to leave here with some insight on what it means to us to be Polish. Thank you!"

Another round of applause resounded as I left the stage. I was about to go see my parents when a group of women intercepted me.

"I can't believe someone so young did something so amazing!"

"You should be proud of yourself, dear!"

"You're a real genius!"

I couldn't help but blush at all the compliments and kept thanking these kind women.

"You know," one of them said, "it was very interesting to learn about another culture. We didn't have many foreigners here before your group showed up, and I'm rather glad you did."

I paused for a second, weighing her words. For years, we had travelled from place to place, desperate for a semblance of a home. After Siberia, each stop was better than the previous, though we still felt secluded from the rest of the world. In Tehran and also in Tengeru, we got along quite well with the locals, but this was the first time someone told me they were glad we came here. We were probably seen as intruders by some, but at least there were others who enjoyed our presence.

"Thank you. That means a lot to me."

"Excuse me! Excuse me, Miss Helena!"

A tall man elbowed his way through the crowd to reach me, and seemed pleased when he finally did.

"Hi, my name is John Smith, and I'm a journalist for the local paper. I saw the ad for this event and came to have a look. I must say, your work is truly beautiful!"

With how he looked at me, I could tell it wasn't just my work he thought was beautiful.

"I'm glad you liked it."

"Do you have a few minutes to spare? I would like to ask you some questions for the article I'll write this week."

I accepted to undergo his interview, though we were often interrupted by other guests who came to congratulate me. It was only late at night that I finally returned to my room. Exhausted, I fell fast asleep as soon as my head touched the pillow.

My 15 minutes of fame lasted a bit longer than I imagined. For days, many of the military camp refugees continued congratulating me on the exhibition. My students also wouldn't stop talking about it and said they wanted to do something similar again. The buzz was accentuated after a certain article was published.

"Did you read the paper, Helena?"

Stefa ran to me, a few rebellious strands of hair sticking out and today's local paper crumpled in her fist.

"No. What does it say?"

"It's talking about you!"

She shoved the newspaper with crazy excitement and pointed to an article on page 3, where the title read: "A Taste of Poland in Yorkshire." I immediately recognized the name of the writer: John Smith. I skimmed through the article, where he recounted the event. It all seemed just fine until I reached the paragraph where he wrote of me.

"This brilliant exhibition was led by none other than the very clever Miss Helena Fąfara. Being only nineteen years old, she supervised the creation of the traditional costumes, also creating a few pieces of her own. This beautiful young girl with luscious blond hair and mesmerizing blue eyes brilliantly demonstrated her amazing talent! Many labelled her a pure genius, and Saturday night Miss Fąfara undoubtedly showed a lot of promise with her immense potential."

I couldn't believe what I had just read, and my friend was just as surprised.

"Did you pay this guy to write all this?"

"Of course not! You think I'm that full of myself?"

"Well, with all the exaggerated compliments, I thought something was up. Oh, wait! I figured it out."

She gave me a knowing grin, and I responded with an eye roll; As if someone would fall for me after talking to me for two minutes! Stefa read my mind and said: "You never know! You're quite popular with men, and I don't think he's the exception."

It all sounded like nonsense to me, but a few doubts emerged as I reread that paragraph. Something caught my attention in just a few seconds of reading; John Smith had written that I was blond with blue eyes.

"My eyes are brown…" I mumbled.

"Excuse me? Are you Miss Helena Fąfara? You are, aren't you?"

The excitement was clear in the face of the young man who approached our table. He was already the third guy to ask me this question, and I was getting annoyed.

"Yes, it's me."

"I thought so! I read about you in the paper!"

Of course, you did! I wanted to answer. News had travelled fast, and soon enough, everyone in the military base read that article. Because of it, many men kept trying to ask me out. I had made the mistake of coming to this week's dance, and now they wouldn't leave me alone.

"Wow, you really are as beautiful as they say. Would you care to dance?"

"No, thank you, I'm a bit tired."

He was disappointed, but not ready to give up.

"How about I bring you a drink?"

"Sure." I was glad to be rid of him, even if only for a moment.

"You sure have become popular now, haven't you, Hela?"

I could sense the jealousy in my sister's voice. Since she had a day off today, she agreed to accompany Mama and I, but clearly, she was regretting it.

"It's not my fault Mr. Smith wrote what he did."

"Are you sure you didn't do anything to incite him to write that article?"

"What are you implying?"

She didn't have time to reply, because right then the man came back.

"Here's your drink, Miss Helena."

"You know what? I think I would like to dance after all."

His eyes widened, and his smile broadened. He extended his arm and I grabbed it, letting him lead me to the dance floor. I looked at Jadzia just in time to see her glare at me.

We danced, and the man tried to make conversation, but I was disinterested. I don't think he picked up my hints though, because he didn't stop.

"Miss Helena, I'll be honest with you. I think you're a beautiful young lady, talented and hard-working. And, well... I'd love it if you could become my wife!"

I paused, and so did he, anxiously waiting for my answer. I felt bad simply turning him down and thought I'd have to come up with an excuse.

"Um... I appreciate your feelings, but..."

His shoulders slumped, and his face fell before I continued. I decided to quickly give the final blow and put an end to this awkward moment.

"I'm already engaged to someone in Canada." (Little did I know then that this last-second fib would turn out to be my future.)

"Really?"

"Yes, I'm sorry."

He seemed sad but also comprehensive.

"Well, it can't be helped then. Thank you for at least accepting to dance with me."

With that, he left me on the dance floor. Little did I know, I had just discovered a very useful excuse.

***

"Here's another one, Hela."

Mother tossed me the white envelope; I already knew what it contained. Unfortunately, John Smith wrote two more articles about the exhibition and, of course, about me. Because of that, many boys were writing to me from different parts of England. They all wanted to marry me. Quite frankly, it was becoming annoying.

"That's already the third one this week. And it's only Tuesday!"

"Sure, it is hard to be a celebrity, isn't it?"

I rolled my eyes as I ripped the envelope. I skimmed through the content - just as I predicted - and grabbed a piece of paper and a pen to write my response. I had been using the excuse that I have a fiancé in Canada so these men could leave me alone. Luckily, my tactic worked, and they didn't bother writing to me a second time.

"You know, maybe that lie you keep telling is actually true. After all, aren't you interested in moving to Canada? Maybe that's where you'll find the man of your dreams."

"You think so?"

"I said maybe."

Indeed, I had been very interested in moving to Canada. Ever since my Uncle Sowa offered to bring us there, I developed a liking for this foreign country and read more and more about it. The fauna and flora seemed beautiful, and since it was pretty a new country, there would be many opportunities to build it up. My Uncle also made it seem like a wonderful place when he wrote about it in his letters, and I was getting impatient.

"Mama, when are we going to move to Canada? Tata said he wanted to gather all his children first, and here we are. Isn't it the perfect time to leave?"

"Hmm… I guess you're right. I'll have to talk about it with him."

At that moment, we heard a knock on the door, and Janek appeared.

"Hi, you two!"

"Oh Janek, I didn't know you were coming today."

"I was visiting a friend and decided to stop by."

He let himself fall on the sofa, his back sinking into the cushiony fabric. With my salary, I had been able to afford better quarters, so now we had two separate rooms with nice furniture.

"What are you working on, Helena?"

"I'm just writing another response."

He was already aware of all the attention I'd been receiving. It seemed his friend Marek regretted not making a move earlier, because now I was too desired. Ah well!

"By the way, is that Mr. Smith still writing about you?"

"He wrote two more articles and kept sending letters for me to my supervisor at work. I'm fed up with it!"

"Well, you should be careful with that man. One of my coworkers knows him and told me he's married."

"Married?"

Both Mother and I were surprised.

"Yeah, so I don't know why he's complimenting you so much and sending you all those letters. He seems like a flirt to me."

"Thank you for telling us, Janek. Helena, I hope you understand you shouldn't waste your time with this man."

"Yes, Mama."

I was already disinterested in him, but this news only gave me another reason to stay away from John Smith. Why a grown man - a grown *married* man – would be so interested in a young girl like me? I couldn't think of any good reason.

I think Mr. Smith fell in love with me and caused me so many problems. He kept on writing about me in papers and showing up at my door.

Since I didn't go to John Smith, he came to me. I was having a quiet night at home when a knock came on our door.

"Hi, Miss Helena!"

"What the..? What are you doing here?"

"I came to visit you, of course!"

"But... How did you know where I live?"

"Oh, I just asked around."

Mr. Smith stood at our door, and it all seemed really strange. His hand was in the pocket of his nicely-ironed black pants, and the other was playing with the short strands of hair behind his neck.

"I noticed you haven't responded to my letters and was wondering why."

"You can figure out where I live but you can't figure out why I'm ignoring you?"

He paused, offended but not defeated.

"I was just hoping I could get to know you better."

"Well, all you need to know is that I don't want to know you at all!"

With that, I slammed the door shut. Unfortunately, he came back two or three times, but after Father had a good *talk* with him, he finally left me alone. I thought all the buzz around the exhibition was finally over, but I was wrong. One day as I finished a class, two men were waiting for me outside the building.

"Excuse me, are you Miss Helena Fąfara?"

I was tempted to lie but decided not to.

"Yes, I am."

"Oh good!"

The men seemed relieved. One was stout with thick black hair, and the other was lean with freckles all over his face. The skinny one took a step forward.

"We're miners from Huddersfield, and next month is going to be our mine's anniversary. Our boss asked us what we should do to celebrate, and since the workers are pretty diverse, we suggested having a representation of each of their countries. My friend and I are both Polish, and we read in the papers about what you did in that elementary school, so we were wondering if you could do the same for us."

"That sounds like a nice idea, and honestly, I'd love to do it. I just have to ask permission first from my superiors."

The men smiled, and we discussed the details of the event. Immediately after we parted, I wrote a letter to my management officials in London, asking if I could be allowed to take on this project. Since my first exhibit went so well, they didn't hesitate to give me permission once again, as well as a subvention. They even accepted to pay for my accommodations in Huddersfield. When I told my students about this, they were all excited to contribute.

There weren't too many costumes to make, and since the ladies now had some experience, the work went smoother than the first time. I chose two of my students to accompany me to Huddersfield, and we arrived there the day before the event.

"Oh, I'm so very excited for tomorrow!" Lena said.

She was one of the students who worked the hardest, so I had to take her with me. However, I was slowly regretting my decision since she couldn't seem to calm down.

"I'm sure it's going to be as great as in Yorkshire. Or maybe even better!"

She rambled on, imagining how the event would go, which distracted her from her task.

"Lena, remember we're supposed to help with the decorations, and you aren't doing much decorating right now."

"Oh! Sorry, Miss Helena!"

She smiled apologetically before focusing on the flowers she had to arrange.

The exhibition was to be held the next day, so I wanted to make sure everything was perfect. We kept working until late at night, finishing the last-minute preparations. I was enthusiastic about the event, and I also had another reason to look forward to tomorrow.

The next day, we woke up early and got right to work. I double and triple-checked everything to make sure there were no mishaps, that all the costumes fit nicely, and all adjustments were complete. The public filled the room in the afternoon, admiring the decoration. Blue and yellow balloons contrasted with white Canterbury bells. Several tables draped in white cloth were spread on the wooden floor, and a banquet on the left side provided the crowd with refreshments. A wooden stage was in the center of the room with a black curtain in the back, behind which the mannequins hid, awaiting their cue.

Just like in Yorkshire, everyone was bewildered as they saw the costumes. Since they were for adults this time, we decided to make them a bit more special with more complex embroidery and a wider variety of colours. As I enjoyed the evening, I felt a hand touch my shoulder. I turned around and saw Lena smiling.

"The people love your creations!"

"*Our* creations! Don't forget you also helped."

"True, but you supervised it all!"

We chatted a bit, and then the manager of the mine went on stage.

"Excuse me everyone, could I please have your attention?"

It took a few seconds for the chatter to die down.

"I hope you all enjoyed your evening. Tonight, we wanted to commemorate the fortieth anniversary of the Huddersfield mine. Since we have workers from different ethnicities, we decided to highlight each of them. You have been able to enjoy foods, performances, and even clothing from each of these countries."

His speech continued, but it was only when he mentioned my name that I really paid attention.

"I would like you all to welcome on stage Miss Helena Fąfara, the young lady who created the traditional Polish costumes."

Applause arose as I made my way on stage. It was at that moment the manager added something I wasn't expecting.

"I would also like to mention that today, September 19, is Miss Fąfara's birthday! Just as the mine is celebrating its fortieth anniversary, she is celebrating her twentieth!"

More applause! I looked in the crowd and spotted Lena smiling broadly. I figured she told him, but didn't mind; it gave us another reason to rejoice. This event was also a complete success, and I was more than happy to return home without having been interviewed by anyone.

My younger brother Andziej and I at the beach.

My portrait,
Helena Fąfara.

My Mother's portrait,
Anna Fąfara

My Father, Ludwig Fąfara.

My portrait as a young lady, England.

My girlfriends and I at one of the many dances we attended in England. I am third from the left.

My Father, Ludwig Fąfara, England.

My wonderful husband, Tadeusz Zbygniew Robaszewski.

My photo, Helena Fąfara.

Zbyszek's Mother, Franciska Robaszewski Gawroński.

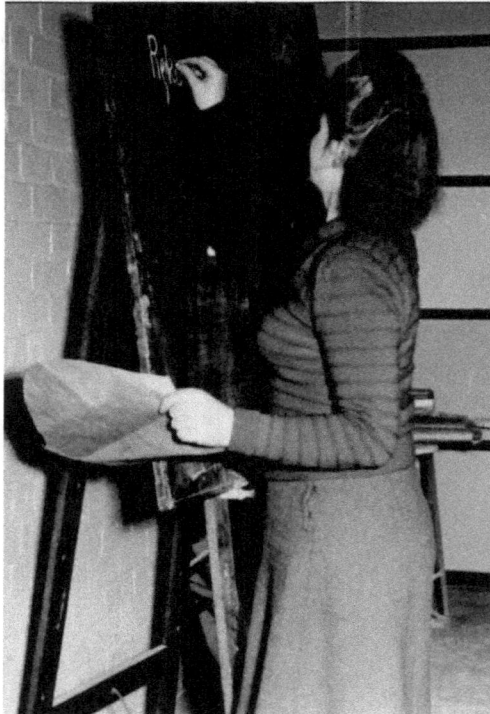

Beginning my lesson of the day as a sewing teacher of costume and clothing design.

Sewing exhibition, England, after WWII.

**One of the many beautiful dances we attended in England. From
the left is me, my brother Janek, and our friends.**

Janek and I dancing together, England.

Photo taken of me, Helena Fąfara in England.

My sewing exhibition showcasing the beautiful work of my students

Picnic at the park, England.

My two young models, showcasing the Polish national costumes of the mountain regions.

My younger brother Andziej Fąfara and myself Helena Fąfara.

Me and my workmates I am second from the left, England.

My photo, Helena Fąfara

Photo of me, Helena Fąfara.

Part 7

Canada

Halifax-Edmonton-The Farm in Vilno-Toronto

CHAPTER 19

Departure

A s time passed, my eagerness to move to Canada only increased.

"Tata, don't you think it's time for us to leave England? Maybe Uncle Sowa won't keep his offer on the table much longer."

"I understand, Hela, but I'm having doubts about moving there. I heard it's so cold that even potatoes can't grow!"

It took me a tremendous amount of effort not to roll my eyes.

"That's only in the winter! I read a lot about Canada, and it's a truly beautiful country. It has nice big lakes, dense forests, and wonderful mountains. Just ask Uncle Sowa since he lives there."

Tata still wasn't convinced, so I tried to get allies. The whole family had gathered for Easter, and since this was one of the rare occasions when we were all together, it was my chance to get everyone on board.

"Don't you all think we would be better off moving to Canada? We could finally have a stable life again."

My sister was the first to object.

"I don't want to go there. Not when I finally have a boyfriend here."

"I agree with Jadzia, Janek said. Things are going well between me and Emily, and I don't want to repeat the same mistake as with Paula."

"Who's Paula?" I asked.

"Don't you remember? The one who was going to Brazil and that I wanted us to follow."

We all rolled our eyes simultaneously. Had Janek truly believed the whole family would move to another country simply so he could follow his girlfriend?

"Anyway," Jadzia said, "we're not leaving."

I could tell from her tone her mind was set, but I was desperate for allies. I looked over at Andrzej, who hadn't said anything so far.

"And what about you? Wouldn't you want to leave?"

He shrugged. "I don't mind either way. I don't have a beautiful girlfriend or an amazing job keeping me here."

Since he technically wasn't against the idea of leaving, I counted him as being on my side.

"And you, Mama? What do you think?"

"Well… we have all moved quite a lot in the last decade, so I'm not too sure how I'd feel about moving again."

"We'll have to move either way. You know we can't stay in the military base forever," I explained.

"That's true, but settling here in England and settling in Canada are two different things. I'm tired of long trips and am definitely not looking forward to boarding another ship."

She made a point, and I wasn't looking forward to the long boat ride to Canada. However, as much as I enjoyed my teaching job, I didn't want that to be it for me. Somehow, I seemed to be the only visionary in the family. For now, I decided to step back and hope that the others would eventually come around.

"That's it for today's class. I'll see you all Monday."

I waited until the last student exited the room before doing the same. In the hallway, I was intercepted by Stefa.

"Oh, Helena!

"Hi!"

We walked side by side as we left the building to return to the military base. I immediately noticed the wide smile on her lips and knew she eagerly awaited me to ask her why she was in such a good mood.

"Did something happen?"

At the sound of her cue, her smile broadened.

"Something happened, alright. Something big! Eryk finally proposed!"

"What?"

"Yes! It happened last night. Oh, it was so romantic!"

For the next 20 minutes or so, she explained in great detail how she had been proposed to. Her smile was so wide I couldn't help but wonder if her cheeks hurt, but then I thought she probably didn't feel any pain since she was so happy.

"And what's great is that we'll move together to Australia!"

"Australia?"

"Yes! Isn't it fantastic?"

"It is, but... why there?"

"Well, we heard they have some pretty good opportunities, and many other Polish people will also be going there. Besides, it's not like we can stay in the military camp forever. At some point, we need to move forward in life, right?"

"Yes, that's true."

She flipped her long hair back, and her blue eyes lit up as she continued to speak. However, I didn't pay much attention to what she said afterward, since I was still pondering her words. We were already in August 1950, which meant we had been in England for about two years. Was it going to be like Tengeru, where we stayed for nearly six years? Or was England only going to be a transition to where we should be headed?

"Hey, Helena! Are you listening?"

I snapped back to reality at the sound of my friend's voice.

"Oh, sorry. I missed that last bit you said."

She pouted, but was in a good mood to stay mad for long.

"Anyway, I was simply saying that we'll leave in October of this year."

"That's pretty soon, only a few months."

"True, but sometimes taking too long can result in us missing an opportunity. It's time for us to take our lives back. We can't afford to wait around any longer. Besides, it's not like we have much keeping us in England."

Her words hit home; at that moment, I was more resolute than ever. For the next few days, I informed myself of the procedures to follow in order to leave the country. I was ready to go to Canada no matter what, even if it meant going alone. I decided to take the first step and get my passport. The problem though, was that I wasn't 21 yet and couldn't legally travel alone internationally. Maybe from there, I'd be able to convince the rest of my family to join me.

On one of my days off, I travelled to London to go to the Canadian embassy. The building had a tall ceiling and the marble flooring was so shiny that I was scared to step on it. The employees looked slightly intimidating in their polished blue uniforms, but I shook off my uneasiness. I decided I wouldn't leave without my passport. I had decided I wouldn't back down from my resolve, so with a somewhat confident look, I marched towards the receptionist.

"Hi, how can I help you?"

The man seemed nice, which helped me ease up a bit.

"I would like to get a passport. I'm planning on moving to Canada."

"Alright, then."

He explained to me the immigration process and which papers I had to fill. With practiced movements, he took out some sheets and showed me where to sign and what information to insert. It took me a couple of minutes to complete it, but he waited patiently for me to finish.

"Here you go."

"Thank you."

He quickly reviewed the sheets in order to make sure everything was in check. He nodded a few times as he went from page to page. I stood there awkwardly, not knowing what I should do or say.

"This is just out of curiosity, but will you be travelling alone?"

"I fear I might. I would like to bring my family along, but they don't want to come."

Surprise was evident on the man's face.

"Why don't they want to move to Canada?"

"For various reasons."

I ended up ranting to the receptionist about how my family wasn't able to realize the great opportunities they'd have in Canada and that they were giving petty excuses; especially Jadzia and Janek.

"You know, they really should leave now."

"Why now?"

He leaned forward as if he wanted to tell me a secret.

"Until the end of this year, the Polish government will be covering traveling expenses for all the ex-soldiers and their families who wish to settle elsewhere. If you wait after that, it might be too expensive for you to leave."

"What? Really?"

He nodded and went back to my dossier. I gathered more information about us having to travel this year, then left with the papers in my hand; I now had another card to play in my favour.

Thankfully, my Uncle Sowa hadn't stopped corresponding with us and trying to convince my parents to move. The piece of information I brought to the table was the final blow.

"Mama and I have decided we will be moving to Canada."

"What?"

"No!"

"Yes!"

There were all sorts of reactions when we heard the news. Obviously, Jadzia and Janek were against it and explained why we shouldn't leave.

"Didn't you say it's so cold in Canada that even potatoes can't grow? Haven't you had enough of the cold in Siberia?"

"Janek is right," my sister added. "Nothing good will come from going there. And we don't even know for sure that we'll be able to build stable lives there."

"If you want to reason that way, we don't know for sure we'll build a stable life anywhere, including here," Tata answered.

I was glad he came around and simply sat back as I enjoyed the show.

"But things are going well here. Why should we have to risk this nice situation for the unknown?"

Jadzia's temper was quickly rising, and I apprehended the moment she would blow. Thankfully, Father stayed calm.

"Jadwiga, you heard what your sister said. If we don't leave this year, we might not be able to leave at all."

"So what? I don't see what's so bad about staying in England."

"You don't see anything at all because you're blinded by love, you foolish child!" Mother retorted. "You can't just think about what's in front of you. You have to think about the future as well."

My sister exaggeratedly rolled her eyes. She sank down on the sofa and thought it wise to simply sit quietly and pout in her corner, instead of saying something she'd regret; That's when Janek intervened.

"I understand what you're saying, Mama, but... are you all sure this is the right thing to do? Will there truly be more positives than negatives if we move to Canada?"

"Well, what about England? What are the positives in staying here?" Mother asked.

"For starters, all the children have jobs, which means we can afford to eventually bring you out of the military base and get you your own house. Plus, we've made many friends here. We've known many other refugees since we were in Siberia, and after what we went through, our bonds are inseparable."

Mama's expression showed that she believed he made valid points. I began to fear Janek might win her over. He caught on, and quickly added:

"We could very easily settle right here in Yorkshire, buy a nice house, and live a comfortable life. And the best part: you won't have to deal with any boat ride."

He glanced at me, and I noticed the smirk in the corner of his lips. He knew Mom and I didn't want to ride a boat for weeks, so that argument could settle things. At that moment, I felt I had to step in or else I'd lose my case.

"Everything you're saying, we can do in Canada as well. We can get jobs over there and buy a house. It's true we won't be with the same friends anymore, but they're all leaving anyway. And we can make new friends in Canada, plus there is a lot of lands there."

"Some bonds simply can't be replaced," my brother answered.

"Oh please! You wouldn't be talking like that if you didn't have a girlfriend here."

"What did you say?"

Our argument was getting heated, so Tata interfered.

"That's enough! Both of you."

We piped down on the spot. He looked at us sternly before letting out an exasperated sigh.

"I understand your positions and why you want or don't want to leave. However, this is an opportunity we can't pass up. My cousin will help us get back on our feet, so I'm willing to take the risk of moving to another country. If we fear to do something because of the risk it entails, then we won't ever do anything."

We knew there was no point in adding anything now, which I was contented with. Janek and Jadzia on the other hand, were clearly disappointed. I wondered how they'd break the news to their romance partners. It was then Andrzej got up and clapped his hands, immediately getting our attention.

"Well, we better start packing!"

A smile broke my lips.

"Indeed!"

We were now a few weeks away from our departure, and I had to resign from my teaching job.

"Are you sure you don't want to stay, Miss Helena? You've been doing such great work." The disappointment was clear on my supervisor's face. However, my mind was set.

"I'm sorry, sir, but my family has already decided we will be leaving in December."

"But... We were planning to offer you a scholarship!"

"Scholarship?" I gasped!

Noticing he had piqued my interest, the man went on.

"Yes! You could continue working here, and we would also fund your studies at one of our most prestigious universities! How about it?"

"Well... I truly don't know."

Since I had technically already gotten a diploma in Tengeru, I didn't see the point in pursuing my studies. However, I also feared my diploma might not be acknowledged, which would cause me trouble when looking for a better job.

"Maybe you should think about it and come back to us, OK?"

I nodded and left. On the way back home, I wondered if this was also an opportunity I shouldn't pass up.

"Welcome back, Helena! How was work?"

"Not too bad. I gave my resignation letter today."

"How was it? I'm sure they were sad to lose you."

"Yeah. My supervisor even offered me a university scholarship so that I could stay."

"A scholarship?"

She was packing clothes and stopped in her movements in stunned surprise.

"Yes. He said they'd pay for my studies at one of their most prestigious universities, so now I'm wondering if I should stay or not."

"Weren't you the one who was so eager to leave?"

"I was, but then again, I thought my college diploma might not be acknowledged elsewhere, and then it'll be hard to find a good job."

Mother paused for a moment, pondering my words. She knew I wasn't wrong for thinking the way I did, and she didn't want me to take this scholarship, which also included English classes. My heart was with my family, though. After all this time we've had all my family apart, and now with all of them together, I couldn't be apart again.

"We're already preparing to move. Tata and I are going tomorrow to get our papers. Since everyone is going to Canada, you should come too. Besides, you'll get lonely staying here by yourself. And who would give you advice for your dates? Plus, haven't you told all the boys you *have a fiancé in Canada*? You must go to him"

She winked, and I couldn't help but smile.

"Yes, Mama, you're right."

"If you want more time to think about it, that's fine. But for now, I need you to help me pack."

Without wasting another moment, I got to work.

The next day, I told my students about my resignation. As expected, they were sad I was leaving but happy for me; I also had mixed feelings. This wasn't our last class yet, but the thought that soon it would be was hard to digest. At the end of the day, my manager's assistant requested I see him.

"Yes, sir?"

"Ah, Miss Helena. I wanted to talk to you about your resignation."

I wondered if he'd also try to convince me to stay, but it wasn't the case.

"I know you'll be leaving us next week, but you're only moving to Canada in December. Since you'll have a bit of time before your departure, I thought maybe you would like a small job to make some pocket money."

His thick glasses gave him wide brown eyes, and he stared at me with an inquiring look, wanting to know if I was interested or not. I nodded, which was his cue to continue.

"A friend of mine works for the White Cross and owns a Polish club. He was looking for a receptionist, and I thought you would fit the bill. What do you think?"

"I would love to do it! Would he be willing to hire me for such a short period of time?"

"Yes, it wouldn't be a problem. They're short-staffed at the moment and need someone right now. While you're there, it'll at least give them time to search for someone who'll work long-term."

The assistant manager gave me more information about the job, and I decided to accept. That's how barely a week later, I was at the reception of a beautiful Polish club. The place had high ceilings and shiny wooden floors. There was also a restaurant with round tables draped in burgundy red cloth. The second floor had rooms usually rented out to students. Polish artifacts, such as tapestries, vases and dolls, were displayed to accentuate the decoration. All in all, the place was wonderful!

The time of our departure was fast approaching, and I was getting more and more excited to leave. Jadzia and Janek had a hard time breaking off their relationships, but eventually, they did. By the time everyone got their papers, there wasn't much time left before it was time to depart. We packed all our belongings and soon enough, were on an enormous ship, waving goodbye to England. I couldn't help but remember when we left Tengeru in the same manner. That camp had brought its share of laughter, sorrow, growth, and bountiful life, just like England did.

The two years I spent there were now behind me, and looking back, I truly had an amazing time. I was able to meet great people and live out fabulous experiences. Despite all the fun and friends, I knew I had to move forward. Canada was calling me, so I had to go.

Unfortunately, the trip was just as unpleasant as I had feared. Mother, my sister and I all got seasick. It was quite windy, and the boat was constantly swaying.

"Merry Christmas!"

"Blurgh!"

The Holiday season in 1950 was one I'd always remember, since we spent it on the floor. We were feeling incredibly nauseous and didn't enjoy the festivities at all.

"Tata, I think we'll need to bring the mop," Janek said.

"Again?"

The men were also getting sick; sick of seeing us in such a pitiful state! Andrzej and Janek kept mocking us, whereas Tata actually took care of us.

"Whose brilliant idea was it to come to Canada?" Jadzia asked in a fury, her arms holding her stomach in order to keep in what was ready to burst out again.

Her menacing eyes darted in my direction, but I was too ill to be scared. My head hurt a lot, a throbbing pain pounding against my skull, so I laid down in an attempt to feel better.

"I knew getting on this boat was a bad… a… blurgh!"

"Mop!"

Father walked into our cabin with the mop, grumbling all the while. He handed it to Janek, who had been snickering all day.

"Here, you do it this time."

"Why me?"

"Because I told you to get them a bucket, but you forgot, so this is your fault."

The roles switched, and my older brother grumbled while Andrzej snickered in a corner. Every time I tried to relax for a moment, the boat was violently shaken by big waves again. I didn't know how the others weren't getting seasick. We were constantly swaying from side to side, but the captain assured us everything would be fine. I wanted to believe him, though I was starting to fear for our safety. Nonetheless, he accomplished his promise and brought us to our destination.

Canada.

CHAPTER 20

Firsts

That's it? That's Canada?

I couldn't help but be disappointed at the sight. Everything was covered in thick blanket of snow. I knew the winters could be harsh, but I didn't expect it to be this bad.

"My children, we are back in Siberia."

Mother couldn't stop sighing as she shook her head, clearly just as disappointed as I was. Indeed, looking around, the scenery reminded me of the long-frigid days and waist-high snow I soon wanted to forget.

"Well, standing here and freezing all night won't do us any good. We need to get to the train station, remember?"

We all nodded and let Tata lead the way after getting directions from the boat crew. When we were still in England, Janek told us he wanted to visit his friend in Toronto; it was Bolek Dzierzek, the one who took care of him after he was wounded in the war. We arrived in Halifax and took the train to Toronto. It was December 29, 1950, and we welcomed the New Year by the time we made it to our destination.

"Janek! Good to see you, my friend!"

"Bolek!"

The two men embraced, clearly happy to see each other again. At the heartwarming scene, my regrets and doubts quickly dissipated. We made the right choice to come here.

"I present to you my family! Here are my sisters, Jadwiga and Helena, my brother Andrzej and my parents, Ludwig and Anna."

"It's a pleasure to finally meet you all! Janek wouldn't stop talking about all his family members when he was in the hospital, and it was driving me nuts!"

We laughed as he invited us into his cozy home. The walls were painted beige and were nicely decorated. There was a fireplace in the living room on top of which various military medals were neatly aligned. In the dining room stood a showcase with beautiful china displayed. Frankly, I wasn't expecting such elegance from a man living alone. Bolek had cooked us a nice dinner, and we all sat at the table to catch up.

"How was the trip?"

"It depends on who you're asking. We men had a great time. But the ladies..."

Janek shot us a side glance and smirked. I started getting nauseous simply at the thought of the rocking boat and big waves, but somehow I managed not to spill my dinner. We talked for a while - well, Janek and Bolek did most of the talking - and eventually asked our host how life was in Canada.

"Honestly, it isn't easy. This country technically isn't even 100 years old yet, so it's still growing. (Between 1950 and 1951, the population of Canada grew by nearly 1 million) It's hard to find job opportunities, but here in Toronto, it's better than in some other places."

I wasn't encouraged at the sound of that. We had come here to build our lives back, but if we wouldn't even get the chance to do so, maybe we had wasted a trip.

"And what about Alberta?" Tata asked, trying to mask his concern. "Are there good opportunities there?"

Bolek rubbed his hairy chin and pondered before answering.

"I'm not too sure. I think they have a lot of farms, but not too many developed cities like Toronto, so it might be tough to find work."

Tata's shoulders slumped slightly. I was also disappointed after hearing such an answer. It seemed so many obstacles kept getting in our way each time we tried to finally make a life for ourselves. Eventually, we moved on to another topic, but that short conversation kept replaying in my mind.

"We're not leaving you here, Janek."

"But Tata, listen!"

"I listened to what you said, and I don't approve of it."

The following evening, my brother and Father had a bit of an argument. Thankfully, Bolek had gone out to run an errand, so he didn't witness the scene.

"I just think it's better if we children stay in Toronto since there aren't that many job opportunities in Alberta. You heard what Bolek said! We're better off here than over there."

"I did hear what your friend said, but the reason I had initially pushed back our departure to Canada was because I wanted to gather all my children first. Now, I want all of us to make it to Alberta. From there, each of you will be free to go in your separate ways."

Janek didn't seem too convinced, but he didn't get the chance to retort since his friend came back at that moment.

"Sorry I took so long! There really is some crazy snow out there!"

My brother went to help him carry the bags he brought back, and that was the end of that conversation.

We only stayed at Bolek's house for a few days before boarding the train once again, this time in the direction of Alberta.

"Is *that* what we're getting on?"

Jadzia wasn't being picky. Our means of transportation *was* in pretty bad shape. There was rust eating the train everywhere, thick layers of dust rested on the railings, stuffing stuck out of the seats, and a foul smell forced us to constantly cover our noses. I wondered if it could safely travel through three provinces.

"It looks like it's about to break. How old is this thing?"

Andrzej started kicking the train, but stopped when Tata reprimanded him. We didn't have much choice and boarded, praying we would make it safely to our destination. On the plus side, the wagons weren't too packed, so at least we had our own space. The trip lasted four days and three nights. Sleeping on the hard and uncomfortable seats was nearly impossible, so we were very tired when we arrived at the train station in Edmonton. We stretched our limbs and dragged our luggage to a bench, where we waited for our connection.

"I'm going to walk around," Andrzej suddenly said.

"What for?" Mama asked.

"To explore. We have some time before we need to take our next train, and I want to see what Edmonton is like."

My younger brother rose before we could stop him, and I decided to follow since I had nothing better to do. We stepped outside the station where the sky was dark, and the city was still because it was six in the morning. The icy wind shook off all tiredness from my eyes, and all my senses were alert.

"Make sure you don't go too far! The last thing we want is for you to get lost."

We barely paid attention to Father's warning and left. I was eager to explore, but that eagerness quickly disappeared. We barely walked ten feet when Andrzej stopped dead in his tracks. I stopped too, knowing it was for the same reason.

"Helena."

"Yes?"

"It's way too cold."

We were already shivering and with a simple nod, decided to turn back.

"Oh? You're already done exploring?" Dad asked.

"It's too cold to go exploring!" Andrzej answered as he rubbed his frozen hands.

Janek and Jadzia both laughed at us. I hadn't thought I would one day end up in a place nearly as cold as Siberia, but here I was. We stayed in the semi-warm station before taking our next and final train. Half awake, I watched the moving landscape through the window. Snow-covered mountains contrasting with tall, dark green pine trees were the dominant elements constituting the scenery. As I flirted with sleep, I imagined how my Uncle would be, how my cousins would be, and how my new life in Canada would look like. I imagined getting a prominent job and a beautiful house. I thought of peaceful days spent near the cozy fireplace and with loved ones around.

When the train stopped and we stepped off, a whole family welcomed us.

"Oh, there they are! Welcome Ludwig!"

"Sowa!"

The two men embraced each other, initiating a series of hugs and kisses. Arms and bodies were confused in a huge pile of warm reunion. Our smiles unfroze our faces and laughter was heard all around. Once the euphoria calmed down, the presentations followed.

"Here is my wife, Rose, my son Julian who is 18, and my daughter Alvina who is 16."

Father followed the same protocol, pride evident on his face as he presented his loved ones. Each family contemplated the other as if they are seeing a celebrity in the flesh.

One thing I noticed right away was that they were all blond. Alvina was quite short, maybe around 5"4. Julian had deep blue eyes just like his mother, whose short hair nicely framed her round face. Uncle Sowa was stout and had a loud laugh. When everyone knew who was who, we departed. During the whole trip to their house in Spedden, my uncle and his wife kept repeating how overjoyed they were that we came. Their children were very nice, and I immediately felt at ease.

Their home was a modest bungalow with a fireplace in the living room and an outhouse in the back. A faded white coated the walls, and the wooden floor squeaked at some spots. They didn't have many rooms, but somehow, we managed to find space for everyone. After we settled in, it was time to eat.

"I would like to say a few words before we share this meal."

We all turned our heads towards my Uncle (Tata's cousin), who was beaming.

"Ludwig, I can't express how happy I am to see you with your whole family present at our table today. Throughout the war, my family and I were bent over the radio every evening to hear what was happening in Poland. Even though I don't know exactly what you went through, I know there were many hardships in your life, but the Lord brought you through them all. It is truly a blessing that each of you made it here. That's why today, we celebrate!"

That was our cue, and soon, we had our cutlery in hand and food on our plates. The atmosphere was lively as we shared jokes and funny anecdotes. They were very interested in hearing our stories and learning about the different countries we visited, and I felt a sense of pride as I recounted our adventures. We had a wonderful evening, and I was truly grateful to be here. Slowly but surely, Canada was becoming my new home.

"Hey, everyone! There is a New Year's party in town. Let's all go together!" Julien announced at the dinner table.

Julien was Uncle Sowa's Son. He was around the age of my siblings and I, so he fit right in.

"Oh my goodness - Yes!"

Jadzia was very excited, and so was I. This would be our first big celebration out on the town since we arrived in Alberta. The energy grew each day as the party date came closer.

In my family, it was tradition to believe that however you live on New Year's Day will predict how the rest of your year would go. So we would all dress in our best clothes and share kindness with others and be merry in hopes that the rest of the year will be just as happy.

My brothers planned to wear their best tuxedos and long jackets. Though Jadzia and I took more time to decide on which dresses to wear.

"No, Jadzia! I get to wear this dress because I made it for myself. I tailored it to my body." I said sternly. My sister was always interested in my clothes and what I was wearing to parties.

Jadzia rebutted, "Well, that's not fair! I'm the eldest girl, and I must have the best dress".

"Please, you have other dresses. Here, I even made this one for you." I pulled out a floor-length maroon dress from her chest.

"I think this dress compliments your dark hair beautifully, and this long ribbon out the back is so elegant."

"Fine. This will have to do." Jadzia sulked.

I was never one for parties, but I always liked to dance. I remember practicing how to dance to songs on the radio or record player whenever I had the chance.

In Poland, my Mama taught me how to practice dancing when I was little. She gave me a pair of fluffy socks and a broom. Then she showed me how to swing my hips to the rhythm of the music using the broom as my partner. I can see now that Mama had succeeded at occupying her child and cleaning the floors at the same time! Though I didn't care, I enjoyed it, and now I have developed a good rhythm.

The time was about 9:30 pm when Julien got the car ready. My siblings and I waited in the living room.

"Oh Helen, you are wearing a dress? And you men are wearing tuxedos?" Uncle Sowa had a confused look on his face.

"Well, of course we are! It's a New Year's Party!" Jadzia responded as she twirled around the room in her dress.

"My dear, it is -20 degrees outside. That's why I told Julien to get the car! Don't you realize that your celebration will be in the Town Hall?"

Now we were all confused. Why was Uncle Sowa opposed to our outfits? It's a New Year's Party. This is when you should be welcoming in the New Year with your best foot forward!

Uncle Sowa explained himself. "I understand that you want to look nice, but the Town Hall does not have any heating! Also, you live in Canada. These people do not have the same traditions as you."

Jadzia stopped dancing. "So you mean I can't go in my dress?"

"You can go in your dress. Please do my dear, you look stunning. Just know that the others will probably be wearing big parkas and cowboy boots."

Julien came in soon after.

"Car is ready! Let's go!"

Even if we wanted to change clothes, it was too late now.

We realized that Uncle Sowa was right when we arrived at the Town Hall. The big hall was decorated nicely, but the people were *not* in their Sunday best. Even the people dancing were wearing parkas.

"Well, here we go," John said as he picked out a table for us all to sit at.

The energy was so lively! The people were dancing and laughing, and the music was upbeat. Every once in a while, when a popular song played, everyone rushed to the dance floor.

"It's called line dancing, but western style. So the steps and pattern fit in with their band's music." Julien explained

After some time, it seemed nobody wanted to ask me or my sister to dance.

"Ugh, this is horrible. Everyone is looking at us funny. It's not fair that all the girls dressed in simple clothes get a dance but not me!"

Jadzia was very upset.

I turned to my cousin, "Julien! You're not doing much. Why not take me to the dance floor?"

Julien looked uninterested.

"I'd rather not. With all these girls here, you want me to dance with you?"

"Oh, come on, you have two feet -and hopefully some rhythm. You can show us off! These boys just don't know we can dance."

"Well, alright Helen, let's see what you got!"

Julien and I danced. It was great! I never knew songs with fiddles could be so fun! Soon the song ended, and we went back to our table. Julien went to get some punch.

"Act natural," Jadzia whispered to me.

"What? But I am acting natural." I said.

"Say, Miss! That's a beautiful dress you are wearing tonight."

I turned around to look at who owned this low and manly voice.

"Thank you, Sir."

A tall, brown-haired man owned that voice. He wore a red plaid shirt, dark-washed jeans, and embroidered square-toed cowboy boots.

"I was wondering if I could take you 'round for the next song. My name is Richard."

"I would like that very much, Richard. Thank you."

I was smiling because a good-looking man asked me to dance, and also because my plan worked.

Again, I was dancing to an upbeat song with a fiddle.

"I must ask, Richard. Are you a real cowboy?"

Richard furrowed his brows and made a face. "If I'm a real cowboy? What? So, what do you think you are then, exactly?"

"Oh, dear. I am very sorry. I don't mean to offend you. My family and I are DPs from Poland, and we just arrived from England. I've just... I've never seen anything like this before."

Richard was still not amused.

"Please Sir, I really don't know! The only thing I know about cowboys is from movies. They all wear plaid shirts and well, cowboy boots!"

Richard looked down at his leather boots. "I can see where you got this idea from."

The time was around 11pm, and our family was all sitting at the table. "I'm cold. Is it okay if we go home now?" John asked.

"Yeah that's fine with me, let's go be with the rest of the family." I said.

Back at home, my parents, Wujek, and Ciocia were sitting around the kitchen table playing cards.

"Well, well, well! How was your evening, kids?" Tata Exclaimed.

"Helen danced with a *real cowboy*!" Jadzia said with a teasing tone.

"Well, I had to ask because he was wearing plaid and cowboy boots. He got offended, but he was wearing the outfit, so it was a fair guess."

Mama laughed "Hahaha! Maybe he is a cowboy but he doesn't realize it yet. That's alright, pull up a chair. Your Ciocia is losing our card game!"

We spent that New Year's together as a family; Warm, comfortable, and still in our fancy clothes.

In the spring when it was warm, I moved to Edmonton to look for a job. I received a phone call from Uncle Sowa.

"Oh Helen, I forgot to tell you! Remember your cowboy friend with the red plaid shirt? He came to the house last Saturday looking for you."

"Richard came to your house?!" I replied in surprise.

"Yes, you must have really caught his eye. Imagine all the footwork he had to do to get our address."

"He must have asked a lot of people..."

"Well, I think it was very sweet of him. He also left me his number to give you. Are you interested?"

"Ummm... Alright, but I do live kind of far now."

Until this day, I haven't called the cowboy back.

Our Wujek (Uncle) Sowa told us it would be better to find jobs in the spring, so we simply enjoyed our stay till the end of winter. Honestly, he and his family were simply fantastic! Not only had they welcomed us in their home, but also in their hearts. We were the only family they had in

Canada, so in a sense, we were the representatives of all their relatives. Each day, they brought joy into our lives with fun activities and taught us about our new country. My first impression of Canada was that not only was it cold, but it was also empty. There weren't many people around, and large patches of land separated houses, which made us feel more isolated. It somewhat reminded me of my home in Poland.

During winter, I didn't go out much, unlike Tata. Even though he disliked the cold, he never passed an invitation from his cousin to go ice fishing.

"Julian, how does ice fishing work?"

I kept hearing about it without actually understanding what it was. To me, fishing on a frozen lake was too mystifying to comprehend.

"You have to make a deep hole in the ice to access the running water underneath, and then you fish."

"A hole? But what if they fall?"

My cousin simply shrugged.

"That sometimes happens, which is why ice fishing can be pretty dangerous. Every year we learn of people who drowned and froze to death after they fell in the water."

"What?"

Hearing that automatically made me fear for Tata's safety. Especially since that time they had gone with their wives.

"How could anyone possibly do something so risky?"

Various scenarios surged through my mind, and I imagined one of my parents or both falling into the lake. They weren't as experienced as Wujek Sowa and Ciocia (Aunt) Rose, so surely they were more likely to have an accident. Julian noticed my panic and laughed. I stared at him, confused, not understanding what was funny about such a dangerous practice.

"Relax, Helena. I'm just messing with you! Obviously it's dangerous to fall in a frozen river, but my Tata knows what he's doing, so you have nothing to worry about."

I didn't want to believe him just yet, but he seemed so carefree about it I thought maybe he was right. Besides, almost anything was risky when we went outside in such weather. The temperature was far below zero degrees Celsius, and snow wouldn't stop piling. Thus, I kept my outings to a minimum.

I was very happy when the adults returned safe and sound later that day.

"We brought you guys something!"

Tata proudly showed us their catch - one bull trout and two rainbow trout - and Andrzej was already licking his lips. The women quickly got to work and cooked dinner. The evening was merry as we all enjoyed the fish.

"Thank you so much for the meal, Ciocia Rose! It was delicious!"

"I'm glad you liked it, Andrzej! This kind is also Alvina's favorite."

"By the way, how is she?"

"We went to see her yesterday, and she seemed a bit better but still coughing a lot."

Not long after our arrival, my cousin, Alvina got sick. She had gone to see a doctor who said she only had a cold, but her condition worsened. That's why my Wujek brought her to a hospital in Edmonton where she was diagnosed with tuberculosis. The treatments she was receiving were slowly bringing her health back, but she still couldn't come back home just yet.

I brought her one of those canvases where you paint by colour, so that she can pass the time.

I can imagine how bored she must be over there.

"I'll come by next time you visit her, Ciocia."

With that, we cleared the table and moved on to another conversation topic.

My Wujek had been in Canada since 1929, so he knew quite a few people. In fact, one of his friends owned a big farm, and there was also a house on the property. After he heard of our arrival, he offered us the place, saying he only used the farm and lived elsewhere. We couldn't believe it, but my Wujek was dead serious and explained this was his friend's way of helping us settle into our new country.

We were overjoyed at the news and immediately started packing our things. I was sad to leave my cousins, but at least we wouldn't live too far from them. We cleaned and redecorated our new home. The men worked on renovations, while the women worked on decorations. For my part, I took care of all the curtains, sewing beautiful designs.

Since we didn't have jobs yet, we spent our days working on the house and cleaned it up in record time. When we finally moved in, it looked amazing!

"I wish I lived here!" Alvina told us as they came to visit.

She had finally been discharged from the hospital and was slowly recovering. Her brother nudged her elbow after hearing her remark.

I was happy to finally have a place to call home. After over a decade of wandering, we eventually had our own place to call home. It was a great feeling.

I came back to visit my wonderful Uncle, Aunt, and cousins often. All the Canadian things I was experiencing were so exciting!

"What are you making, Ciocia Rose?"

"A pie."

"A pie? What's that?"

"You've never seen a pie before, Helena?"

I had come to visit my Ciocia and cousins and was intrigued by this foreign recipe.

I shook my head, and she seemed undignified as if it was a shame I didn't know this pastry.

"Pies are deserts that are made of crust and filled with different things. You can make blueberry pie, a cherry pie, and so on."

Fascinated, I watched her work. She kneaded the dough for the crust and then carefully placed it in the pie pan. Next, she prepared the filling for her blueberry pie. She explained each step of the recipe, and I was excited to see the final result.

"Now, we need to bake it for about 30 minutes. After, we'll let it cool down for a bit and then we can eat it."

I was disappointed I had to wait all that time to taste the pie, but knew it couldn't be helped. As if he knew I didn't know what to do while I waited, Julian asked me if I wanted to go outside and do some blueberry picking and visit the magnificent forest nearby.

"I'll show you some really special pine trees too."

Without hesitation, I followed my cousin out the door. The warm weather made me forget about the cold months that welcomed me when I arrived in Canada. I used to dislike going outside, but now I couldn't get enough of the fauna and flora. The emerald-green grass stretched towards the blue sky, sunrays creating white highlights contrasting with the dark brown bark of pine trees. Wild flowers added hints of purple and pink as they populated the ground. Black squirrels ran away once they spotted us, disappearing in thick bushes or tree branches. The woods were fairly quiet, and all we could hear was the sound of the wind playing in the tree branches, punctuated by the rhythmic sound of our footsteps. I kept looking around, taking in the view. The sky was completely washed of any clouds, and a magnificent blue radiated the sky.

"It's nice, isn't it?"

Julien had read my mind – or simply noticed me gazing at the scenery like a tourist.

"You know, this reminds me of Siberia. In the summer, we always went out to the forest to pick mushrooms and berries. That dense forest used to scare me, but I'm not feeling afraid right now. Actually, I just find all of this beautiful. I think the fact that my mind isn't in survival mode allows me to enjoy what I would've missed otherwise. Maybe that's what it means to live in peace."

He smiled and kept moving forward, bringing me deeper into the woods. At some point, a peculiar smell stung my nose, ruining the enchanted scene, and I was really disturbed by it. I looked at Julian, who kept walking and decided to stop. He noticed I wasn't following him and turned around.

"What's wrong?"

"You know what's wrong," I said, covering my nose.

A puzzled look furrowed his brown eyebrows, and he came closer, but I immediately took a step back.

"Don't! I know you farted!"

"Farted?"

"Yes, and it smells really bad."

"Helena, what are you saying?"

He kept coming closer, and I warned him not to. It was then that he paused and sniffed the air.

"You're right. It does smell bad."

"Don't play innocent."

"I'm serious, it wasn't me."

He looked around, and his eyes stopped on a small creature nearby. I followed his gaze and also spotted the black and white animal. It wasn't moving much and seemed to be staring at us.

"That's what smells bad. It's the skunk," Julian whispered

I vaguely remembered having read something about skunks in one of my books about Canada but I didn't know much about them. However, judging from my cousin's very slow movements, I guessed we shouldn't mess with them.

Is it going to attack us?" I also whispered, fearing that speaking too loud would make it mad.

It might if it thinks we're a threat.

"Skunks use their bad smell as a weapon, you know."

"Weapon?"

I didn't wait for more explanations and quickly ran back home.

"Helena?"

"I don't know about you, but I'm not going to wait around for that skunk to attack me and get sprayed!"

I tried to sprint through the forest as fast as I could, not knowing how quickly skunks moved. Julian was right behind me, and we decided to simply go back home. So much for those pine trees and blueberries!

"Welcome back, you two! The pie is almost finished cooling down."

I had forgotten about it, and so the excitement from earlier quickly came back. About fifteen minutes later, I was sitting in front of my first piece of pie with a fork in my hand. I took a bite, and my Ciocia waited for my reaction.

"So, do you like it?"

I took the time to swallow first before answering, but she had probably already guessed with the beaming smile on my face.

"Delicious, Ciocia!"

With the coming of spring, this new season also marked a new beginning in my life. Following Wujek's advice, I had waited for the cold months to leave before looking for a job. I went to an employment agency, feeling both nervous and enthusiastic. I was a pretty competent worker, and my English wasn't too bad. However, I had the Yorkshire accent, but hoped it wouldn't cause much of a problem. Either way, I was a fast learner and had gained a lot of experience throughout the years, so I believed my chances of getting hired were pretty good.

I went to the office and filled out some paperwork. Then the secretary looked over my file before giving her verdict.

"I am sorry, but we don't even have enough jobs for our own people, so there's nothing I can do for you."

I paused, blinked and replayed her words in my head before sinking down in my chair. I was prepared to face some challenges, but this sort of response was unexpected. Before I could think or say anything, tears rolled down my cheeks, which startled the secretary.

"What's wrong?"

"Are you seriously asking me what's wrong?"

She didn't answer, most likely realizing the stupidity of her question, but I still explained myself.

"You're telling me there aren't enough jobs for your *own* people. Canada accepted us, so we're Canadian too. Those who are considered to be 'your own' people have roofs above their heads and food on their table, but we have nothing, yet we still have to take care of ourselves and our families, just like you do. I'm not asking for pity. I'm asking for a job so that I can support myself and not be a burden to the country."

At that moment, I couldn't help but think of all the hardships and challenges we had gone through. The grain we stole in Siberia, the villagers to whom we begged for food, and the badly-maintained boats on which we sailed to better lands. We never asked to be caught up in a war, or exiled and reduced to a state lesser than human. Those who had prominent jobs and enticing lifestyles had lost prosperity, family, and inevitably a part of themselves. We had fought to get through today, hoping tomorrow would be better. We had bled and cried, been beaten and bruised, but still found the strength and courage to get back up and keep pushing. We could've given up at any point along the road, taking the easy way out and committing suicide if diseases or famine didn't kill us first. And now I was being told that despite all the challenges I overcame, it didn't matter because I hadn't had the privilege to be born and grow up in a country free of war. Thinking of such injustice, I couldn't help but cry.

"Oh! Miss Fąfara... I'm so sorry, I didn't mean to hurt you."

"You know, when I first read about Canada, I was very excited to come, but if all or most Canadians will be treating me this way, I probably should've stayed in England."

I knew the lady was feeling uncomfortable, which I was glad about. I didn't want her pity, but simply for her to understand how frustrating it can be to be discriminated because of circumstances we can't control.

"Maybe I can find something for you after all. Let me take a look."

She went through some of her files, and I sat there patiently, wiping away my tears. After a short while, she smiled and presented me with a job offer: nurse at the Misericordia Hospital.

CHAPTER 21

Job hunting

The Misericordia Hospital was in need of nurses, especially to treat patients with tuberculosis. The nurses benefitted from dormitories and paid dinners, so I lived there.

"Hi, you must be the new nurse!"

"Yes, my name is Helena."

"I'm Janina. Pleasure to meet you!"

Janina Hotkiewicz (now Muszynska) was an assistant nurse, and we quickly became good friends. We didn't have the same tasks, however. I was in charge of delivering food to patients and washing dishes, since I had no real medical knowledge, whereas she dealt directly with patients. Canada needed people to work. It wasn't the greatest job, but still, it was something. I had been there for about a week now and was enjoying my dinner at the cafeteria one evening, when my new friend joined me.

"How was your shift?"

"Not too bad, though I do get tired of standing all the time washing dishes. I wish I could at least move around like you."

"Don't envy my job. Treating patients is no easy task."

Janina had brown hair falling to her jaw, and her light grey uniform (with a pressed apron and a little white hat) floated around her skinny body. We chatted a bit, and as one thing led to another we talked about how we came to Canada.

"I arrived at the beginning of the year. We had been in England before."

"Wait, were you with the other Polish people who had been brought to England?"

"Yes, how did you know?"

"Because I was one of them!"

I was pleasantly surprised to hear such news. I knew Janina was Polish, but I thought maybe she was like Ciocia Rose, who was born here.

"In that case, you must have also been in Africa before coming to England."

"Yes, I was in Kenya. And you?"

"Tanzania."

From there, we had a long conversation about our time in Africa and the great journey coming here. It felt nice talking with someone who experienced similar events. The other nurses were nice and all, but they couldn't fully understand where I was coming from. Even though Janina and I hadn't been in the same camp, we had gone through more or less the same journey. Time flew, and I was very surprised when I realized we were the only two left in the cafeteria.

We had to pass through an underground tunnel to go from the nurses' dormitory to the hospital. It was dark and slightly ominous, but I was brave enough to pass through it. One evening, I went to Janina's room to chat. We were having a good time until she brought up the tunnel.

"Are you afraid of it?"

"Not at all. I've seen worse."

She knew I wasn't kidding but she still continued.

"The other day, a nurse was found dead. They placed her in the morgue which was located in the tunnel."

"What?"

"Yes. She died from tuberculosis."

"You're kidding."

"I'm serious! It was the nurse two rooms down. Everyone has been talking about it."

All of a sudden, my bravado faded away and gave place to fear. I knew dealing with patients meant being exposed to their diseases, but I didn't think someone would die. The incident happened not long after I had been hired, so I started to second guess my choice. Maybe the high risk of infection was why there were so many vacant positions.

"Janina, do you think it's safe to stay here?"

"Not really. But a job is a job, and we need the money."

She was right, though I didn't believe my life was worth the few dollars I received at the end of the week. In all cases, I knew I at least had to be more careful and take necessary precautions to remain healthy with this job.

With my first paycheck, I bought my parents a cooking stove.

"Oh, God Bless you, Dziecko! (Child) This is exactly what we needed!"

My parents were overjoyed by the gift, and I was glad I could help them. It was a small way to pay them back for everything they had done for me.

"I can't wait for all the delicious meals you're going to cook now, Anna!"

Tata smiled at his wife and winked. Mama shook her head and moved on to something else.

"So Helena, how is your new job?"

"Honestly, not so great. I dislike the tasks I'm given, and the place is a bit dangerous too."

"Dangerous?"

I told them of the recent events, and Mom was the first to panic.

"You need to leave that place right now! Who knows when you'll be infected?"

Father tried to calm her down, but he was also worried.

"You know Helena, doctors can't do much against tuberculosis. If you get it, it could most likely be fatal."

I knew they were both right, but I also thought of how happy they were when I gave them the cooking stove. I wanted to support my parents, and that's why I had gotten this job, but then again, I wouldn't be able to do much for them if I contracted a disease and died.

"You know what, Mama? You're right, I think it's better if I leave that hospital."

"Good! Besides, I'm sure you'll be able to find an even better job."

I trusted Mama's words.

Valentine Dombrowski, Georgie Leizert (Fąfara), Woselina, and me, Helena Fąfara.

I decided to live in Edmonton and found a room for $24 a month. We were five girls living in a bungalow and got along quite well. All my roommates were Canadian, and I was the only foreigner, but it didn't matter because we were like one big family. Oftentimes, we gathered in someone's room after dinner and talked the night away; I always had a great time.

Soon enough, I found my second job: fixing army tents. My sewing background made it easy for me to get the job done. My supervisor, on the other hand, wasn't as skilled. Unfortunately, she didn't know much about sewing and constantly ruined the material, which meant she always had to order new ones.

"How was your day, girls?"

"Ugh! Don't get me started!"

Valentine, one of my roommates, also worked with me fixing army tents. However, she wasn't very patient with our supervisor and often complained about her.

"Can you believe she threw out a piece of fabric this long?"

She sized up about one yard. Times were difficult, so you always used what you could; material was always scarce. It was the evening, and we had all gathered in her room.

"This woman is always ruining everything! Oh, and the other day…"

From that point, she went on a rant, and being good friends, we listened. Georgina, whom we all called Georgie, was the one who could put up with Valentine's rants the best. She was very social, and everyone loved her. We spent the rest of the evening chatting about all sorts of things and only went to bed late at night.

"Wow, Valentine. That sounds really rough.

"It is! Maybe I should find another job."

"I think you should continue with this one. But if you really want something, I'll help you look for work."

"Thanks, Georgie."

Valentine was a bit more at ease, and that's when Mela spoke up.

"Oh! I almost forgot to tell you guys! I have a date tomorrow!"

"Oh, Wonderful!"

As typical young women, we all got excited and started helping our friend pick out her clothes and jewelry. That night we stayed up late, gossiping, prepping, and planning for Mela's date.

I was a bit nervous when Mr. Hargrave, my manager, called me into his office. I tried to recall ever performing poorly, but I believed to have always produced quality work. I fiddled with the hem of my skirt as I waited for him to arrive.

"Miss Fąfara! Sorry I am a little late."

"That's ok, Sir."

He sat down, invited me to do the same, and crossed his arms over his desk.

"I wanted to talk to you about a certain… issue."

My heart rate went up as I waited for him to proceed.

"I think you might have noticed there has been a lot of wasted material lately."

I nodded.

"About that, I was thinking maybe it was time to have a new supervisor to... do things differently."

I knew this was his subtle way of saying the current supervisor wasn't doing a good job, but I still didn't know what that had to do with me. Mr. Hargrave rested his chin on his hands and leaned slightly forward.

"The other day, I asked the employees if they knew someone who was good at sewing. You weren't there, but your friend Valentine told me you had experience teaching how to sew, so I thought maybe you would be a good fit for the job."

I caught on and realized he was offering me a promotion, to my delight. However, there was one hiccup.

"I would love to become supervisor, sir. It's just that I noticed you measure in centimeters in Canada, but I'm used to inches. It will be hard for me to constantly do the conversion."

"Don't worry. I can do the conversions for you."

Something had changed in his eyes, and he looked at me intensely. I probably took too long to answer, because then he added: "Please Helen![15] If this keeps up, I'll go bankrupt!"

He dropped his diplomacy and went straight to the point. I could tell he really wanted me to take the job, and since I didn't have much reason to refuse, I accepted.

"It's great that you'll become the new supervisor, Helen!"

"It's all thanks to you putting a good word in for me."

---

15   English version of the name Helena

"In that case, I better get a percentage on your new paycheck!" Valentine and I laughed as we walked back home. Soon enough, all the other employees had been informed of my promotion. I was very happy to have moved up a rank, feeling a great sense of accomplishment. Plus, I would be able to better support my parents.

"But joking aside, Helen, you should also be careful."

"Careful of what?"

"The other girls weren't too happy to hear about your promotion. Most of them are jealous."

"Really? How do you know?"

"I heard them gossiping. They don't want to have to take orders from you."

I knew Valentine was telling me this for my good, but it still hurt to know my colleagues were against my success. I then started to wonder if this position was worth taking. I didn't want a better job and better pay if it meant constantly being hated by my subordinates. I carefully took the time to think about it before making my decision.

"I wanted to tell you all that I won't be taking the supervisor position. My English still isn't great, and it's hard for me to convert inches to centimeters, so I thought someone else would be a better fit."

"What?"

"Really?"

"Helen!"

All the employees were surprised by my sudden announcement. I had taken the time to think and came to the conclusion that I didn't want to work in a toxic environment because I wouldn't even enjoy it anyway. If the other girls hated me that much, then I didn't want anything to do with them.

"So now what? You're going to stay a regular employee?" a lady asked.

"No. I'm leaving."

More surprise. Valentine scurried towards me, clearly shocked. "You never told me you were quitting!"

"I thought you might try to dissuade me, so I decided to tell you at the same time as everyone else."

"But Helen! You're about to pass up a great opportunity!"

"Why are you trying to stop her? Let her leave!"

Valentine turned around to glare at the girl who just said that. She smirked, clearly happy I wasn't going to be around anymore.

"Yes, bravo. Thank you for the announcement!" another one added.

"Hey! You shouldn't be saying that!"

There was another girl apart from Valentine who wasn't happy about my departure. She argued with the other two, and soon enough, things got worse. Actually, they got violent! In a matter of minutes, hairs were being pulled out, and high-pitched shrieks resounded throughout the factory. Some accused others of always being jealous, and then were accused of never doing their work properly. Secrets were spilled as everyone denounced the other, fueled by rage. The whole thing was rather petty, but I knew I had to do something. I rushed to the phone and called Mr. Hargrave.

"Hi, Miss Fąfara, what is it?"

"Sir, you need to come right now."

"Why? Did something happen?"

"It's better if you simply come."

With that, I hung up and hoped he would be here soon. Thankfully, it didn't take him too long to arrive, and he was very surprised by the ongoing battle.

"What is going on here?"

At the sound of his voice, all the girls stopped fighting and lowered their heads in shame. They were quite sorry-looking, with their messy hair and slightly torn clothes. Some tried to fix their appearance a bit, though it didn't do much. Mr. Hargrave glared at them severely, eyes wide and menacing.

"Well? Is someone going to tell me what happened?"

Since no one had the courage to speak up, Valentine did.

"Sir, ever since the others found out Helen was going to become supervisor, they've been jealous because she's a DP."

"Is that so?"

Mr. Hargrave then turned his attention to me.

"Miss Fąfara, did you know about this?"

"I knew the other girls were jealous, but I didn't know it was because I was a DP. Actually sir, I don't even know what that means."

"DP stands for a displaced person," he calmly explained. "It's someone who is forced to leave their home country because of war, persecution, natural disasters, and the likes."

"Well, you should know that it's because of our wealth, level of education, and property, that my family was targeted by the Soviet Union and deported to Siberia, so I don't feel inferior because I'm a DP."

He smiled, satisfied by my answer, and then turned his attention back to the beaten-up employees.

"You, Miss Schmidt. Where do your parents come from?"

She was startled by the sudden question and stuttered as she answered. "Um… G-Germany sir."

"And you, Miss Kravets."

"From Ukraine, sir."

"And you, Miss Jones? Ireland?"

He went on to ask each girl where their parents were from, and they all originated from European countries. At the end of his interrogation, he smiled at them and said:

"It seems everyone's parents are displaced people. And I guess I am one too since I'm from New Zealand. You shouldn't think you're better than others simply because you were born here."

The girls kept quiet, shame and guilt evident on their faces. After that fiasco, everyone went back to work.

"I'm very sorry about all this, Miss Fąfara. I hope you'll change your mind about leaving."

"I don't think so. I indeed would have liked to stay and become a supervisor, but not in this atmosphere. Thank you again for everything you've done sir."

With that, I grabbed my purse and left.

"I passed by a women's clothing store the other day, and they are hiring."

"Oh, that's very interesting!" Even though I had quit my previous job, I needed to find some work if I wanted to be able to pay rent and support my parents; that's why I paid close attention to Georgina's news.

"Yes. They do alterations and things like that, so I think it should interest you."

"Thank you for telling me! I'll go there tomorrow."

I looked forward to this possible new opportunity, but my friend didn't share my enthusiasm.

"You should watch out, though. I often see that store post ads in the newspaper, so there must be a reason why they are always looking for people."

"Do you think it's because the employees quit or they get fired?"

She shrugged.

"I don't know. But in any case, you should be careful. Don't take the job right away, take some time to check it out first."

I kept her advice in mind as I went there the next day.

"Hello, Sir."

Behind a cluttered counter stood a short man with thick glasses. He turned around and looked at me.

"Can I help you?"

"Yes, I heard you were looking for workers, and I came to apply for the job."

His expression eased up and merged into a smile, exposing two golden teeth. "Indeed, we are hiring. I am Mr. Felderman, the manager." He extended his hand, and I shook it.

"Nice to meet you. I am Miss Helen Fąfara."

"Well, Miss Fąfara, how about you come to my office for a quick interview?"

I nodded and followed the man into a separate room. His office was small and clustered, and I felt slightly claustrophobic in such a tiny space.

"So, Miss Fąfara. Do you have any sewing experience?"

From there, he asked a series of questions and always seemed pleased with my answers since he often nodded. The interview lasted about 15 minutes, and he concluded with a smile that I was hired.

"You have a great background and are just the person we are looking for."

"Thank you very much."

"Is it OK if you start next week?"

"Yes sir."

After that, I handed him a document with important information such as my SIN number, status, and things like that. It was like a certificate needed for job applications. I breathed a sigh of relief as I exited his office, happy to get fresh air and because things had gone so smoothly. It was at that moment I noticed one of the workers nearby. She stared at me curiously, and I decided to approach her.

"Are you going to work here?" she asked right away.

"Maybe."

I decided to play it safe and not tell her the news I received. I then remembered what Georgie had told me and tried to get some information.

"How is the job here? It seems this store often posts ads in the papers looking for employees."

"Well, you'll find out soon enough."

Her answer wasn't in the least bit reassuring, and she quickly left, not giving me the time to inquire further. I walked home that day with mixed feelings.

The next day, Mr. Felderman called me in. I had barely closed his tiny office door when he snapped.

"How dare you talk about me in such a way? Instead of rejoicing that I gave a job to a foreigner like you, you start badmouthing me!"

"Excuse me?"

Saying that I was confused is an understatement. I was completely baffled! I had no idea why the man who was so eager to hire me the previous day was now yelling in my face.

"Don't play innocent! I know you were talking behind my back!"

I didn't know when he thought I had time to talk behind his back since I had just been hired yesterday. I still tried to comprehend what was happening as the insults kept fusing.

"You no-good foreigner! I should've known not to hire the likes of you!"

"Alright, that's enough!"

I decided to put a stop to this nonsense. Why was he accusing me of badmouthing him? I barely even knew the man! But now I knew enough to know I didn't want to know more.

"I have no idea what you're talking about. I never said anything bad about you, especially since I met you just yesterday!"

"Don't try to fool me! Emilia told me everything!"

"Who?"

"Emilia. The one who works at the front."

It then clicked that Emilia must have been the employee I spoke with the previous day. However, I still didn't understand why she lied about me. It's not like I had done her any wrong. I realized that if trouble was going to come so early on, this job was not worth taking. That's why I decided to get up and look straight at Mr. Felderman and say,

"You know what, sir? I'm not going to take this job."

"What?"

His fury quickly gave place to fear. He needed employees, but I guess he hadn't realized he would lose one if he insulted her in such a way. I was truly mad and hurt, hearing him call me a no-good foreigner and all. Why did it have to be so difficult to find a decent job where people didn't hate you because of the soil on which you were born?

"You heard me. I'm not going to work here, so give me back my papers."

Mr. Felderman seemed troubled but tried to hide it.

"You are the one at fault here."

"No, you are, for believing stupid and baseless lies. Now give me back my papers!"

His guilt technique didn't work. There was no way he'd make me feel bad about something I didn't do. He quickly realized I wasn't going to change my mind and finally gave in.

"Alright, alright. But I don't have them with me. Come back tomorrow."

I wasn't satisfied with his answer, but knew there wasn't much I could do about it, so I left.

The following day, I had barely closed the door at the entrance when Mr. Felderman ran to me.

"Oh, Miss Fąfara!"

His attitude was completely different from that of the previous day, and I wondered if he was bipolar.

"I am so sorry about yesterday! You were right. I had believed lies! It's all Emilia's fault. She always tells me newcomers are badmouthing me, so I chase them away, but she was the one lying all along! Honestly, I've been trying to replace her for a while because she is also very inexperienced. She figured it out, and that's why she always makes sure I don't hire anyone else. I'd fire her."

He continued in that manner, apologizing with great fervor, but I wasn't impressed by his little show. How was it that he never questioned his employee, no matter how many times she told him newcomers were talking behind his back? Clearly, this man didn't have any common sense, so I knew he would make a poor supervisor.

"Mr. Felderman, you believed her lies before hearing what I said. That speaks a lot of your character, so I don't want to work here."

He knew I made a valid point and didn't continue his spectacle. He went into his office and reluctantly brought me what I had come for. With my papers in hand, I exited the building without looking back.

CHAPTER 22

T for Toronto

My next job was at GWG,[16] where I made jeans for 50 cents an hour; the price of one loaf of bread. My pay increased if I produced more, so I always felt the pressure to work hard. The job was demanding, and soon enough, I realized I was miserable working in that factory.

"How was your day?"

"Terrible Georgie!"

I sank down on the living room couch, exhausted. My friend noticed my fatigue and made me a cup of tea.

"Is it because of your job again? It seems quite rough."

"It is! For some reason, not long after I started working there, my stomach and the back of my head have been hurting."

"Hmm… those clearly don't seem like good signs."

I was always very anxious going to work, had long shifts, and small pay. Plus, my forelady kept watching me in order to point out a mistake - which seemed to be the only satisfaction she got out of this job. If I did something wrong, she made me correct it right away, adding pressure and making things worse.

"I'm beginning to wonder if staying there is worth it."

"Well, there aren't that many job opportunities in Edmonton, so you might not be able to get much better."

---

16   Great Western Garment Company

Georgie was right, and I sighed heavily at the thought of not being able to find better employment than this. I was nearing my mid-twenties and didn't want to waste my youth in such a depressing place.

My roommate was braiding her brown hair, sitting cross-legged on the couch.

"If you still feel pain, maybe you should go see a doctor. It could be that the work you're doing isn't good for your health."

"Yeah, you're right."

Valentine entered the living room, followed by our two other roommates.

"Hey girls! What are you talking about?"

I explained my situation, and they could all empathize, since at one point or another, they had to deal - or were still dealing - with a crappy job too. We talked for a while before Valentine decided to change the subject.

"You know what? It's Friday night. Let's stop thinking about work and talk about something else."

We nodded in agreement, and Georgie - who had just finished braiding her hair – suggested, "Oh Helen, you should tell a story!"

"A story? Oh, common, why me every time?"

"Because you always tell the best ones!" (Which is true to this very day), Valentine added. The other girls were also pressing me on. Indeed, throughout my stay in our shared home, I sometimes told funny anecdotes. It's true that I often talk about various events that occurred in my life; I enjoyed it tremendously. It was also a good way for me to practice my English, so I accepted to be the storyteller for tonight.

"I don't think I told you about the time I puked in a lady's bra."

Right away, I hooked their attention, and they listened carefully as I recounted my trip across the Caspian Sea when we sailed to Iran. Even though I was quite sick, that one incident was pretty funny. As I told my story, the girls laughed at all the right places. Encouraged, I continued until I finished the tale. I had gotten thirsty and got up to get a glass of water, but Georgie held me back, still laughing.

"What is it?"

"You can't leave until you tell us the story!"

"But I just did."

"Tell us in English!" The girls burst out laughing, but Valentine was able to calm down long enough to tell me I had unconsciously told the entire story in Polish.

"Really? And here I thought my English had become so good that you all understood me perfectly."

I sighed and sat back down. Take two.

The pain in my stomach and head didn't go away, so I followed Georgina's advice and went to see a doctor.

"Hi, Miss Fąfara. What can I do for you today?"

I explained my symptoms and answered the doctor's questions. He kept nodding and listening to me with great attention, which put me at ease. After his short interrogation, he kept quiet for a while before talking again.

"Well, clearly, you're under a lot of stress, and that's why your body is reacting this way. Is there something that concerns you? Perhaps some trouble with your boyfriend?"

"Boyfriend?"

I knew he was asking a genuine question, but I still thought it was ridiculous. I leaned slightly forward and looked him straight in the eye.

"Doctor, I'm barely alive, working long shifts and trying to make ends meet, and you think I have time to preoccupy myself with a boyfriend?"

He raised his hands innocently and quickly added: "I was simply asking."

I leaned back in my chair, and he pondered shortly before speaking again.

"So from what I understand, it's your job that is stressing you this much?"

"Yes, it's going to kill me!"

For the next few minutes, I ranted about the small pay, long hours, and evil forelady that all made my life miserable. The doctor nodded and listened all the while, often fiddling with his goatee. He started seeming more like a therapist than a medical doctor at this point. When I was done venting my frustrations, he looked at me tenderly.

"Child, I think you're better off quitting that job."

"I understand, but there isn't much work offered in Edmonton."

He took a few moments to think, and then his eyes widened as he found an answer. "You could go to Vancouver! It's a beautiful city, and they have a lot of jobs there."

He described the coastal city, and hearing about it got me excited. I thought Vancouver might actually be the place for me. Unfortunately, my excitement was short-lived, because the man soon changed his mind.

"Wait! No, you can't go to Vancouver."

"What? Why?"

"Because there are too many sailors there, and..." He paused and winked at me. "... You're a pretty girl, so they'll be all over you."

"Doctor!"

"I'm serious! It truly is a bad idea for you to go to Vancouver."

I decided to trust him, since he was a nice man who genuinely cared about my well-being.

"How about Montreal? Even though it's an island, they don't have sailors like in Vancouver. Maybe you should go there."

This time, I wasn't enthusiastic at all, because even though Montreal was a nice city, there was one major problem.

"Doctor, I read about Canada before coming here, and I know that Montreal is in the Quebec province, where they speak French, but I don't know any French."

"Hmm... that is a problem." He slumped back down in his chair and thought for a bit before suggesting one last option.

"Toronto, yes. There are no sailors and no French!"

Indeed, the metropolis seemed like the best option and worth considering. It was far from my family, which I didn't like as much, but at this point, I had to do what I could to get by. "Thank you doctor, I'll think about it."

"No problem Miss Fąfara. I hope things will work out for you."

He got up, and I realized it was the end of the appointment, so I took out my purse.

"How much will that be?"

He raised a hand to stop me and smiled.

"Free of charge! I think you mainly needed a listening ear."

"Oh, but…"

"I insist! Don't worry about it."

He escorted me back to the front desk and told me one last thing before he left.

"You should watch out. If you let stress and anxiety build up, it can have permanent consequences, so think wisely about which job you are willing to take."

"Thank you, doctor."

He smiled one last time before disappearing back into his office.

The rest of that afternoon and the following days, many thoughts buzzed around in my mind. I evaluated the pros and cons of going to Toronto in order to decide the best course of action. I then remembered that my friend Janina, with whom I had worked at the Misericordia Community Hospital, was now living there, so I decided to write her a letter. About a week later, I received her reply in the mail:

Dear Helena,

I am sorry to hear about the difficulties of your job and the negative impacts it has on you. On a more positive note, Toronto is a great place for you to live, and there are many opportunities, so I would highly recommend you

come here. Also, since I have gotten to know the city, I could always help you if
you need guidance with anything.

All the best,

Janina

This letter was the confirmation I needed, so my mind was set at that point; I was moving to Toronto.

"You're moving to Toronto?"

"Yes, Georgie."

"But... why so soon? I thought you would stay here a little longer."

"I would have liked to, but you know how difficult my job is and how hard it is to make a living in Edmonton. I think it would be smarter for me to move someplace better."

My friend was clearly sad, and I was a bit sorrowful, but this was for the best.

"Don't worry. You'll still have another Fąfara around to comfort you."

I wiggled my eyebrows and she immediately knew what I was talking about. As a matter of fact, my brother, Janek and her had gotten rather close lately, so it seemed that soon enough she would become my sister-in-law. Georgie smiled and looked away.

"I don't know what you're talking about."

"Actually, I think you know what I'm talking about very well."

"We sure are going to miss you, Helen. And your stories!"

"I'll miss you too, Valentine. And don't worry, I'll continue to write to you."

My roommates and I spent the rest of the evening talking and laughing. Over time, they had become my second family, and I knew I would miss them very much. I had also informed the rest of the family about my move. By this time, my sister, Jadzia already lived in her own place. She had gotten married in 1953, to the son of a Polish family living close to my parents. Speaking of which, I went to visit my parents one last time before my departure.

"Hela!"

"Hi, Mama!"

Mother pulled me in a warm embrace, and even though I was almost 27, I was still as attached to her as when I was seven. My parents were progressing very well. Mama and Tata continued living in Wujek Sowa's house for a while. Then they lived in the house next to the hospital in Vilna. Mama milked the cows of that house to provide milk to the small hospital kitchen, and Tata maintained the heating boiler of the same hospital. They had met other people who spoke Polish and were there to support them; they were quite happy.

I went to the living room where I found my Father resting on the couch. He got up and welcomed me with open arms.

"Ah, Dziecko (Tata and Mama always called me, 'my child')! I can't believe you're leaving!"

"It's not like I'll be gone forever. I'll still be in Canada, so I'll come to visit from time to time."

Tata let go and took a long look at me, a semblance of a smile twisting his lips. He then invited me to sit down, and Mama brought us something to drink.

"I know I said this at Jadzia's wedding too, but it's crazy how fast you all have grown. Sometimes, I feel like you've always been adults."

"Don't worry. There was a time when we were kids too. It's just that it was cut short."

He took a sip of tea, and I did the same. Even though I had been living in my own place in Edmonton, I was still very attached to my parents. However, this time, I would be hundreds of miles away, meaning I would see them less often. I must admit, the thought of being completely on my own was a bit scary.

At that moment, we heard a knock on the door, and Mother went to open it.

"Ah, Janek!"

"Hi Mama!"

She embraced her son and invited him inside, where he joined Tata and I in the living room.

"It's good to see you, my son. I'm glad you could come!"

"Well, I had to see Hela one last time before she leaves us forever."

"Don't make it seem as if I'm going to die in Toronto."

He shrugged and smiled.

"I heard it's a jungle out there."

I rolled my eyes and took another sip of tea.

"By the way, I received a letter from Bolek yesterday. He said he'll pick you up at the train station at 8:00 am."

"Alright, sounds good."

We had decided that since I was moving to a different city and province, it would be wiser to first stay with someone I knew, and Janek's friend was our best option. By now, Bolek was married to his wife Magda, and they had a beautiful daughter, Marysia, who was three years old. I didn't mind since I wasn't going to live with him forever, and he had been very kind to us when we arrived in Canada.

"Everyone is going their separate ways now, huh?" Janek added, and we nodded in agreement.

"I'm so proud to see how independent each of you has become. It makes me believe we didn't fight for nothing."

Mother already had tears in her eyes. To comfort her, I went and sat by her side.

"Of course, you didn't fight for nothing, Mama. None of the sacrifices you made for us were in vain. It's thanks to you and Tata that we made it this far."

I sincerely believed each word I said. My Mama was my everything, and I knew that I wouldn't be where I was if it hadn't been for her.

"Still, it will be a bit lonely after you leave. And who is going to give you relationship advice now?" she asked with a half-smile.

Indeed, she had been my advisor in all things love-related, so I would miss her guidance.

"I'm sure I'll find someone. I can still write you letters."

"Let's hope I'll answer you before your date!"

"Don't worry, Mama. She won't need any advice because all she ever does is refuse proposals."

"That's not true."

"It sure is! And Tata can testify."

Father slowly nodded his head, and I rolled my eyes again. Indeed, many men had courted me. I hadn't shown any interest in the proposals I received both in England and Canada, but it was because I wanted to get my life together first, and that's why I was going to Toronto; love would come after. I quickly changed the subject, and we moved on to something else. I don't regret having that mentality because I ended up with the best man. But that's an episode I'll recount later on.

It was finally my departure day. I bid my family and Alberta farewell and went on to start my life anew. I had lost count of how many times that had happened already. Once again, I was back at the beginning, but this time with a bit more tools up my sleeve.

"Helen! I'm glad you made it!"

"Hi, Bolek. It's nice to see you!"

"How was the trip?"

"Long," I admitted.

"Ha, ha! I'm sure you must be tired. I'll try my best not to exhaust you too much."

With that, we drove off towards his house. Bolek had changed a bit; His strong physique had morphed into a stout man, and his dark brown beard had grown. Over time, he got married and now lives with his wife. Their house had many rooms, so they rented a few. During the car ride, I reflected on the five years that had passed since I arrived in Canada. The first place we stayed at was Toronto, and I was back here again, but this time wiser and more experienced. It was at that moment I realized everything I had gone through since 1951.

Soon after I settled in, I started job-hunting. I didn't want to waste time and hoped to soon become independent. I consulted many different agencies but had no luck. A few weeks passed, and my worry grew, fearing I would stay unemployed.

Seeking advice, I decided to meet up with my friend Janina.

"Helena! I'm so happy to see you again!"

"Me too!"

We held each other in a tight embrace before sitting at our table in the cafe. My friend looked beautiful in her dark green shirtwaist dress. She had tied her brown hair in a low ponytail, giving her a mature look. We chatted as we waited for our orders to arrive.

"So? How have you been?" I asked her.

"Busy! We still have some work to do around the house, mainly renovations in the kitchen and living room."

"Oh, that's true. You told me you had bought a little rundown house, right?"

"Yes. We chose it because of its great location and spaciousness, but it's a real fixer-upper."

Janina fiddled with the golden ring on her left hand, a soft smile hovering above her lips. Even though she complained about all the work she needed to do in her new home, I could tell she was happy since she had recently started her marital life with the man she loved. I was also happy for her.

"And how about you Helena? Anything new?"

"Not really. The truth is, I'm having trouble finding a job."

"Is that so?" Janina took a sip of coffee, pensive. "Did you try going to job agencies?"

"I went to a couple, but couldn't find anything."

"Hmm…"

She then suggested a few more ideas, and I took note of them. After that, we talked about everything and anything. At some point, Janina told me about a Polish Scouts club she was in. "It's a club for adults. We meet monthly and do all sorts of activities. Sometimes we go out, do community work, or organize events. It's quite fun; you should join!"

"It does sound interesting."

She gave me more information about it, and I was sold. My family was far now, so I often felt lonely. However, joining a scouts club - and a Polish one - would give me a sense of belonging and community. Janina promised to take me with her during their next meeting.

Soon enough, the sun was setting, so we parted ways. As I arrived home that evening, I noticed a few empty cans of beer on the kitchen counter and sighed disappointedly. *Here we go again!*

"Ah, Helen! Welcome back!"

I found Bolek in the same position I always found him in when he started drinking; lounging on the couch, a hand resting on his exposed hairy stomach, and another one holding his drink. His head was usually tilted towards the small television, and he lifted it at a certain angle each time he took a sip.

"Hi, Bolek."

It hadn't taken me long to realize this man had a drinking problem. Almost every other night, he opened a can or bottle of something. And once he got going, I didn't know when he would stop. He wasn't violent and became obnoxious, swearing at the TV because something happened, an actor wasn't doing a good job, or the media kept repeating the same boring news. His wife didn't do much about it, probably fed up at this point, and simply went to bed. Another tenant was living with us, but he worked at night, so he didn't witness the scene.

I scurried to my room, trying to avoid what usually came next.

"Hey! Why don't you come to grab a drink?"

Too late. Slowly, I turned around, trying to smile as politely as possible.

"Sorry, I'm a bit tired tonight."

"Aw, don't be like that!"

It took him a few tries to get up from his drinking position, and he staggered towards me. "Just one drink. Come on!"

He reeked of alcohol, so it took me a tremendous amount of effort not to cover my nose. He kept insisting, but by now, I had mastered the art of being stern yet still respectful. Eventually, he gave up and left me alone. After barely a month, I decided to move out. I didn't feel comfortable and found myself a small apartment elsewhere.

Soon enough, I joined the Polish Scouts and loved it right away. The people were nice and welcoming, making me feel at home.

With the scouts, I went skiing for the first time and quite enjoyed it. It was scary at first but pretty nice once I got the hang of it.

I went inside the ski lodge (in the Kaszuby, Renfrew County, west of Ottawa, Ontario) to warm myself up. Even though the sky was blue and the sun was shining, it was rather cold since we were in the middle of February. I sat by the fireplace, coffee in hand, sipping slowly and relaxing by the fire.

"May I join you?"

"Helena! Nice to see you!"

"Nice to see you too, Jurek!"

I turned around and noticed Jurek, one of the other scouts. I scooted over on the dark brown leather couch to make some room for him, and he sat down.

"So? How do you like skiing?"

"It's not too bad. Today's my first time ever."

"Mine too."

We simultaneously took sips of our coffee and stared at the fireplace.

"By the way, you were part of those who were still in Poland during the war, right?"

Jurek's parents had settled in Canada in the mid-20s, so he had spent his whole life here.

"Yes."

"And... how was that?"

Inevitably, those who went through the war were asked about it and what happened afterward. Some needed to talk about it as a coping mechanism, whereas others preferred to keep quiet, burying the dreadful memories deep within their subconscious. Then there were those like Jurek who hadn't dealt with the horrors of the war but still needed to know how it affected their people and ultimately, their history.

"Well, if I learned one thing during those hellish times, it's that it could've been us. So many people died, but we survived. So many soldiers were amputated, but my brothers made it through with all their limbs. So many families were broken, but we're all together."

The greatest lesson is this; whatever isn't already within you can be taken away. Whatever is in your heart, your head, and your soul, nobody can take that away.

He nodded his head in agreement.

"Oh, that is so true! What a profound and impressive thing to say."

We lost everything in half an hour, and so when I look at where we are now, I can't help but feel blessed. We didn't do anything better than the others to survive and make it this far, but at least we were resilient and persevering. I think that and how our hard work greatly contributed to our outcome."

"Is your whole family in Toronto right now?"

"No, just me. I left Alberta, where the others are, to try to find work. I'm working at a factory sewing skirts right now, but it doesn't pay much."

Jurek paused to think, scratching his short blond hair, before talking again.

"Are you good at math?"

I was surprised by the question, but still nodded.

"A friend of mine works at an insurance company, and he says they have a pretty decent pay. You simply need to know some basic math. Positions often open there, so you should wait for that job. I'll give you their contact information."

I was excited at the news because this opportunity seemed promising. The rest of the afternoon went by smoothly. I talked with Jurek and skied a few more times. Before we knew it, evening fell upon us, and it was time to leave.

"Before you all go, I have an announcement to make."

One of the people in charge of our club gathered us in the lobby. I noticed he was holding a newspaper.

"I know there are many among us who have been caught up in the conflicts of war and were spread all over the earth. Well, I wanted to tell you that a big reunion will be organized for those sent to refugee camps. I saw the ad in the newspaper and had to tell you!"

Enthusiastic chatter arose, and the man went on to give more details. In a flash, I saw all the places I had been to, all the people I had met, and all the unique bonds we shared. Recent memories were revived, and mixed feelings filled my chest.

CHAPTER 23

We meet again

I listened to Jurek's advice and, sure enough, got myself a job at the Independent Order of Foresters, a life insurance company, in the accounting department. Indeed, the pay was good, I could support myself well, support my parents, and I could even afford to visit my parents in Alberta, which I very much needed after not seeing them for a long time.

"Hela, my dear!"

"Hi, Mama!" We shared a nice long hug, and I heard her sniff back tears. Many months had passed by since I last saw her, so we were both joyous. Tata also welcomed me with open arms, and it was great to be with my family once again.

It was then Georgie ran to me and held me in a tight embrace. She was as beautiful as always, her light brown hair tied in a low bun, giving her an elegant air. Janek walked slowly behind her with a smile on his face.

"It's been a while."

"It sure has, big brother."

My brother looked more mature now that he was married. Georgie and Janek got married before I moved to Toronto, and I was one of the bridesmaids. He seemed to always think before he did or said something, and put other people's needs - especially his wife's - before his own. Jadzia and Andrzej were also present, so the whole family was together.

"It feels great to see all my children again. Now that you've all grown and moved out, I'm stuck with your Tata!"

"Hey!"

We all laughed, and Mama teasingly nudged my Tata's elbow. We ate and talked; it was very lively at the dinner table. Each person added to the conversation, and we sometimes cut each other in order to tell our story.

"You know, Janek, I don't think I ever told you, but there was a time when I plagiarized your work for a school assignment when we were in Africa."

"What?"

I recounted the tale of how I used the letters he sent us in Africa to write my essay. He wasn't undignified but instead laughed out loud as he heard this for the first time.

"You sure were a smart girl, Hela!"

"'Were?' I still am, mind you!"

"You may be book smart, but not street smart. Why else would you still be single at your age?"

"Jadzia, don't start!"

Our little dispute didn't go far, and the joyful atmosphere quickly returned.

"Oh! I have to tell you about what Ludwig said the other day!"

We turned our attention towards Mother, who shot a side glance at her husband.

"I was at work and trying to bring the cows back to the barn, so I said *Camun! Camun!*[17] But then Ludwig came to tell me the cows won't understand because of my Yorkshire accent, so I have to speak with the Canadian accent and say *Caman! Caman!*"

We burst out laughing, and Tata shrugged, trying to show he was unbothered.

"You know I was right."

"Oh, please! As if the cows could understand anything we say."

"Not with that accent, they won't."

---

17   Come on! Come on!

Their bickering continued for a bit before we moved on to something else. The rest of the evening went the same way. We kept reminiscing about old stories and telling recent ones. It was only well after midnight that we finally went to sleep, somehow finding room for everyone in my parents' small house.

The next day, I woke up early to help Mama in the kitchen with breakfast.

"Good morning, Hela! How did you sleep?"

"Good, and you?"

"Not too bad." She took out some eggs and let out an exasperated smile.

"Here, let me help you," I offered.

As I washed my hands, Georgie entered the kitchen. "Good morning!"

"Good morning, Georgina!"

"I came to help with breakfast."

Though we appreciated her intentions, but we were getting cramped in the small kitchen. My parents now lived in Vilna, in a different house than the one they were in before I left for Toronto. It was smaller than the previous one, though they were still content with it.

"So Georgie, how's married life?"

I grinned at my friend and noticed the corners of her lips curve upwards. I hadn't seen her since the wedding, almost a year ago, so this was a good time to catch up.

"Well, Janek is simply amazing, so everything is going great."

"He sure loves you a lot," Mother commented, which made Georgie blush.

"I know it's rather demanding for him to work at the mine, but he still comes home with a smile, and then we talk for hours. This man is full of stories!"

"We all are, my dear," Mama answered.

There was a short pause, and I noticed from the corner of my eye that Georgina's smile had faded slightly. I was going to ask her what's wrong when she spoke again.

"You know, he told me about what happened to you all in Siberia and I want to believe him, but… I have a hard time imagining someone could go through something like that. And I can't help but wonder if the same thing would've happened to me had I been born in Poland and not Manitoba."

She looked at me with worry, and I understood her concern. Our story wasn't easy to tell or to hear. It was a great burden for both parties, but it couldn't be kept silent. I was glad Janek had found someone to whom he could entrust the less glorious parts of his life with, but at the same time, I knew it must have been hard for Georgie to shoulder such a story. It was almost like his scars and pains became hers after they got married, so now we could only hope she would be strong enough to bear them.

I wrapped my arms around her and held her in a tight embrace. Georgie responded by wrapping her arms around my back in return, and let out a long sigh.

"I'm sure it wasn't easy for Janek to tell you everything, but since he did, he must have had a pretty good reason to."

I looked down at her, our eyes locking.

"You're the one he chose to be by his side, and I have no doubt you're exactly the kind of support and wife he needs."

Her soft smile returned, and she was about to respond when the man in question arrived.

"Good morning!"

"Oh, good morning Janek," I answered.

"What were you girls talking about?"

He sat down at the breakfast table and yawned.

"About how you snore like a horse!" I replied teasingly.

"What?"

His fatigue vanished, and he turned towards his wife.

"Georgie! You told them?"

We paused for a second, and then burst out laughing.

I returned to Toronto after my family visit. For some time, my work was going well. However, one day I was called into my manager's office.

"Hello, Miss Fąfara, please take a seat."

I did so quietly.

"I'll be brief. You know that Mrs. Rockwell left us because of her pregnancy, right?"

I nodded.

"Well, she was in charge of the French reports, and since we don't have anyone to replace her, I decided to give you the task."

My eyes opened wide in surprise.

"Mr. Steward. I can't speak French."

He was unfazed by my remark and looked at me straight in the eye, leaning forward a bit on his desk.

"You're a foreigner. I know you'll do it."

He was serious in his tone very forceful, and discriminatory but I felt I should ride this out and see exactly how it could turn out, and so I quietly nodded. As I closed his office door, I let out a long sigh, realizing my predicament.

"What's wrong, Helen?"

I turned to see one of my colleagues who was passing by. She was one of the secretaries in the building, and I got along with her pretty well. I decided to tell her about my problem, hoping she'd help me find a solution. Thankfully, she did!

"I can translate those reports for you."

"Really? That would be amazing!"

"It's no trouble at all. My family is originally from Quebec, so I'm fluent in French."

I was more than relieved to have found a solution so quickly. The secretary kept translating the reports for me until we found a proper replacement.

As time passed, my official day was drawing near: my Canadian Citizenship acceptance!

"Good morning, Miss Fąfara. My name is Mark White, and I will be in charge of your interview today."

I sat on the small metallic chair with a thin fake leather layer. I tried my best to remain calm, reminding myself that I had studied for this and was ready.

"I will ask you a series of questions about Canada. It can be about the history, geography, politics, etc. If ever you need me to repeat a question, just say so. After that, a decision will be made based on your performance as to whether or not you should receive your Canadian Citizenship. Do you have any questions?"

"No sir," I answered with confidence.

After the mountain of paperwork I had to fill out and hand-in just to reach this point, I simply wanted to get it over with. The man then went on to ask the questions to which I knew the answers all too well. Everything I studied was still fresh in my mind, so I had no issues during the interview. He asked the final question, and I gave the final answer; all I had to do now was wait for the verdict.

Mark looked over his papers and then at me with a stern look;

"I am completely shocked! Never in my entire career, in this office....!"

I was taken aback, not expecting that reaction.

"What did I do?"

The confidence I felt only a few seconds ago was quickly disappearing, and I feared that maybe I had been overconfident.

"No, it's not what you didn't do!"

His face relaxed and revealed a contagious smile. My heart rate dropped back to normal, and I started breathing properly again.

"You knew all the answers and didn't make a single mistake. Even many Canadians wouldn't have done so well!"

I was flattered by the compliment and explained that my interest in this country had made me study it closely, and that's how I had been able to know all the answers. He nodded to show his approval, then paused for a second.

"But you know.….I can't help but wonder why a bright young lady like you isn't married."

He pointed towards my naked ring finger.

"Ah well, I just haven't found the right person yet."

Honestly, I didn't feel like talking about my love situation with a perfect stranger.

"Hopefully, you'll get married soon and have children. Canada really needs more people. Especially if they are as smart as you."

He smirked, and I couldn't help but do the same. After that, he told me what the following procedures would be. All I had to do was follow protocol until I was officially a Canadian citizen.

"Thank you very much, Mr. White."

"Don't thank me," he said. "You're the one who did all the hard work; it was a delight to interview you. Take care now!"

With that, we parted ways. As I arrived home, I couldn't help but wonder if I should've asked him if he was married. After all, he was pretty young and didn't have a ring. Oh well!

July came along with the usual summer heat and the excitement of two months of warm weather. I looked forward to the hot season because my upcoming reunion with my friends from Africa drew near. We were to meet in Orchard Lake Village, Michigan. For about a week, we would stay at the SS Cyril and Methodius Seminary, which was usually vacant during July and August since it was summer break for the seminarians. On my way there, my heart kept pounding with enthusiasm. I had travelled with some Polish people from my scout's club, so we arrived together at the imposing and beautiful Seminary building.

"Welcome! Welcome, dear friends! We are so glad you were able to respond to our invitation!"

A couple of priests in black clerical shirts guided us inside, and there were a few registration documents to fill out before we were assigned to our rooms. The building had high ceilings and thick wooden walls. Almost all the windows were made of stained glass, reproducing the image of a saint. Our rooms were modest in decoration, with a single bed big enough for one. There was a wooden cross on the beige wall and a small wardrobe. Though the space wasn't big, it was cozy.

After all the formalities, we gathered outside, where some were already present. Actually, the reunion had already started, as many people embraced each other, thick tears flowing freely down their cheeks. Emotions rose up in my throat, and I heard a voice call out my name.

"Helena? It is you!"

I turned around and spotted a familiar face that had slightly changed due to time.

"Irena!"

My friend and I hugged each other, and I couldn't stop myself from crying. The last time I had seen her was in England.

"Wow! You've grown so beautiful!"

"You're one to talk, with your fashion model figure!"

We laughed and cried, with mixed feelings welling up in our chests. Irena's blond hair had grown and nicely framed her face. Her cheeks weren't as chubby, but her dimples still showed. She looked wonderful in her blue buttoned shirt and floral skirt. Chatter came to us naturally; It was quite contagious, actually, and hard to stop after we started. Our brains had so much to process, and our spirits had so much to say.

"Oh! Irena, is that you?"

We were interrupted by a deep voice and simultaneously turned around. Both our eyes widened, but for me, it wasn't only due to the surprise of seeing an old acquaintance.

"Karol Kołodziej?"

He had retained remnants of his childish face, his eyes were still just as big and his ears stuck out. The man turned towards me with a confused look. It took him a few seconds to remember who I was, which irritated me.

"You're Lena, right?"

"Helena," I corrected him.

He smiled apologetically, which only made me madder. It wasn't that I still had a grudge against him for kicking me with his metal shoe and nearly breaking my leg, but it was pretty infuriating to realize that despite all the pain and problems he caused me, he never formally apologized.

"Wow, you two ladies sure changed a lot."

This time, it was Marek Lawrence who spoke. He had come out of nowhere and suddenly joined the conversation. He was much taller than me, quite lean, and fiddled a lot with the hair on his nape.

"I can't believe it's been so long since we last saw each other. Our time at the Tengeru camp now feels like a distant memory in another era!"

Our conversation flowed as we reminisced about the past. Every once in a while, I caught Karol or Marek discreetly wiping away a silent tear. Because of that, I momentarily forgot how rowdy they used to be as children and realized they suffered just as much as the rest of us, so fighting was probably their way of coping with it. It was at that moment I spotted someone from the corner of my eye.

"Regina?"

My old friend turned around at the sound of her name, and our eyes met. Immediately, a broad smile stretched our lips, and we ran to embrace each other.

"Helena! I'm so happy you made it!"

"I'm glad to see you too!"

The repetition of the same scene had been looping since the beginning of the reunion. We yelled each other's names, hugged, smiled, and cried. After the first wave of emotions, we calmed down to ask about the formalities.

"How have you been? What are you up to now?"

"I live in Toronto now."

We went on a never-ending conversation before being interrupted by the arrival of another long-lost friend. And the same scene restarted once again.

"I still can't believe everything that happened today. It feels like a dream!"

"Oh yes, it truly does! We were just kids in Tengeru, but now we're all adults. Most of us are even married!"

A group of girls had gathered in one of the rooms to continue talking, and by the looks of it, we definitely wouldn't be going to sleep anytime soon, even though it was very late and most of us were exhausted from the trip.

"By the way, who is still single?" someone asked.

A few girls raised their hands, and I did the same.

"What? Helena, you too?"

Stefa, my friend from England, was the most surprised.

"But you were so popular! You girls should've seen her at our dances. She wouldn't be left alone for two minutes before some guy asked her to dance."

"You're exaggerating!"

"You know I'm right. It was to the point where I didn't want to attend those dances with you anymore because I kept feeling like a third wheel. But then, I met Eryk!"

Some girls pressed her for details, and Stefa became all dreamy-eyed, whereas others rolled their eyes. Afterwards, we discussed all sorts of topics, but inevitably ended up on what united us; our one story, our journey.

"When I think about it, we were quite resilient children. We were taken from our homes and lived under inhuman conditions. We kept moving from place to place until we were brought to a land we knew pretty much nothing of. I'm not saying it was easy for us to adapt, but despite the challenges we faced, we ultimately overcame them and became who we are today."

We nodded in agreement with Regina, and then Teresa spoke.

"I think it was just as heartbreaking for a parent to see their child suffer under such conditions than it was for a child to watch their parent sacrifice everything for their survival. There were countless times when I asked myself if all this was worth it. Why did we bother struggling so hard to live - or should I say to survive - in such circumstances? We begged for bread left and right, knowing all too well it wouldn't be enough to satisfy us anyway."

"I understand what you're saying, Teresa and I felt the same way. Our parents also thought that, but they had a reason to persevere us; their children."

I paused for a moment, not realizing how emotional I was getting over this topic.

"Mama did everything she could for us, and I mean everything. She was a genius at managing our little food, ensuring we were fed every day, and meeting our basic needs. Mama believed we would get out of Siberia alive, so her determination and hard work motivated us children to fight for survival. She knew that if we overcome this challenge, we could overcome anything in life; and we did. Our parents knew we had to make it out alive because we were worth saving, so I'm glad they didn't give up, especially not on us."

There wasn't a dry eye in the room, so silence reigned, occasionally ruptured by sobs and sniffles. It was after I spoke those words that I realized their weight. Our parents obviously didn't plan the war but had to submit to it, which meant we had to submit to it. Despite that, they didn't stop fighting for us to be able to start life in the best possible conditions. There were countless stories of parents starving themselves to death in order for their children to eat. My parents also sacrificed a lot for our well-being, and now it was our turn to make something out of ourselves with this opportunity they had given us.

Our talk continued until late, and before we knew it, the sun shyly pierced through our small stained-glass window.

CHAPTER 24

Stuffed peppers and suitors

Vacation was over, and Orchard Lake Village was behind me. I took the contact information of many people during my stay there and kept corresponding with them. My family members hadn't been able to attend the event since the location was far, that's why I gave them a full report of my trip. They were happy to hear about the people we knew in Africa and how they were doing.

Sometime after our reunion, my friend Stefa visited me.

"Welcome to Canada!"

She ran to me excitedly and hugged me tight. "Helena! It's been so long!"

We didn't stop talking on our way to my apartment. There was much to catch up on and, of course, many memories to evoke.

"You remember when Marek and your brothers came over to play cards, and you threw everything on the floor to make them leave?"

"Ah, I was hoping you forgot about that."

"How could I? You completely embarrassed yourself in front of the guy you liked."

"I never should have told you that story."

Stefa kept laughing, and I couldn't help but crack a smile at the memory. Thinking back now, I honestly don't know what had gotten into me, but oh well. It didn't do me any good to worry about it now.

"Maybe if he didn't think you were crazy, he would have asked for your hand in marriage."

I brushed off her comment and took a sip of tea.

"By the way, how is your son doing?"

"He's fine and full of energy. When I see him playing around, I almost forget all the issues he had when he was born."

"Issues?"

"Didn't I tell you? About his blood system having to be changed?"

"No, you didn't!" I put down my cup of tea, intrigued but also worried. "What happened?"

"Don't worry, he's fine now, but he did give us quite a scare a few years back. I have Rh-negative blood, and my husband has Rh-positive. Our son also had Rh positive so he needed to have an exchange transfusion where they replaced his blood with mine."

"Are you serious?"

"Yes! I was very worried, but the doctor told me the real problem would occur if I tried having a second child. My blood lacks the Rh protein and came in contact with my son's blood which has the Rh protein. Because of that, my blood will create antibodies to attack the protein since it doesn't recognize it. If those antibodies get into my second child's blood, they could become crippled, so the doctor told me to stop having children.[18]"

I never knew having Rh-negative blood could cause so many complications. Stefa went on to explain what happened afterwards, but I was only half listening.

At some point, she noticed my troubled expression.

"What is it, Helena?"

---

18   Modern science prevents complications by giving Rh immune globulin injections to the mother. Those injections make sure the mother's blood doesn't create antibodies that could attack the child's blood.

I paused before answering.

"It's just that… I also have Rh-negative blood."

Her eyes widened in surprise.

"With what you just told me, I absolutely have to marry someone who has the same blood type, since I do want to have children. Plus, in Canada, couples have to get a blood test before they get married. If they aren't compatible, the marriage won't be approved."

"Really? That's a law?"

"Yes."

Suddenly, I felt very discouraged. I knew I had Rh-negative blood, and it wasn't common, but after hearing Stefa's story, I felt like my chances of finding the right spouse had significantly decreased. Once again, my friend noticed my worry and placed her arm on my shoulder to show support.

"Cheer up. I'm sure you'll find someone."

"How? I can't just ask guys to tell me their blood type right after we meet."

"True, but I'm still positive things will work out for you. They always do."

I smiled at her; she was right. Somehow, things always worked out just fine, so it should be the case this time too, right?

Things were working out just fine. Or at least, it still continued to. There was an old lady living with her son across from my parents. Mama always brought her food because she was ill, and the lady was very grateful for that. Unfortunately, she passed away not long ago. Her son decided to sell us the farm cheaply to thank Mom for all she did. That's why all of us children pitched in to buy it. I sent them all my savings, and as happy as I was for my parents, I realized I now had quite little funds. So, came my next challenge to find a 'working out just fine', scenario.

"So Miss, Fąfara. What did you want to discuss?"

My manager sat heavily on his black leather chair and looked at me with tired eyes. I had revised over and over the speech I would give in order to convince him. My financial situation hadn't been so great lately, as I tried to support my parents with their newly bought farm, so I needed more money.

"Mr. Steward, please Sir. I came to ask for a raise because I can't make ends meet. I have to support myself and also help my parents in Alberta." I explained my situation, and he listened calmly. I didn't think I was asking for much, and also believed I deserved a raise since I was producing quality work.

"Well, Miss Fąfara, I'm sorry to hear about all this, but unfortunately, I can't give you what you're asking for. As you already know, we are currently building a new office, so we don't have those kinds of funds right now."

"I understand, but I can barely make ends meet with my current salary. If this keeps up, I'll have to look for a job elsewhere."

He raised his bushy brow.

"I'm sure you don't need to go *that* far."

"Don't get me wrong. I do enjoy working here, and I like this job. I feel at home, but what I'm receiving simply isn't enough."

I was aware of how bold I was, but didn't have much choice. I looked him straight in the eye and noticed a smirk on the corner of his lips.

"You're free to do as you please. However, I hope you will also consider the consequences of your actions."

I had a feeling he didn't believe I would quit, so he didn't bother giving me the raise. Furious and upset, I left his office.

"Why the long face?"

I turned around to see William, one of my work colleagues. He was an older man who always checked up on me to see if I was alright.

Oh, well…. A few things happened."

I told him about my recent exchange with Mr. Steward, and he wasn't impressed in the least.

"That cheapskate! He'll never give you that raise."

"I figured that much out."

William scratched his beard, taking a few minutes to think, then his eyes lit up.

"I know! One of my friends said there was an opening in his company, and they have much better pay than here. Maybe you should apply? I can even put in a good word for you."

"You'd do that?"

"Sure thing! I'm always happy to help a damsel in distress."

He winked at me and smiled.

Somehow, William worked his magic, and I got the position. It didn't take me long to learn the ropes, and I was fully integrated. Or at least I hoped. Everything was fine except for one small detail; the other employees didn't speak to foreigners.

I noticed it right away. They were always cold and avoided any sort of contact with me. I wasn't the only victim. An Indian lady, a mathematical professor in Nairobi who wore the most beautiful sarees, also worked there and only received silence or standoffish replies from the others. No one ever complimented her about her apparel either. As a fellow foreigner, I thought we should stick together, so I chatted with her during my breaks.

One day, I bumped into her in the hallway.

"Hi, Prisha!"

The lady turned around with a strange look in her eyes, and I noticed she was experiencing something bewildering. She stared at me, then stared back out the window. "Helen, what's that white stuff falling from the sky?"

"It's snow."

"Snow?" Her lips twisted bizarrely, as if she disliked pronouncing such an unusual word. "But… where is it coming from?"

"The air. It's like rain, but colder."

Confusion was still evident on her face as she admired the seasonal phenomenon.

"How is it that there is so much falling? It's even piling up."

"That's how it is each winter. Snow keeps falling until we reach spring."

She asked more questions, and I patiently answered each one. Prisha was amazed to witness her first winter in Canada and seemed rather excited to see how much snow we would get that year. Eventually, we changed the subject, and I asked her how she liked the job. Her excitement faded, and she lowered her head.

"It's nice but... no one likes me here. The other employees always avoid me."

"Don't worry. No one likes me either!"

She looked up at me with empathy in her gaze. We both smiled, and her mood improved.

"I've been in Canada for a while now and noticed they don't like foreigners much because they're afraid we'll steal their jobs, but you'll be alright."

"Thanks for the encouragement, Helen. I know I shouldn't always worry about what others think of me, but since I spend most of my day here, I would like for it to be pleasant so I can return home in a good mood."

"I understand. It's unfortunate, but the best we can do is produce good work. Some employees might then realize we're just as competent as they are - maybe even more - and stop treating us differently because we were born on a different patch of dirt."

"Yes, you're right." A shy smile made its way onto Prisha's face. With that, we went back to work.

Mama and Tata were settling in very well; each had gotten jobs in Vilna. Mama worked on a farm, milking cows, and Tata, even though he still barely spoke English, found a job taking care of the heating in local churches.

I got out of Janek's car and stretched my tired limbs. Now that he could drive, he was my ride each time I came to Alberta. On the way, we also picked up Andrzej and Jadzia to visit our parents. When he heard us arrive, Tata welcomed us to the barn with the cows; however, when he approached us, a foul smell stung my nose. I thought maybe it was because he had been spending too much time with the animals.

"Hi, children, how are you?" He clicked his tongue with his head hung low.

"Hello Tata, we're good, and you?" I asked, trying to ignore the smell.

He looked to the side.

"Ah, you know…" I stopped in my tracks, not expecting such a gloomy welcome. Tata barely looked at me.

"What is it?" Janek inquired.

"It's Anna. She won't let me sleep inside the house."

"What? Why?"

"Go ask her."

He stomped back to the barn to continue milking the cows, leaving us perplexed. Without having to say anything, my siblings and I all walked to the house, hoping Mother would provide us with answers. We were welcomed by the appetizing scent of turkey fresh from the oven, luring us into the kitchen.

"Hi, Mama!" I said.

"Oh, children! I didn't hear you come in." She wiped her hands on her apron and hugged us. She then began chopping a few vegetables and was about to say something when Jadzia asked what we all wondered.

"Tata says you won't let him sleep in the house. Why is that?"

Her hands froze, and she put down her knife before letting out a few chuckles, to our astonishment,

"Is that so?'

"Yes, and we are wondering why?'

"Well, you should go ask him!"

We were more than confused, but Mom picked up her knife and continued her work without adding anything else. I looked at my other siblings, and then Andrzej got up, throwing his arms in the air.

"I guess I'll go ask him then!"

We followed him to the barn where Tata was gathering hay.

"Mama told us to ask you why she won't let you sleep inside."

Father let out an annoyed sigh before finally revealing what was going on.

"Yesterday, I went hunting and saw this beautiful animal. I thought its fur would look very nice on Anna, so I shot it and brought it back. But when I showed her my trophy, what was her reaction? She chased me out, saying she didn't want it!"

"Why would she react that way?" I asked.

Father hesitated before answering, and I noticed a hint of pink creeping up his cheeks. He leaned forward and whispered:

"Well... turns out that animal was a skunk, and it smelled pretty bad."

"A skunk? Why would you shoot it?" Jadzia inquired.

"I didn't know it stank so much! Anyway, your Wujek Sowa told me to bathe in tomato juice, but they didn't have any when I went into town to buy some. So now I can't sleep inside because I stink too much."

He seemed quite mad and upset with himself, so it was hard for me to hold in my laughter. It had already been about a decade since we lived in Canada, and I was surprised he was unaware of such an important fact, especially since he lived out in the country.

"You know, I even buried the clothes I wore that day and dug them out later, but the smell was still there. I can't believe myself."

At that point, I couldn't hold it in anymore and burst out laughing, quickly imitated by my siblings.

"What... children!"

I tried calming down, but his confused expression only made things worse.

"What's all this noise?"

Mama came out to join us and seemed just as perplexed as her husband.

"He just told us the story!" Janek managed to say between chuckles.

Eventually, all six of us were laughing.

"So, how have things been in Alberta?"

"Ah, same thing."

My Father's bad smell had worn off so we could all sit at the table.

"I hold you about Andrzej's engagement, right?"

"Yes, and how it didn't work out?"

"Such a shame."

My Mother shook her head, disappointed. My Father however didn't seem too surprised.

"Humph! And I hold him that girl wasn't the right choice. Didn't I tell him?"

"Yes, you did."

Mama let out a huge sigh, most likely because she had already heard this same speech countless times.

"And how is he?"

"Well....not so great. But what really worries me is that job of his. I want him to quit working in the mine. What happened to Janek should be enough to dissuade him, right?"

"He probably thinks he won't get injured like his older brother. You know how he is."

"And that's the problem! After his injury, Janek was compensated and became a barber instead. But that's only because he's a veteran. "

"I don't think Andrzej would receive the same treatment."

As always, Mama was worried about her children, even though the youngest one was already in his thirties.

"He's a responsible adult, Mama. He knows what he's doing."

"Can't you find him a job and a wife in Toronto? He visits you sometimes, so maybe you could find something that could make him stay there. Anything to get him away from that mine!"

"I'll try the next time he comes."

With that, we continued our meal.

I was startled by the sudden sound of the phone ringing and quickly dried off the dishwater from my hands before answering.

"Hello?"

"Hi, Helena! It's Nina."

"Hey, how are you?"

"I'm good. I called to ask if you were doing anything tonight."

"No, I don't have any plans."

"Perfect! Come over, I made really good stuffed peppers!"

"Alright. I'll get ready and head out."

"See you later!"

"Bye!"

I hung up and looked around for something to wear. Nina and Lodzia were two sisters I met again at a Polish dance in Toronto. I had recognized them from Tengeru, and since then, we became good friends. They sometimes invited me over, which was great because being a single lady living alone meant I often didn't have much to do on Saturday nights.

About half an hour later, I arrived at my friends' place, and Lodzia and Nina welcomed me with open arms.

"Smells nice!" I said as I closed the door behind me.

"You're going to love this, Hela! I tried a new recipe, and it turned out great!"

My mouth was already watery, and I was excited to eat.

"Kasia (Kay) isn't here?" I asked, noticing my friend's third sister wasn't around.

"No, she went for a ride with a guy from her choir. He had promised her she'd be his first passenger after he got a new car. You want something to drink?"

I sat down on the vinyl leather couch while my friend fussed around in the kitchen. Two other girls were present, and we chatted for a while until we were interrupted by the front door opening.

"We're back!" Kasia entered the small apartment, followed by a handsome man.

"How was the ride?" Lodzia asked.

"Great! Zbyszek's (Tadeusz Zbigniew) car is so nice. Though it is a bit cramped."

"Hey! There's a year and a half worth of savings invested in that car!" the man retorted. The two friends kept chatting as they made their way to the living room. Kasia was the first to notice me.

"Oh, Helena! I didn't know you were coming over."

"Nina practically begged me to come try her new recipe."

"Not true!"

We laughed, and Kasia introduced me to her friend.

"Zbyszek, this is Helena. Helena, Zbyszek."

The man extended his hand, which I shook.

"Nice to meet you."

I didn't get the chance to reply because Lodzia pressed us to sit at the table so we could eat. We enjoyed the meal - it turns out those stuffed peppers were worth the trip - and later on, we played card games and told stories. I had a wonderful evening, as usual, but as the clock's hands ticked forward, I realized it was time for me to leave.

"Well, everyone, I need to get going."

"Already?"

"You know I don't like getting home too late, Kasia. I'm going to call a taxi."

I got up, but then Zbyszek intercepted me.

"Wait, where do you live? Maybe I can drop you off."

"Unbelievable! You've had your car for five minutes, and you're already driving people around?"

"Kasia!"

She raised her hands innocently, and Zbyszek turned his attention back to me. I told him my address, and he said it was on his way, so he offered me a ride. I half believed him, because I thought it was a bit too convenient that both our houses would be in the same direction. Nonetheless, I accepted his invitation, since it was cheaper than paying for a taxi.

We said goodbye to the sisters and left. On the way in the car, I chatted about this and that to make conversation.

"Do you have any hobbies?"

"I enjoy hunting, but not many of my friends like it, so I often go alone. Do you know anyone who likes to hunt?"

"Actually, yes. My friend's husband."

"Is that so? Maybe you could give me his number so that we can hunt together."

"Well, I can't just give you his number like that. I have to ask him first."

"Oh right, that makes sense." He paused for a second before adding: "But wait. How will I know you got his number? I would need your contact too so you can tell me."

I gave him points for using such a smooth way to ask for my number, but I still wasn't willing to give it to him. Since there had been three other girls at Nina's place, I didn't know if he was dating one of them.

Zbyszek stopped in front of my house, and I was about to get out when he placed his hand on my forearm. I looked at him, puzzled.

"Um... so... will you give me your number?"

"I don't think so. You're probably in a relationship with one of the sisters, and I don't want to interfere."

"I'm not in a relationship with either of them!"

He clearly wanted me to know he was single, and I believed him. However, there was still something that made me hesitate.

"Look. Maybe we shouldn't exchange contact info right away. After all, we just met this evening."

I couldn't help but remember my talk with Stefa and how she had complications because of her blood type. Even though Zbyszek seemed like a nice guy, I didn't want to give myself false hope.

"Oh. I guess you're right."

He lowered his head and let go of my arm to scratch his short blond hair. Defeat and disappointment were evident on his face, so I decided to give him a chance.

"You know what? Ask Kasia to give you my number."

"Kasia? But why?"

"She knows you better than I do, so if she thinks it's OK for us to be in contact, then I guess it is."

He was still confused, but accepted my proposition. In reality, I also felt that my friend liked him more than just a friendly manner. I noticed it by how she smiled when she talked with him and wouldn't stop laughing at his jokes. I didn't want to make it seem as if I was going behind her back, so if she thought it was fine for Zbyszek and I to see each other, I wouldn't feel any guilt.

My heart rate dropped back to normal as he drove off after I closed the door of my apartment.

CHAPTER 25

Happily ever after...

Eventually, Zbyszek got my number; he surprised me with a call one afternoon.

"Hi. Helena? Pani Helena Fąfara?"

"Yes, who is this?"

"It's me, Zbyszek Robaszewski. Kasia gave me your number after all!"

He tried to keep a composed tone as he asked about my day, and we talked of mundane things for a while until he got to the reason for his call.

"I was wondering if you would like to go mushroom picking with me." His voice was hesitant.

I was excited he was asking me out, but I wasn't too comfortable going on a date with him just yet since we only met once. Plus, the blood type issue kept nagging at the back of my mind, reminding me not to get too eager.

"I'll go if someone else is there too."

"Someone else?"

"Yes."

He sounded disappointed but didn't give up.

"Come on, we aren't kids anymore. We can go places by ourselves."

"That's true, but I at least want one other person to join us."

He sighed and pondered for a bit. I wasn't trying to play hard to get; my blood type wasn't the only reason I was taking things slow. I didn't believe in getting close to someone too quickly. I wasn't playing hard to get, and I was being smart and safe. There are steps to go through, and time to spend together so we can know each other better. I was already over thirty, so I didn't need some fleeting crush in my life.

"Alright. How about we go with my mother?" Maybe he was joking or serious; Nonetheless, I accepted his proposition, to his astonishment.

"Yes, that would be nice."

He released a big sigh. Was he holding his breath? Well, we sorted out the details, and then I hung up.

"Hello, Mrs. Robaszewski! It's nice to meet you!"

"Mhm."

The lady barely glanced at me before turning her attention back to her son.

"Zbyszu, are we going or not?"

"Yes, yes!"

The young man grabbed the baskets in the trunk before joining his mother, who was fanning herself.

"It's quite hot. Couldn't you have picked another day to go out?"

"Well, Saturdays are when Helena doesn't work, so..."

"Yeah, yeah."

Without adding another word, Mrs. Robaszewski began walking towards the thicket. I glanced over at Zbyszek, who smiled apologetically.

"Don't worry. She'll warm up to you."

I only hoped he was right.

We marched on, keeping our eyes peeled for our prized mushrooms. I had already thought of a few recipes to make with our treasures.

"So Helena, Zbyszek tells me you weren't born here."

Surprised and excited to receive the lady's attention, I quickly answered.

"Ah, yes. I was born in Poland, in Miratycze, but when the war started, we were deported to Siberia and…"

"Yes, yes, I know. Us too."

A short but heavy silence loomed over us. Even though I still didn't know much about these two individuals, we were connected by our similar stories. Mrs. Robaszewski didn't want to talk about what scared us, so she quickly changed the subject.

Mrs. Robaszewski was after Tad all the time, so I went on my own to find more mushrooms and away from their chattering noise. As I bent down to reach for a plump mushroom, my knee locked, and I was stuck; I was alone for so long. I thought that Zbyszek and his Mother had forgotten me and I would die among the mushrooms. I didn't want to call out because I didn't want anyone strange to find me. Then I saw a figure walking towards me from a distance, so I kept quiet behind a tree. Then I realized it was Zbyszek! My saviour! Coming back to the car, Mrs. Robaszewski was angry because she thought maybe I was playing games.

The rest of the afternoon went on without many mishaps. Mrs. Robaszewski didn't talk to me much, which was awkward at times, but at least Zbyszek's smiles and side glances reassured me. When our outing ended, he offered me a ride home.

"Thanks again for inviting me out. Now I have enough mushrooms for the whole week!"

"Good to know! And next time we can…"

"Zbyszek, I want to go home now."

His mother stared straight ahead in the passenger's seat and seemed rather eager to leave. Her son acquiesced and smiled apologetically for the umpteenth time that day.

"I'll call you later, have a good day Helena!"

That was all he said when he arrived at my apartment before he drove off.

Zbyszek wasn't the only man in my life during that period. I had also gotten acquainted with a good friend of his, Kazik Moneta. The two had attended cadet school together in Egypt and stayed as friends since. I met him at a Polish social event and, just like I did with a lot of people who went through the same journey as me, kept in touch.

Kazik was a nice young man, but his mother was unbearable! After the few times I met her, I could tell she didn't want me around. She was too attached to her son, who was already in his thirties, for Pete's sake! There's a limit to how much one can indulge their child.

One day, I received a call while listening to the radio.

"Hi, Kazik! How are you?"

"I'm good, and you?"

"Not too bad."

We talked about how our week was going, and soon he got to the heart of the matter.

"A few days ago, my mother's cousin came to Chicago, so now she wants to make him visit America. I wanted to warn you that she'll probably invite you to join us."

"I thought she didn't like me."

"She doesn't, but she'll hope you can split motel fees with her."

I rolled my eyes. How cheap was this lady to spend time with someone she disliked simply to lower her expenses?

"I simply wanted to let you know. It's up to you to decide if you want to come or not. Of course, I'd be happy if you did join us, but I didn't want to keep quiet about my mother's real intentions."

He gave me more details about the trip, and I told him I'd think about it. They were planning on driving from Chicago to New Mexico. I had already been to Chicago a few times to see some of my girlfriends and my great aunt who lived there, but I hadn't been to New Mexico yet. I wrote to Mama in order to have her opinion, and she advised me to go since it would be a good opportunity to see if Kazik was the man for me. Thus, my mind was set, and I started packing.

The sun wrestled to stretch itself above the tall skyscrapers of Chicago. The usual movement agitated the city, and a perpetual buzz mixed animated conversations with honking horns.

"Helena! So nice to see you!" Kazik's mother smiled as she hugged me. "Here is my cousin David. David, this is my son's friend, Helena."

A tall man from Poland - seeming much more welcoming and cordial than his cousin - approached me and smiled sincerely.

"It's nice to meet you."

"Nice to meet you too, sir."

'Oh please, just call me David."

Presentations were done, and we launched our tour with the main attractions of Chicago. We went on a day cruise to get a general sense of the place, then visited various sites such as the Arts Institute and Lincoln Park Zoo. After that, we filled the car's gas tank and hit the road. We stopped a few times along the way to take pictures of the beautiful scenery; the journey was really nice. The trip would have been perfect if not for one thing.

"Mother, is it OK if we continue for another hour?"

"No, I need to stretch my legs. Take the next exit."

"Alright."

No one dared mention that we had stopped only 30 minutes ago. The problem wasn't all the pit stops; it was Kazik's relationship with his mother.

"Mother, can I go buy drinks at the corner store?"

"Alright, but make sure you also get me some nuts, unsalted."

"Of course."

After travelling with them for a few days, I was very sick of this. Kazik was a complete mama's boy! He needed to ask her permission for every single thing, and I was slowly regretting coming on this trip.

"Helena, do you want to come with me?"

"I don't know. Will your mother let me?"

"Um…"

He actually turned around to ask her, but I stopped him.

"It's fine. I need a bit more fresh air anyway."

"Oh, OK."

He entered the corner store alone, and I let out a long sigh. Someone came up behind me, and I almost jumped in surprise.

"Oh! It's only you, David."

"Ha, ha! Sorry to scare you!"

In practiced motions, he took out a cigarette and his lighter and took a few puffs. He was a very handsome gentleman. David had this habit of looking out to the horizon each time he smoked. His eyes were fixed on something no one could see, as if he was receiving some revelation.

"I hope you're observing all this."

"What?"

He brought the cigarette to his mouth and then moved it away to let a grey cloud escape his lips.

"If you're planning on marrying Kazik, I hope you're observing his behaviour. Notice how close he is with his mother. This is the sort of thing you'll have to deal with."

He detached his gaze from the horizon and turned his head towards me, a grin stretching his lips.

"He'll start asking: 'Mother, can I sleep with Helena now? Mother, can I start a family with Helena now? Mother…'

David purposely imitated a child's voice, which made me laugh.

"What are you guys talking about?"

My conversational partner and I immediately became silent as we noticed Kazik arriving, a plastic bag in hand.

"Oh, nothing. We're just observing the great scenery. Come on, let's get back on the road."

The young man shrugged and followed his cousin. In the car, David shot me a knowing look, and without saying a word, we both smiled.

The days passed, and soon our trip neared its end. I had a great time, but a certain thought kept itching in the back of my mind. Finally, I decided to simply deal with it.

"Kazik, could I talk to you for a moment?"

He diverted his attention from his mother, with whom he had just finished a card game, and looked at me.

"Right now?"

"Yes."

He turned back to his Mama, who was clearly displeased but didn't say anything.

"Um... Mother, is it alright if..."

She said, "Yeah, yeah," pretending to be more focused on shuffling the cards. Kazik got up and followed me outside the motel.

"What is it?"

"Well... you've been very nice to me and invited me on this trip, so I didn't want to make it seem like I was taking advantage of you or playing behind your back. I simply wanted to let you know that lately I've also been seeing your friend Zbyszek."

"Zbyszek? You mean the one from cadet school?"

"Yes. We met a little while ago and have gotten to know each other. Anyway, I just wanted to let you know."

Kazik didn't say anything for a few seconds, which worried me, but then he suddenly started laughing.

"Huh? What's so funny?"

I had mustered the courage to be honest with him, and this was his reaction?

"Sorry Helena, it's just... I was scared you were going to say something serious or sad, like you were leaving or something like that."

"Well, isn't this serious too?"

"I guess so."

I still didn't understand his attitude. Maybe I had imagined things, and Kazik had zero interest in me, so it didn't bother him if I was spending time with one of his good friends.

"Zbyszek is a great guy and all," he finally said, "but I'm not worried."

"Why?"

"Because his mother will never let you marry him!"

The Polish reunions at Orchard Lake Village were held every other year, and I attended each one, always spending a great week with longtime friends. Andrzej, who had visited me a few times in Toronto, ended up permanently staying here after he got married. My parents lived modestly and happily on the farm in Alberta; I always loved visiting them. Janek and Georgie already had children, so they were kept busy. I was still the only child who wasn't married, but that would soon change.

"What is this?"

"Exactly what you see."

Kazik had invited me out to the park, and the last thing I was expecting as we sat down on a bench was for him to pull out a wedding ring.

"But… I don't understand."

"What is there not to understand?"

"You never mentioned marriage or anything of the sort. I didn't know those were your intentions.

"Well, I thought my intentions were pretty clear. Don't you know that I love you?"

He was trying to allure me with a charming smile and tender eyes, but I wasn't buying it. Kazik was a nice person, but I think it was a problem that he didn't mention anything regarding a potential romantic relationship and suddenly appeared with a wedding ring.

"Actually, I don't. You always made it seem as if we were only friends."

"Come on, Helena."

He tried to persuade me, but all to no avail. This wasn't my first time turning down a marriage proposal, so I knew how to be firm. As much as I enjoyed spending time with Kazik, I didn't picture myself spending the rest of my life with him or with his overprotective mother. Thinking of the long run, he didn't seem like the right fit for me, especially since his mother consumed all of him all the time. Of course, he was very disappointed by my rejection, but he also knew he couldn't make me change my mind.

I left him alone on that bench, and I was glad I did because someone better still awaited me.

Since Zbyszek and Kazik were friends, I figured they might eventually talk about the ring incident, so I decided I'd rather tell him myself.

"I wanted to let you know that I've also been seeing Kazik."

"Kazik? My classmate from cadet school?"

I nodded, and Zbyszek seemed more miserable than ever.

"What's wrong?"

"Well, nothing if you ignore the fact that now I have no chances since you're already in a relationship with such an amazing guy."

"I've been spending time with him, but we aren't in a relationship."

"Not yet, you aren't."

Zbyszek looked rather discouraged, and I was about to say something, but he didn't give me a chance.

"Kazik is handsome, tall, and smart. He's so knowledgeable too. There's no way I could compare. I'm sure it's only a matter of time before you end up together."

"Calm down now."

I put my hands in front of him to bring him to a halt.

"There is absolutely nothing romantic between us. We're just friends."

"Just friends?"

"Yes."

He finally regained composure and a puffed-out chest as his ego became triumphant.

"Besides, my main concern is finding a husband with Rh-negative blood, not someone with good looks."

I had said that nonchalantly, but Zbyszek's eyes lit up.

"Helena! Helena!"

I didn't understand his emotion and was quite startled by the sudden switch in his mood. We were in a café, and other customers stared at us, perplexed.

"You can't marry anyone, just me!"

"Just you? Why?"

"Because I also have Rh-negative blood!" he declared, full of pride as he puffed out his chest.

At first, I didn't know how to react. This was the answer to my prayer. A man who was responsible, dependable - good looking too - and, on top of all, had the same blood type as me! His face beamed, and my heart raced.

"You can only marry me, Helena," he repeated in a much calmer tone this time.

He stared straight at me, his affirmation sounding more like a question. He grabbed my left hand and locked his eyes with mine. I knew he was waiting for an answer, and I also knew that this time, my answer would be different than the previous times I was asked the same question.

"Yes."

Zbyszek proposed at the Polish New Year's Ball, organized to celebrate the end of 1965. A friend of mine in Chicago sent me beautiful sequenced fabric with which I created a stunning navy blue ballroom dress, floor length, sleeveless with a low back and long gloves past my elbows to match.

Tad was my date, and we arrived together at the grand hall. Round tables draped in black cloth were accentuated by tall white flower vases serving as a centerpiece. There was a large rectangular table on the side with refreshments, and the marble floor glittered under the shiny lights.

I recognized some friends, so we sat with them. However, I didn't get much time to sit since I was continually being asked to dance.

"Isn't this already the third one, Helena?" Janina asked as a tall man led me away.

I shrugged in response and followed my partner. That night, I felt transported back to England, attending dances on Friday evenings. I remembered Stefa, who rolled her eyes nearly each time a man approached me until she finally got her own.

Music poured out from the live band performing on stage, each gentleman looking sharp in their black tuxedos. Smiles were pinned to our cheeks, and laughter flowed with the melody. Arms and legs moved around in rhythmic motions, high heels hitting the floor on the beat. I received many compliments on my outfit and was proud of the work I had created.

Though I had many dance partners throughout the evening, my heart was fixated on a particular individual. Despite our recent conversation about him being the only one I could marry, nothing was set in stone.

Speaking of which, Zbyszek quickly grew annoyed - or worried - by my popularity on the dance floor. I felt like 'the star of the night'. Apparently, he couldn't take his eyes off me, admiring me from the table at dinner and across the room of the dance floor. After the first dance of the New Year, Zbyszek escorted me to the table.

"Helena, I would like to speak with you for a moment." He leaned in close as I sat down.

"Oh, OK. What is it?"

His blue eyes glanced at Janina, who didn't seem to miss one bit of our conversation.

"I would prefer talking outside."

"Outside? But it's freezing!"

"It won't be long, I promise."

I trusted him and followed him out of the building. The air was icy as we approached the end of December. My hands continually rubbed my arms, hoping the friction would provide some heat. However, Zbyszek seemed unbothered by the weather, clearly preoccupied with something else.

"So... I noticed you've been asked to dance quite a lot tonight, and I've heard a lot of men compliment you on your looks."

He scratched his short blond hair, and I wished he would hurry up because the frozen breeze made my legs shiver.

"Also, we talked about how we both have Rh-negative blood so that we would be a good match, but nothing was made official."

"Yes, Zbyszek, what are you trying to get to?"

He looked up at me and realized I was freezing, so he finally popped the question.

"Will you marry me?"

My mind was already set, and my answer came right away.

"Yes! Yes, Zbyszek, my love! Of course, I'll marry you!"

His eyes opened wide as a smile stretched his lips.

"Really? You accept?"

I had technically already accepted his proposal when he mentioned his blood type, but maybe he wanted to formulate the question and receive an official answer properly.

"Yes, I do! Now come on, let's head back inside; it's so cold!"

Zbyszek leaped forward and hugged me tight, his body heat transferring into mine. Though it was bitterly cold, warmth filled me up as I realized the man embracing me was now my fiancé.

Zbyszek's proposal came two years after we met. Once we were engaged, there was a lot to do. Zbyszek and I were both low on funds, but believed we would manage somehow. We tried figuring out which house to buy, thinking an older one might be the cheapest option, but that discussion was still ongoing. Another big issue weighed on my mind, and I talked about it with him.

"Don't you think it's time we told your mother about our engagement?"

He bit his lower lip and diverted his eyes.

"Well... I don't know if that's a good idea. I told you she's very over-protective."

"Yes, but I'm also wondering if it's a good idea to keep our relationship secret. Won't she be even more furious when she finds out on her own?"

"OK, fine, I'll tell her, but I'm already letting you know she won't like it. It's not because of who you are. She would have hated whoever I ended up with."

"Isn't that her job as a mother-in-law?"

Zbyszek chuckled.

" Yeah, I guess so."

He paused for a second, and his smile faded.

"You know, she wasn't always like this. She used to work with sick people and loved helping others. It's just... the war. It changed her."

He paused, and I placed my hand on his shoulder to show support. Since we were about to get married, he figured I should know his family story.

"My father was a Hrabia (count), and a General (four-star) in the army, and was away a lot. After the war began, he was one of the first killed among other men because of his high military rank. He ended up in the Katyń Forest with the others."[19] One of the Russians main missions as the war began was to eliminate all the wealthy, intelligent, and people with power in Poland so that they don't interfere with the Russians' plan of

---

19   In 1943 Nazi troops discovered mass graves of Polish officers in the Katyn forest near the city of Smolensk, in western Russia. Later on, historians discovered that Katyn was one of the many sites of mass murder by the Soviet regime between 1939-41.

taking over. Mr. Robaszewski was a General in the Polish army who was murdered in the Katyń Forest with hundreds of Polish people of rank.

He looked grim, and I wondered if he should stop here, but he continued.

"As you can imagine, my Mother didn't take that loss quite well. I'm the only family she has left since she never had other children, so she doesn't want to lose me too. I know it's not an excuse for her to be so mean to you, but..."

He fiddled with the hem of his sleeve and sighed.

"You never know. Maybe I'll be able to change her back."

I said to reassure him. My tactic half worked, and I decided to change the subject.

"By the way, did I tell you about my new job?"

He seemed relieved to talk of something other than the horrors of the war.

"No. You just said some guy found something that could interest you, but I didn't know you got the position."

"It's the same man who had gotten me my previous job. He came to check up on me one day, and I told him the place was nice, but no one talked to me since I was a foreigner. He then got me a job in the head office of Loblaws.

"Wow, that's great!"

"It sure is! The only problem is the boss' secretary. She's his mistress, and for some reason sees me as a threat. As if I would want to sleep with the boss to get a promotion!"

"I hope you don't want to sleep with the boss to get a promotion."

"Zbyszek! Of course not!"

"Just checking!"

I nudged his elbow, and he chuckled. I loved hearing him laugh!

"Besides, why would I want him when I have you?"

He stared back at me, the corners of his lips curving upwards.

"That's a very valid point you make."

He wrapped his arm around my shoulders and held me tight.

CHAPTER 26

Our legacy

Preparations for the wedding advanced, and there was one element I absolutely couldn't neglect; my wedding gown. Since I had a lot of knowledge in fashion, I made sure to choose it wisely. I found a beautiful design, bought the material, and then took it all to a skilled seamstress, who took care of the rest. There was a belief in Poland that a woman shouldn't make her own wedding dress, because the amount of times she inserted the needle in the fabric would equal the amount times she'd cry over her marriage. I could plan and assist as much as I wanted, but my hands were not to sew even one stitch!

There was another task I had to take care of. I went to see my boss in his office, and he invited me to sit down.

"Hi Miss Fąfara. What did you want to discuss?"

"As you know, I'll be getting married in about a month and a half. That's why I wanted to ask for some time off so that I can go on my honeymoon."

He nodded; however, there was something in his expression that wasn't quite reassuring as he crossed his thick fingers on the desk.

"Yes, I am happy to hear the news. I can give you a week off."

"One week? We plan on leaving for ten days, so I'll need at least two."

"I'm sorry, Miss Fąfara, but you're still very new, and we need you here. This is as much time as I can offer."

"I understand I'm in no position to ask for time off since I started recently, but I can't let my husband go on the honeymoon alone!"

"Listen. I'm only giving you one week, and that's final. If you decide to extend your leave, keep in mind that you might lose your job."

I didn't like the look in his dark brown eyes and asked myself if I really wanted to keep working for such a man. Most likely not.

Our conversation ended with quite a bitter taste. Without another word, I got up and left.

"So? How was it?"

"Terrible." I met up with Zbyszek at a cafe to discuss table arrangements. We received our orders, and I realized how hungry I was. Despite it being short, my conversation with my boss drained me. Between bites, I recounted my discussion to Zbyszek.

"So now I might lose my job," I said as I sighed heavily.

"Hmm… that is no good, my dear." He nibbled on some fries before adding: "But don't worry. Even if you lose your job, I'm sure we'll get by, and everything will work out just fine. Don't forget I'm working as an engineer now, so money shouldn't be too much of a problem.

"That's true."

We moved on from that topic to discuss another problematic matter; his mother.

"You remember how I bought her a dog because she kept complaining that she'd be alone after I got married? Well, now she's complaining about the dog!"

"Really?"

"Yes! She doesn't like taking care of it because it's a lot of work, and she says it's too violent. When she takes it out for a walk, it's actually the opposite that happens, and the dog ends up walking or dragging her!"

I couldn't help but chuckle as I pictured Zbyszek's tiny Mother being dragged around by her huge Dalmatian dog.

"She's even saying I bought it for myself because the dog is a hunter. Maybe I should have gotten her something smaller."

"Zbyszu, you know she would have complained no matter what you got her."

"True. She does like to complain, especially about you."

I rolled my eyes. Unfortunately, Mrs. Robaszewski was set on preventing me from marrying her son. Tad told me she constantly tried to dissuade him from getting hitched, but he didn't listen. His friends also warned me to watch out for her, knowing she could be unpredictable. Honestly, I was sad and disappointed to have such a toxic relationship with my future mother-in-law, but I could do nothing about it.

"You know what? Maybe I will keep that dog after all. Since he's a hunter, I could take him out with me."

Zbyszek looked at me for approval, and I shrugged.

"Sure, I don't mind us having a dog."

"Yes!"

A childish smile stretched his lips. After that, we finally started working on what we were supposed to do; table arrangements.

People often say their wedding day was the most beautiful day in their lives. As I finally had mine, I couldn't help but agree. It was July 2nd, 1966. I married Tadeusz Zbigniew Robaszewski. My wedding dress turned out beautiful, and my husband looked as handsome as ever. All my family came to celebrate this special day. Zbyszek also invited his friends, but there weren't many guests. Unfortunately, my mother-in-law didn't come.

As I stood in my dazzling white dress among the people I loved, I realized I could have been an old maid. For so long, I rejected marriage proposals. However, I didn't dwell much on what didn't happen because I had a ring on my finger and a husband by my side.

We had a feast after the ceremony at church. The atmosphere was festive, and Zbyszek and I kept receiving congratulations from the guests. Eventually, my Tata came to chat with us.

"I can't believe my youngest daughter is married at last, and of course, she had to pick such a shrimp!"

Tata laughed out loud, but thankfully Zbyszek didn't feel offended. Indeed, he wasn't very tall, about 5"8, but at least, his days in the cadets gave him a nice physique.

"All jokes aside, you chose yourself a good man, Hela. Looks fade, but personality always remains. I simply hope you'll take proper care of him."

Tata gave me a real and true blessing to marry Zbyszek. His good, beautiful and true personality shined through, just like the diamond on my finger.

"Father, you're telling her to take care of me, but I should be the one to take care of her," Zbyszek replied.

"Ha! Ha! Ha! Son, I'm saying this because I know her!"

Tata continued to chat with us for a bit and eventually Mama joined us before they both left. Then Mietek, Zbyszek's best man, came along to congratulate us.

"Good to see you're finally married Zbyszek!"

"Well, it was worth the wait," my husband replied, all smiles.

"It's crazy how far we've come, huh? Back in cadet school, marriage was the last thing we thought about."

"I'm sure you also didn't think you'd become a chemist one day, yet here you are!"

Indeed, Mietek had come to Canada after finishing university in England, and now occupied a prominent position within the science world on a provincial level. I didn't know the exact title of his job, but I knew it was serious business. He continued to chat with us for a while before heading back to his table.

A few minutes later, Jadzia approached us with a glass of champagne.

"Wow, Hela. You had so many handsome boyfriends in Toronto, yet you chose this fine fellow?"

I crossed my fingers that my growing family would all get along well. I had already warned Tad of my sister's challenging nature, and I still feared her remark hurt him. As I was about to answer, he did it first.

"I'm charmed to finally meet you, Jadwiga. Helena chose me; quite frankly, that's all I care about."

My sister was taken aback and immediately understood the request. Growing up, I looked up to my sister because she was older and so pretty, but through the years, she had become more and more bitter, so the admiration I once had for her had dissipated some.

I enjoyed my day thoroughly. The atmosphere was jovial, and the guests were merry. We took many pictures, and I often had to stop what I was doing to smile at the camera. I was at the epitome of joy, and it was the same for Zbyszek too; we were blissfully happy. We had been able to buy our house before the wedding, so that night was our first in our new home.

A lot of movies often end after the wedding. However, in real life, that's only the starting point. Married life begins after we say 'I do,' and the next chapter begins.

We had a wonderful time on our honeymoon. We planned a camping at Algonquin Park.

We both loved nature and the outdoors. In preparation, I managed to get a week off of work and Tad bought a camping trailer that was attached to the back of our car.

At this time, we had a Dalmatian dog named Rex which we inherited from his Mother. I loved Rex so much. I always made sure he was fed, walked, and full of cuddles. Rex probably thought of me as his mama.

One of the nights, Zbyszek and I enjoyed our evening with some wine and music on the radio. We had a grand time. Well, at least Rex and I did.

It started off with some good laughs by the campfire. Then the music took over. Good Vibrations by the Beach Boys was playing, and of course, I was singing along.

....I'm pickin' up good vibrations......

Soon Rex joined in on the fun and howled to the tunes. He was so adorable.

....good, good, good, good vibrations... and ouwwwwwww!

"Okay, okay, Helen, quiet down now."

Zbyszek said. But the singing continued. Our howling voices rose up into the night.

"Shhhh! Please calm down!" Zbyszek insisted." Someone is going to think that I'm murdering you! Your singing sounds more like yelling!"

I smirked "Psshhh...it's the dog who's yelling. Ladies can only sing."

It was a beautiful night—one that Zbyszek and I cherished for many camping trips and even more years.

Rex was born to be a hunting dog. Zbyszek had given him to his Mother first. Though, as time went on, Franciszka realized Rex was a stereotypical dog in some ways, but in other ways, he was so naive. He had the strongest urge to chase critters in the park, but when there was a thunderstorm, he would try to fit himself under the couch for protection.

Zbyszek's Mother returned the dog to him.

"This isn't a dog, Zbyszu. Rex is a human trapped in a dog's body," she said.

So on this camping trip, Zbyszek thought it would be the perfect time to familiarize Rex with the world, and maybe train him to be a hunting dog.

There was a lake nearby our camping site where Zbyszek and I went swimming to cool off from the summer heat.

"Come on, Rex. Come on, boy, let's go!" Zbyszek was encouraging the dog to come in the water. Rex preferred to bark up trees.

"Let's go cool off, Rex!" I said gently.

He then changed his mind to follow by my side, just until the shoreline.

"Come on, my boy, let's go!"

I tried encouraging Rex into the water. At this point, I was lying belly down in the shallow water. Occasionally splashing the water to make it look more fun. Rex only managed to put his 4 paws in.

"What is up with this dog? Dalmatians are supposed to love swimming!" Zbyszek growled.

He swam over to the dog, petted him gently, and slowly picked up Rex in his arms. The two of them went out deeper into the water. Zbyszek was gliding Rex around, ensuring his face was above water. Rex seemed to be okay with it as his spotted tail wagged in the air.

Zbyszek reached about belly deep and spoke calmly to the dog.

"Okay, Rex. In a moment, I'm going to let you go so you can swim to your Mama, got it?"

Zbyszek gently loosened his grip and nudged Rex towards the shore where I was.

AROOOOOO!!! AW! AW! AW! AROOOOOO!!!!

Rex immediately howled and hopelessly flailed his legs as soon as he realized he was on his own.

"Rex! Rex! It's okay! Oh Lord, he was doing so well!" Zbyszek said as he held his scared dog.

"Come bring him over here, Zbyszek. We'll sit in the shade together." I said as I turned to straighten out the towels under a nearby oak tree.

The three of us sat together, looking out across the lake and enjoying a moment of silence.

"I can't get over how Canada looks so similar to Poland. This reminds me of the lake near my farm." I said, as I reminisced.

"I would have to agree, but a few things are different. We're sitting on a big rock right now but the rest is pretty much the same."

"I think this rock is called the Canadian Shield. It covers most of Canada!" I replied and glanced toward Zbyszek.

My view was obstructed as Rex sat himself right between us, demanding attention.

"Oh, my poor boy. You don't have to worry anymore. You are safe with me." I wrapped the shivering dog in a spare towel. Once we were all cuddled up, I gave my boys a kiss—one on the snout and another on the cheek.

The camping grounds at Algonquin Park were surrounded by rich forests. This trip was very successful in our haul and brought back 2 large buckets of mushrooms to be washed and dehydrated in our Toronto home.

"Maybe Rex is a mushroom-hunting dog." I giggled to Zbyszek as we started our hunt.

Zbyszek smiled as he released Rex from his leash

"Go on, boy. Find us some mushrooms!"

Rex pranced about ahead of us, sniffing as he made his trail. The trees, the ground, bushes, logs, and rocks. Nothing was left unsearched.

"Whatever he's smelling must be so interesting! He looks so invested." Zbyszek commented.

Eventually, Rex trailed off into the woods.

When picking mushrooms, your fingers can get sticky and stained from the mushroom skins. The deeper the stain, the more mushrooms, and the happier I would be. Zbyszek and I were picking along until suddenly, we heard Rex crying from afar.

"Oh, I hope he didn't get pricked by a thorn," I said to Zbyszek.

"Well, he stopped now, so it can't be that bad."

After a few minutes, it happened again, then again.

That's it. Something is wrong." I told Zbyszek.

I called for Rex with a loud whistle.

Soon Rex returned to us with his nose still on the ground and his tail wagging. However, we noticed that he never really picked his head up. Rex was still dedicated to sniffing. Once he found a good scent, some alarm went off in his mind, and off he ran, bounding to where his next treasure was hiding!

Sniff, sniff, sniff - *BONK* "AROOOOOOOO!!!"

Rex cried out again.

Finally, Zbyszek solved the mystery. He realized that since Rex kept his head so close to the ground, he forgot to look up to see where he was going. Soon enough, Rex smacked his head straight into a tree!

Zbyszek was laughing and shaking his head.

"He's not a country-hunting dog. Rex is a city dog!"

The honeymoon couldn't last forever, so at some point, we had to get off our happiness cloud and come back down to reality. For me, that meant going back to work.

I didn't know how to face my boss that Monday morning. After all, he *had* threatened to fire me if I left for more than a week - which I did. I had been thinking a lot about whether or not I should continue with this job. Since I was now married, I wanted to have children soon, so I didn't know if I would have enough energy to work, take care of the kids, home, and family. Also, since our home was quite big, we rented part of it, which meant I also had to deal with tenants. I thought for sure I would have a burnout in the span of half a year working in so many places.

"Miss Fąfara!"

I turned at the sound of my maiden name. My boss marched straight to me, and I was more than surprised to see he was... smiling? "Oh, sorry! It's not Miss Fąfara anymore, right?"

"Yes. I'm Mrs. Robaszewski now."

"Right, right!"

He seemed very excited for some reason. Perhaps managers enjoyed firing their staff?

"In any case, I'm so glad you're back!"

"Really? But I thought you were going to fire me."

"Nonsense!"

He waved my comment with the back of his hand as if it was the silliest thing he'd ever heard. "Don't worry about that. You can definitely still work here."

"Actually, about that...Sir. "

I suggested we continue our conversation in his office because a few curious employees were eavesdropping.

"What? You're quitting?"

"Yes. I don't think this job fits me right, so I brought my resignation letter."

My boss looked at the envelope as if it was cursed. We had a short discussion, and he tried to convince me to stay, but my mind was made. Since there was nothing else he could do, he finally accepted my resignation.

That evening, my husband asked me how it went at work.

"I got fired."

"Wow, so he really did it?"

"Yeah."

"That jerk!"

For some reason, I couldn't bring myself to tell Zbyszek the truth. We were newlyweds, which meant our finances weren't necessarily the greatest. I knew we needed whatever income we could get, so he might have been mad or disappointed to find out the truth. However, I believed that we'd be fine with the rent our tenants paid and my husband's engineering job.

"Don't worry, dear. We'll manage, everything always turns out just fine. Remember, I love you forever and always," Zbyszek said reassuringly.

"Alright."

Till this day, I never told him the truth.

We did manage. Zbyszek's job was enough to sustain both of us, so I never worked again. Instead, I focused on house chores and dealing with our tenants. Every Thursday, my husband had dinner with his Mother. I was relieved he went because I feared she might kill me if she didn't get to see her son often enough. I admired Zbyszek for being such a devoted son, despite his mother's "rough" personality, to say the least; it said a lot about his character. I was very happy with my husband - and our huge Dalmatian dog.

The year following our wedding was the famous Expo 67 in Montreal, so we drove to Quebec to attend. We had a wonderful time there. All in all, everything was going well.

And then Tad said something startling.

"Maybe it's time to begin thinking of starting a family? "

It was a Saturday morning, and we were eating breakfast when he brought up this topic out of the blue. I nearly choked on my toast.

"What?"

"I mean... maybe one little one be a good start."

"You... you really mean that?"

My husband knew I still wanted children, so I was more than excited that he finally suggested beginning to grow our new family.

"Yes. I know it's important to you, but that's not the only reason. I see how other couples are happy with their children and families, and I want that for us too."

I could tell he was genuine, which brought tears to my eyes. Without thinking, I threw myself at his neck, embracing him tightly.

"But let's just settle for one!"

"Hmm... how about two?"

"We'll see."

I leaned back to look at him properly. A new spark had been lit within me, and I felt like I had fallen for him at a deeper level.

"Also... promise you'll still have time for me?"

"Always!"

With that, I kissed him tenderly.

Two years after our wedding, we had a baby girl. We called her Danuta formally, and called her Danusia. She was a beautiful and healthy baby. Being very new to parenthood, it was rough at the beginning for Zbyszek and I, but we eventually got the hang of it. Actually, my husband even considered having a second child, saying he would name him Arthur if he was a boy. Unfortunately, baby Arthur never came to be, and Danusia was our only child.

It truly is a fantastic phenomenon to give life to an individual. Of course, I cried. It wasn't only due to the beauty of giving the gift of life, but also because of everything I had gone through to reach this point. My parents did their best to give us good living conditions, despite the many hardships and setbacks. We had to start from scratch when we came to Canada, but since our parents were so supportive, we were able to make something of ourselves.

I, too, went through many challenges but didn't want to waste the opportunity my parents gave me to go further than they did. And now, holding this newborn child, I could only hope for her to strive and advance even further in life.

I could have given up at any point and let my circumstances get the best of me. But then what about all the nights I heard Mama cry in Siberia and all the blood Tata shed in prison? What about Mama's fingers turning blue as she made us clothes out of potato sacks, or Father's weakened body beaten by Russian soldiers? All of it would be in vain.

Not everyone starts life at the same level. Some people get a head start, others are held back a few laps, but finishing the race and passing the baton matters. I did my part and gave my daughter Danusia the tools she needed to succeed, and I couldn't be prouder of her today.

Mama often told us "children" to write our stories. It was hard to do so because life events constantly distracted me, but now it's here.

Engraved on this paper and there to stay.

In commemoration of my Mother, Anna, I gave her name to my daughter as her second name, Danusia Anna. She in turn, gave my Mother's name to her daughter, Sophia Anna, and reflected in the name of her son, Michael Anthony.

I would like to give thanks to my beautiful daughter, Danusia, and her two children, Michael and Sophia, for inspiring me to put the story of my life on paper.

I would like to dedicate this my life story book to my Strong, Brave, Resourceful and Beautiful Mother and Father, Anna Fąfara and Ludwik Fąfara, to my sister-in-law, Georgie, and to my cousin Alvina Sowa. I treasure them all, dear to my heart.

Tadeusz Zbigniew Robaszewski, Fishing Trip, Barry's Bay, ON.

Zbyszek on a hunting trip, Barry's Bay, ON, 1967.

Ski trip with my friends from the Polish Association, Toronto, ON.

Cross country ski trip in northern Ontario with the Polish association in Ontario

**Waxing up and getting ready to hit the cross country trails with
my friends from the Polish association in Ontario**

One of my personal sewing designs.

Wedding of my brother John and Georgie. My brother Andziej is standing. Sitting from left is Janek's friend, myself Helena, my Father Ludwig, my Mother Anna and the newlyweds my brother Janek, and his beautiful new wife Georgie

Myself, Helena and my youngest brother Andziej.

Myself in my Toronto apartment wearing one of my original designs.

Me in my Roncesvalles, Toronto apartment

Date at the beach, summer 1965.

Tadeusz Zbygniew Robaszewski and I, dinner date, Toronto, ON, 1965.

Zbyszek and myself, couple's date, Niagara Falls, ON.

Evening at Casa Loma, Toronto, ON.

The evening Zbyszek proposed, with my famous royal blue sequence dress, New Year's 1966.

Mr. Tadeusz Zbigniew Robaszewski

and

Miss Helena Fafara

have the honour of announcing their marriage
which took place on Saturday, July 2nd, 1966

at

St. Casimir's Church
156 Roncesvalles Avenue
Toronto, Canada

Our Wedding announcement.

Our Portrait, at our home 1966.

**My Father, Ludwig Fąfara, walking me down the aisle on my wedding day.
St. Kazimier's Church, Roncesvalles, Toronto, ON, July 2, 1966.**

**My Tata, Ludwig Fąfara, on my wedding day, walking me down the aisle,
St. Kasimir's Church, Roncesvalles, Toronto, ON, July 2nd, 1966.**

Our wedding day, July 2nd, 1966, Toronto, ON.

Our wedding day, St. Kazimierz Church, Roncesvalles, Toronto, ON, July 2, 1966.

Our wedding day, at the front of St. Kazimier's Church. From left, Jasia, Andziej's wife, Jadzia, Jadzia's husband Peter Krudys, my Father Ludwig, the newlyweds myself Helena and Zbyszek Robaszewski, and Jadzia's oldest daughter Donna

Our first dance, Wedding July 2, 1966, Toronto, ON.

Our Wedding Day, July 2nd, 1966, Toronto, ON.

Our wedding portrait, July 2nd, 1966.

Our wedding portrait, July 2nd, 1966, Toronto, ON.

Our wedding portrait with our wedding party. All my bridesmaids and Zbyszek's groomsmen, July 2nd, 1966.

Zbyszek, Rex, and I, camping. Zbyszek is holding an enormous puffball
mushroom which we ate later that evening. Barry's Bay, ON, 1966.

Wilno near Barry's Bay, ON. Same as Vilno, Alberta and Wilno in Poland!

Camping trip with Rex.

Newlyweds at our home, Highview Cres., summer 1966.

Zbyszek, my darling, professing his love to me, Highview, Toronto, ON.

Zbyszek, Rex, and I after our wedding, at the front door of our
home on Highview Cres., Toronto, ON, 1967.

Rex, caught hiding under the bed from the sounds of thunder!

Our beautiful family with Danusia, Fall 1968.

Danusia's Christening Portrait, fall 1968.

Danusia's first summer 1969 at Highview, Toronto, ON.

Danusia's first birthday, October 3rd, 1969, with me and Zbyszek, Highview, Toronto, ON.

Photo of myself, Helena with my oldest brother Janek, at my home, Highview, Toronto, ON.

My older brother Janek Fąfara, my husband Zbyszek
Robaszewski and our, Rex. Highview, Toronto, ON.

Danusia's Christening Fall 1968, St. Kazimierz Church, Roncesvalles, Toronto,
ON. Top row on the left, my younger brother Andziej and his wife Jasia. Second
row Zbyszek's friend who is the Godfather Mietek Ranosz, my girlfriend who
is the Godmother Mela Kubok, Zbyszek, and my older brother Janek.

Dinner at our house with my family, at Danusia's Christening, Fall 1968.

**From left standing: My oldest brother Janek, Jasia-Andziej's wife,
Georgie-Janek's wife, and my youngest brother Andziej**

**From left sitting down: Zbyszek, my girlfriend and Godmother Mela Kubok,
Zbyszek's friend and Godfather Mietek Ranosz and myself, Helena**

Danusia's first camping trip, Summer 1969.

Bounty from the forest and lakes! Camping trip, Summer 1969.

Zbyszek and I on a camping trip with our dog Rex, Barry's Bay, ON, 1969.

My Mama, Anna Fąfara, holding my daughter, Danusia

Danusia with her Babcia, Franciszka Robaszewski Gawroński, Zbyszek's Mother, 1970.

My Zbyszek and I at a New Year's Ball, Toronto, ON, mid 1970s.

My Mother and I, at the family home at the farm in Vilno, Alberta, 1978.

Robaszewski at the family farm in Vilno, Alberta, summer 1969.

New Years party at our good friends house, Stefa and Stefan Kowalczyk, 1982.

Reunion of all the same friends as we were in our village in Africa.
St. Mary's Preparatory, Orchard Lake, Michigan, USA.

Family portrait, 1985.

**Celebrating my Mother's 90th birthday. Myself, my Mother Anna and
my sister Jadzia at Jadzia's home in Edmonton, Alberta.**

Family Christmas portrait with our dog Terra, winter 1986.

Shenanigans at family dinner! Younger brother Andziej having fun with his older brother
Janek. To the right is Jasia, Andziej's wife, at their home at Bloor West Village, Toronto, ON.

My Mother Anna. Babcia with all her grandchildren. From Left: Richard, Rita, Danusia, Donna, Babcia, Teresa, Susan, Barbara, Robert, Ben

Grand Ball, June 4, 1994.

Family reunion, June 5, 1994. From left: Danusia, my cousin Alvina Green, myself, Alvina's daughter Carla Green, and my Zbyszek.

Three generations, my daughter Danusia, my Mother Anna, and myself.

Our two matriarchs, my Mother – Anna Fąfara and her cousin by marriage Rose Sowa.

Visiting my family in Alberta. Me, my cousin Alvina Green and her Mother, Ciocia Rose Sowa. 1995.

Our family home at the farm, Vilno, Alberta, 1995,

Forest bounty of various mushrooms that are being cleaned pealed
and preparing for drying. Highview, Toronto, ON, 2000.

Our growing family with our two grandchildren, Michael Anthony
Robaszewski and Sophia Anna Robaszewski, April 21, 2001.

My grandson's graduation from grade 8. Myself (Babi) Helena, my granddaughter Sophia, my grandson Michael and my daughter Danusia, King City, ON, June 2012.

My photo on my 95th birthday, September 19th, 2024 celebrating with my two grandchildren, Sophia and Michael.

My photo, Helena Robaszewski, on my 95th birthday, September 19th, 2024, together with my wonderful daughter Danusia Robaszewski and my amazing grandchildren, Sophia Robaszewski and Michael Robaszewski

Babi's Apple cake Recipe

Ingredients

4 eggs

2 cups of flour

¾ cup of oil

¼ sour cream

2 heaping teaspoons of baking powder

2 teaspoons of vanilla or almond flavour

4 large baking apples or 6 small apples, sliced thinly

Sugar and lemon juice to taste

Butter and a teaspoon of flour for the pan

13x9 rectangle baking pan.

Directions

Preheat the oven to 350° F.

Place the thinly sliced apples together with a dash of lemon juice and a tablespoon of sugar. Mix the apples slowly.

In a separate bowl, beat eggs and sugar together until smooth. Add oil and beat again.

Mix in flour and baking powder to the batter.

Combine the apple mixture with the batter and mix gently with a spoon.

Prepare the baking pan by thinly spreading some butter along the bottom and sides of the pan. Then add a teaspoon of flour to the pan. Gently tap the pan with one hand as the other is rotating the pan so that all the buttered areas are coated with the flour. Discard the remaining flour.

Pour the apple batter into the pan. For additional taste and presentation, sprinkle sugar on top.

Bake for 45-50 minutes but keep a watchful eye.

Lullabies

1

Na Wojtusia z popielnika
Iskiereczka mruga
Chodź opowiem ci bajeczkę,
Bajka będzie długa.

Była sobie raz królewna,
Pokochała grajka,
Król wyprawił im wesele...
I skończona bajka.

Była sobie Baba Jaga,
Miała chatkę z masła,
A w tej chatce same dziwy...
Cyt! iskierka zgasła.

2

Tosi Tosi łapki
Pojedziem to Babci
A od Babci do Taty
Po korzuszek kudlaty

Kosi kosi lapki
Pojedziem do Babci
A od Babci to Taty
Tam jest piesek kudlaty

3

Sroczka kaszkę warzyła,
Ogonek sobie sparzyła...
Temu dała na miseczkę,
Temu dała na łyżeczkę,
Temu, bo grzecznie prosił,
Temu, bo wodę nosił,
A temu najmniejszemu nic nie dała,
Tylko ogonkiem zamieszała,
I frrrruuuuuu... poleciała!